UK BUSINESS
TAX GUIDE
92/93

UK BUSINESS TAX GUIDE 92/93

STOY HAYWARD

Accountants and Business Advisers
A member of Horwath International

CCH Editions Limited
TAX, BUSINESS AND LAW PUBLISHERS

Published by CCH Editions Limited
Telford Road, Bicester, Oxfordshire OX6 0XD
Tel. (0869) 253300, Facsimile (0869) 245814.
DX: 83750 Bicester 2.

EUROPE	CCH Europe Inc., Wiesbaden, Germany.
USA	Commerce Clearing House, Inc., Chicago, Illinois.
CANADA	CCH Canadian Limited, Toronto, Ontario.
AUSTRALIA	CCH Australia Limited, North Ryde, NSW.
NEW ZEALAND	CCH New Zealand Limited, Auckland.
SINGAPORE	CCH Asia Limited.
JAPAN	CCH Japan Limited, Tokyo.

This publication is designed to provide accurate and authoritative information in regard to the subject matter covered. It is sold with the understanding that the publisher is not engaged in rendering legal or other professional services. If legal advice or other expert assistance is required, the services of a competent professional person should be sought.

Ownership of Trade Marks

The Trade Marks

CCH ACCESS, COMPUTAX and **COMMERCE CLEARING HOUSE, INC.**

are the property of Commerce Clearing House, Incorporated, Chicago, Illinois, USA

ISBN 0 86325 298 2
ISSN 0967–6961

© **1992 Stoy Hayward**

Typeset in Great Britain by The Eastern Press Ltd, Frome.
Printed in Great Britain by The Eastern Press Ltd, Reading.

Preface

This is the first edition of the *UK Business Tax Guide*. Although the book is written specifically for people who are in business or who are thinking of starting a business, professional advisers and students should find this a useful reference book.

We hope that this book will make you aware of how most business decisions have an impact on the amount of tax you pay. It contains examples showing how you carry out a business transaction in a slightly different way so that you pay less tax. The book offers advice on such day-to-day headaches as PAYE and accounting for VAT, as well as explaining the tax effect of more complicated systems, such as setting up an employee share option scheme, buying or selling a business, or seeking a Stock Exchange quotation.

Some of the questions we set out to answer are:

- Having decided to start a business would it be better to form a company?
- Are there ways of rewarding employees without incurring employers' NIC?
- Are company cars still tax efficient?
- How can staff performance and productivity be rewarded in a tax-efficient way?
- What are the benefits of having an employee share ownership trust?
- Now an individual's tax rate on capital gains is in line with his income tax rate, is there any benefit in receiving capital rather than income?
- When making payments to employees, is it always necessary to deduct tax?
- As a sole trader, can I set my business losses against capital gains?
- What are the new rules regarding the carry back of a company's trading losses?
- Can the Business Expansion Scheme still be used to raise finance for trading companies?
- What are the advantages of obtaining a Stock Exchange quotation?

- What do I need to know about the VAT changes that come into effect on 1 January 1993 on the completion of the Single Market?

Because this book has been written for the non-expert, we explain the important technical terms which you are likely to come across and the basic principles which underlie some of the tax rules. However, where possible we have avoided tax jargon and have not given references to the legislation. Where appropriate the explanations are supplemented with worked examples.

Tax is wide-ranging and complex and this book should be regarded as an introduction to the subject. We hope that after reading it you are in a better position to discuss tax saving ideas with your professional adviser.

This book will be updated annually and this edition is based on the law and practice as at 31 July 1992.

Mavis Seymour
Stephen Say
Stoy Hayward
July 1992

About the Publisher

CCH Editions Limited is part of a world-wide group of companies that specialises in tax, business and law publishing. The group produces a wide range of books and reporting services for the accounting, business and legal professions. The Oxfordshire premises are the centre for all UK and European operations.

All CCH publications are designed to be practical and authoritative and are written by CCH's own highly qualified and experienced editorial team and specialist outside authors.

In the UK CCH Editions currently produces a comprehensive series of reporting services on UK and international tax, business and law, and many books covering specific areas of interest for accountants, lawyers and business managers. Irrespective of the subject matter being discussed or the depth and scope of its treatment, the material is always dealt with in the same clear and concise manner.

CCH is committed to you and your information needs, and this commitment is reflected in the constant updating and development of our reporting services and the growth and expansion of our range of publications.

If you would like to know more about our books or loose-leaf services telephone (0869) 253300.

Acknowledgements

The official forms set out in Appendixes 2, 3, 4, 11 and 12 of this book are Crown Copyright and are reproduced with the kind permission of the Controller of Her Majesty's Stationery Office.

Contents

Introduction

Many books have been written on the subject of tax planning but few deal with tax planning for businesses and the people who run them. This book does just that and addresses the specific problems which frequently arise in connection with business taxation.

So let's start by asking what is meant by tax planning. It is certainly not tax evasion which is illegal. If you were to deliberately understate in your business accounts your income from sales, this would be an example of tax evasion.

Tax planning is the ordering of your affairs in the most sensible way to take advantage of all possible tax reliefs, exemptions and allowances, and to avoid the pitfalls that exist in our complex tax legislation. The Inland Revenue accepts that you have the right to reduce your tax bill by tax planning; it is legal.

To take full advantage of the tax planning opportunities available, it is necessary to be familiar with the tax system and aware of the changes that occur, including the decisions of the courts.

In recent years there have been several case decisions which have had a fundamental effect on tax planning. The courts have decided that a transaction can be ignored for tax purposes where it has been inserted into a series of transactions at a late stage and solely for the purpose of tax avoidance or tax deferral. It is therefore very important when planning to do business in the most tax efficient way, always to ensure that you plan well ahead.

In 1992 Lord Templeman provided further guidance on what was acceptable tax planning. He distinguished a tax avoidance scheme, which he said was recognisable by the apparent magic result and was unacceptable, and tax mitigation where, in fact, as well as in appearance, the taxpayer suffers a loss or incurs expenditure.

Finally, although it may seem a statement of the obvious, you must not, in any tax planning exercise, lose sight of your commercial objectives.

1 Have You Started a Business?

Introduction

The first thing to be clear about is whether the activity which you are carrying on will be taxed as a business. The term 'business' is used to describe many activities – professions, vocations, the ownership of property and receipt of rents, for example. However, in most cases, being in business is synonymous with carrying on a trade.

As a general rule, if you engage in any activity from which you intend to make money, any profit you make is taxed as trading profit. There are some exceptions: horseracing is nearly always treated by the Inland Revenue as a hobby and not a trade. As a result, prize money is tax-free but the expenses involved are not tax deductible. There is also a presumption that, where an individual is engaged in speculative dealings in securities, this is not a trade and it is for the General Commissioners to decide on the facts whether the presumption should be displaced. There is therefore some truth in the saying that if you make a profit the inspector will regard your hobby as a trade, but if you are likely to make a loss he will treat your trade as a hobby.

What is a trade?

It is important to be aware of the features which will be taken into account by the tax inspector when he is deciding whether you are trading. His first concern will be whether your profit is a trading profit rather than a capital profit. The distinction is often described using the metaphor of the tree (a capital asset) and the fruit (the income it produces). In the case of a trade, the income is in the form of trading profits which arise from making or buying goods for resale, or the supply of services, at a profit.

If a factory is required from which to carry on the trade, it represents a capital asset. A profit on the sale of the factory is not a trading profit because the trading activity is not the purchasing of factories for resale.

The courts have on many occasions had to decide whether an activity amounted to a trade. The following paragraphs describe the underlying principles that have emerged from these case decisions.

Motive for acquisition

In some cases the motive for acquiring the asset is evident from the surrounding facts and in other cases it can be inferred. For example, if a company buys a property as a capital asset one would expect to see evidence of this in the minutes of board meetings. It would also be difficult to support an argument that a capital asset had been purchased if the purchaser did not, at the time of acquisition, have the means to finance it long-term or pay for its upkeep.

Nature of the assets sold

Assets can be acquired for resale, for investment, or for personal use and enjoyment. If they produce no return, are not likely to appreciate above the rate of inflation, cannot be used by the owner and have little aesthetic value, it becomes difficult to argue that they were not purchased with a view to resale. The quantity purchased may also indicate the motive at the time of acquisition. For example, if an individual sells calculators having purchased 500 of them, it would be difficult to sustain an argument that they were purchased for personal use.

Period of ownership

As a general rule, assets bought as an investment will be held for a longer period than those purchased for resale but there are exceptions, such as timber and whisky stocks that need to mature. There can be a problem where part of what is purchased as an investment is sold to finance the acquisition or upkeep of the remainder. In one case a person who wished to build herself a home was unable to get the owner of a piece of land to sell a small plot. She therefore bought the land, divided it into house plots, and sold the plots that were surplus to her requirements. She was held to have traded. This illustrates that you could be trading unintentionally.

Frequency of transactions

There is a presumption of trading if you sell the same sort of asset on several occasions. The type of asset and the interval between sales would be relevant. For example, if a person sells one freehold property each year for say three years, this has the appearance of trading, but it would not appear to be the case if he sells an item of furniture each year.

Making assets marketable
Irrespective of your motive at the time the asset was acquired, if you engage in any of the following activities to make the asset more marketable this would be seen as an indication of trading:

- Obtaining planning permission
- Carrying out repairs and improvements.
- Splitting large quantities into smaller units.
- Incurring costs on packaging.
- Large scale advertising.
- Opening a place of business.

For example, if your hobby has been the collection of Victorian postcards and you start to package them and advertise for buyers in collectors' magazines, you will have started a trade.

Reason for the sale
This principle is used to support an argument that a person did not sell the asset in the course of a trade as there were other reasons why the sale occurred. For example, it may have been necessary to repay a bank loan or pay arrears of income tax, or perhaps the person was made redundant.

Method of finance
If an asset has an income-producing life of ten years it may well be financed by taking out a ten-year loan. The method of financing could be a helpful indicator if in fact the asset were sold after a year and it became necessary to refute the contention of trading.

Trade knowledge
The courts have found it easier to decide that a person has traded in cases where he has a knowledge of the trade. The cases have largely been connected with estate agents, builders and land dealers.

Start of a trade

The date that a trade starts is important for determining:

- the first year that profits will be assessed to tax;
- the start of an accounting period for corporation tax;
- the extent to which pre-trading expenditure is allowable for tax purposes; and

- the four-month period after which tax relief can be claimed under the Business Expansion Scheme.

If therefore you plan to commence business on a certain date for tax purposes, you need to know what factors are considered in deciding when a trade starts.

As with many other tax situations, the question of when a trade starts depends on the facts of each particular case. There is, however, some guidance in case decisions. The most helpful case was considered by the courts in 1919. It concerned a company that started a trade of making and marketing products from butchers' by-products such as sausages.

A distinction was made between the actual start of the trade and the preparatory work. Over several months a factory was erected, plant was purchased and installed, contracts were made for the purchase of materials and the sale of products, and a works manager was appointed. These were considered to be the preparations for a trade. It was decided that the trade started when the materials began to be processed into the products for sale.

As a general guide, preparation for the trade ends and the trade starts when you are able to offer your goods and services to the public.

Another difficult area is where a business extends its activities, for example by opening another shop. If the facts suggest that there is a new trade the profits relating to it will be assessed separately and this could affect your tax liability.

Notifying the tax authorities

When you start up in business you have a responsibility to notify the local inspector of taxes. It is preferable to do this at the time your business starts but in any event, it must be disclosed in your tax return covering the year of commencement. The fact that you have not received a tax return is no excuse for not notifying the Inland Revenue that you have started in business.

Failure to notify is an important factor that the inspector will take into account when deciding whether further investigation is required.

To set up the appropriate records the inspector requires the completion of form 41G which can be found in the Revenue booklet IR 28 'Tax and Your Business – Starting in Business'. For companies the form is CT41G. These forms are reproduced as Appendixes 2 and 3. On receipt of the form the inspector will set up a file and computer record for your business and obtain a tax collection reference number from the Revenue's computer centre at Shipley.

After you have been in business for 12 months you will receive a standard letter requesting accounts. The letter will either be sent to you or, if you have given the Revenue the necessary authority (form 64-8), to the accountant who is acting for you.

Where accounts are not received 30 days after the issue of the reminder, the inspector will raise estimated assessments in accordance with set guidelines as to the profit expected from various trades. These guidelines are not normally available to the public, the only exceptions so far being the Business Economic Notes for certain trades that inspectors use as background information: see Appendix 1. If you pay the tax shown by an estimated assessment and subsequently it is found that the assessment was too low, the inspector will issue further assessments.

In addition to notifying the Revenue, you will also have to apply to your local Customs and Excise VAT office for VAT registration if your taxable turnover exceeds, or is likely to exceed, the registration threshold. Further details about VAT can be found in Chapter 8.

Finally, if you are setting up as a sole trader or in partnership (but not as a limited company) you will have to contact your local Department of Social Security (DSS) office to arrange for the payment of Class 2 National Insurance contributions.

Tax repayments

If you are starting in business and have previously been employed, you have the option of either claiming a tax repayment based on your allowances and reliefs for the whole tax year or having the balance of allowances set against your trading profits in that year. Unless you make a repayment claim the Revenue will automatically calculate the balance of allowances due. If the first accounts are not submitted for, say, 18 months the use of these allowances is delayed. Therefore, from a tax planning viewpoint it is beneficial to claim a repayment.

Example

Mr Marchant, who is married, ceases his employment with Sugden and Turner Leather Products Ltd on 30 September 1992 and starts a secretarial staff employment bureau on 1 October 1992. Details of his pay to 30 September 1992 are:

Salary	£7,500
Tax paid	£1,178
Code number	516H

Repayment Claim 1992/93

	£
Salary	7,500
Less: allowances	(5,165)
Taxable pay	£2,335

	£
Tax due £2,000 × 20%	400
	84
	484
Tax paid 335 × 25%	1,178
Repayment due	£694

Enterprise Allowance

One of the problems of starting a business if you are unemployed is that initially your business may not be profitable and you may continue to need state benefits. Recognising this as a problem, the Government introduced the Enterprise Allowance Scheme in 1983 which helped over 550,000 people.

The Enterprise Allowance Scheme was replaced in April 1991 by a new scheme called Enterprise Allowance run by the Training and Enterprise Councils (TECs). Their role is to:

- provide practical help to employers investing in the training and development of their employees;

- develop youth training leading to skills, qualifications and new careers; and

- customise adult training so that everyone, including unemployed people returning to the labour market, have the right skills for local jobs.

The previous Enterprise Allowance Scheme provided you with £40 a week for 52 weeks. This amount was added to your other income, if any, and was taxable. To qualify under the scheme you had to:

- be between 18 and the state retirement age, receiving unemployment or supplementary benefit, and have been out of work for eight weeks;

- agree to work full-time in the business; and

- have your business approved by the Department of Employment as a new business, suitable for public support.

The new Enterprise Allowance run by TECs provides similar assistance to the old scheme except that the amount and term of the benefit is flexible and depends on the results of the business.

For further information contact should be made with your local TEC.

2   The Form of Your Business

Introduction

If you start up a business on your own, for tax purposes you will be a sole trader. If you work with one or more individuals or companies and share the profits, you may be in partnership. If you are planning to set up in business in the UK there is no recommended form that the business should take; it is a case of weighing up the pros and cons for your particular circumstances. If, for example, limited liability is very important, you are likely to decide to carry on your business through a company which may be a private company, or a public limited company.

Sole trader

'Sole trader' is the label given to individuals who are carrying on trades, businesses, professions or vocations. If you are a sole trader you may be working completely alone, for example, a singer, or you may have employees.

The law does not require your financial accounts to be audited or to be open for inspection by the public. You are, however, required to do business under your own name or, if you use a different name, to state your name and address on business documents and display your name at your place of business.

As a sole trader you have unlimited liability which means that if you cannot pay your business creditors out of your business assets, they have a right to be paid from your personal resources.

Your profits as a sole trader are subject to income tax on a preceding year basis except in the opening and closing years of business. Further details are given in Chapter 9.

Partnerships

The Partnership Act 1890 defines a partnership as the relationship which subsists between persons carrying on a business in common with a view to profit. If you receive a share of the profits of a business this would be considered as prima facie evidence that you are a partner, although it is not conclusive.

For example, you are not in partnership if you are:

- simply a joint owner of property;
- an employee or agent receiving a share of the profits under your contract;
- just sharing gross returns;
- a dependant of someone who has died and are receiving by way of an annuity a portion of the business profits;
- receiving an annuity or a portion of the profits as part of the consideration for the sale of the goodwill of a business;
- lending money where the rate of interest varies with the profits.

Whether a partnership exists must depend on all the facts but the following can be useful indicators:

- If you have a partnership agreement it suggests that a partnership exists provided it is acted upon and is not a sham.
- If outside parties such as the bank, customers and suppliers have been led to believe that you are in partnership.

If you bring your spouse or minor children into the partnership the Revenue will question whether they carry out the duties of a partner.

In English law a partnership is not a separate person, but a group of individuals or companies, whereas under Scottish law a partnership has the status of a separate legal person. In both countries the tax treatment of the partnership reflects its status under the general law. As a rule a partnership cannot comprise more than 20 partners. Exceptions are made for certain professions such as accountants, solicitors, surveyors and stockbrokers. If the number of partners exceeds 20 and the business is not covered by one of the exceptions, the organisation becomes an unincorporated association. There are no audit or disclosure requirements for partnerships under general law.

Limited partners

Normally, if you are a member of a partnership you have unlimited liability for all the debts of the partnership. It is, however, possible to form a limited partnership but there must be at least one general partner who has unlimited liability. If you wish to form a limited partnership, you must register under the Limited Partnership Act 1907. If the requirements of the Act are breached, every limited partner is deemed to be a general partner. A limited partner does not have the right to take part in the management of the partnership business.

Salaried partners

If someone is described as a salaried partner he is likely to be an employee and will be taxed as such. As far as outside parties are concerned, salaried partners have unlimited liability, although they may be given an indemnity from the other partners.

Partnership agreement

If you are in a partnership the rights and liabilities of each partner should be recorded. You will find this particularly valuable should there be a dispute among the partners. A partnership agreement is likely to include clauses on the following items:

- How trading profits will be shared, e.g. salaries may be paid to one or more partners; interest may be payable on partners' capital and there will be a basis for sharing the balance of the profits.

- How capital profits are shared, e.g. perhaps only one or two partners share in the appreciation of the business properties.

- How an outgoing partner's capital is to be repaid and whether interest will be payable by the partnership, e.g. the partner may be paid in one or more instalments and may be entitled to interest at 2 per cent above the relevant bank base rate.

- The making of an election (a formal claim/application) for the business to be treated as continuing for tax purposes, in the event that there is a change of partners.

The Partnership Act 1890 comes into play only where there is no clear agreement between the partners, for example:

- if there is no agreement on how profits are shared the Act states that they are to be shared equally, without provision for partners' salaries or interest on capital;

- the Act also states that partners are entitled to interest at 5 per cent per annum on loans made to the partnership.

Unincorporated associations

An unincorporated body is a group of individuals who come together for a particular purpose, such as a golf club or a trade association. Profits of an unincorporated association are subject to corporation tax.

Companies

A company is a legal person. It can, for example, enter into contracts and borrow money in the same way as an individual. Its separate identity commences on the date of the issue of its certificate of incorporation, a document which is, effectively, its birth certificate.

Before you can obtain a certificate of incorporation you must send the following documents and pay a fee of £50 to the Registrar of Companies:

- A printed copy of the company's memorandum and articles of association signed, dated and witnessed.

- A statement of the names of the first directors and secretary of the company and their consent to act; the address of the company's first registered office. This need not be the company's trading address but will be the address at which any notices, etc. will be served: form 10.

- A statutory declaration either by a solicitor or an officer of the company, i.e. director or secretary, that the requirements of the Companies Acts have been complied with: form 12.

- Return of allotments: form 88(2).

Provided the documents are in order the Registrar will issue the certificate of incorporation. If you do not want the bother of forming a company you could buy a ready-made 'off-the-shelf' company from a company registration agent. These companies can easily be adapted to your requirements by passing resolutions to appoint new directors, change the name, increase the capital or alter the articles.

A company must state on its letter heading its full name, its registration number and country of registration, its registered office and either the names of all its directors or none of them.

Memorandum and articles of association

The memorandum states the name of the company which (with a few exceptions) must end with 'Limited' if it is a private company, or 'Public Limited Company' if it is a public company, or with the Welsh equivalent of these words. It also states the objects of the company, the fact that the members' liability is limited and the amount of its authorised share capital.

Shares may be issued either fully paid or partly paid. They can be issued at a premium on their par (face) value but cannot be issued at a discount or with no par value.

The articles are the internal regulations of the company, covering the rights of shareholders, the appointment and removal of directors, procedure at meetings, etc.

Directors
A private company need only have one director but a public company must have two. Every company must have a company secretary and in the case of a public company the person must be appropriately qualified. If you are the sole director of a private company you cannot also be the company secretary. You might therefore consider whether your spouse should be company secretary. The power to appoint directors usually rests with the shareholders. The law sets out specific responsibilities for directors which include:

- keeping proper statutory books, such as a register of shareholders, and these must be available for inspection by the public;
- keeping proper accounting records;
- presenting a directors' report and the company's audited balance sheet and profit and loss account to the shareholders at regular intervals, usually once a year;
- filing with the Registrar any mortgage or charge on the company's property within 21 days; and
- filing the audited accounts and the annual return with the Registrar of Companies.

The annual return sets out the authorised and issued share capital, and a list of the present directors, secretary and members. A fee (currently £32) is payable when filing this form. If a company is quoted or listed, the Stock Exchange imposes additional responsibilities on the directors on matters affecting the price of the company's shares.

Public limited companies
A public company is a company limited by shares which states in its memorandum that it is a public company and is registered as such. Before a company which is set up as a public limited company, can borrow or do business it must:

- apply to the Registrar of Companies on form 117 signed by the secretary or a director;
- comply with the minimum share capital requirements; and
- have been issued with a 'Certificate of a public company being entitled to do business'.

A public company is required to have a minimum issued nominal share capital of £50,000. At least 25 per cent of the nominal value of the shares must be paid on issue, together with any premium. The consideration for the shares must be money or money's worth which can include goodwill and know-how. It may not, however, include an undertaking to carry out work or perform services. Where a public company proposes to offer shares for a non-cash consideration it is necessary to obtain a valuation report from an independent expert to justify the amount of shares offered.

There is an advantage to being a public rather than a private company because only public companies can offer shares and debentures to the public. It also means that if they meet the necessary requirements, a public company's shares and debentures can be listed on the Stock Exchange or quoted on the Unlisted Securities Market.

A private limited company can re-register as a public limited company if it meets the minimum share capital requirements. It is necessary for the shareholders to pass a special resolution stating that the company should re-register and making the necessary alterations to the company's name and the memorandum and articles. When the company applies to the Registrar it must include:

- a copy of the revised memorandum and articles;
- a copy of a balance sheet prepared at a date not more than seven months earlier, together with an unqualified audit report;
- a written statement by the auditors that the enclosed balance sheet shows the company's net assets to be not less than the total of its called-up share capital and non-distributable reserves;
- a copy of the independent valuation report, where shares have been allotted since the last balance sheet for non-cash consideration; and
- a statutory declaration that all the legal requirements have been satisfied and that since the date of the balance sheet the company's net assets have not fallen below its called-up share capital and reserves.

The income and gains of a company resident in the UK are subject to corporation tax which is considered in Chapters 13 and 14.

Branch of a non-resident company
If you wish to conduct your business in the UK through a branch of a non-resident company you will need to send to the Registrar of Companies:

- a certified copy of the instrument that constitutes or defines the constitution of the non-resident company, and if this is not in English a translation should be attached;
- the names of the company's directors and the secretary; and

• the name and address of at least one person resident in the UK on whom any legal notices can be served.

The non-resident company must file a copy of its annual financial statements with the Registrar but the detail that needs to be disclosed is limited. The letter heading of the branch must show the overseas company's name, where it was incorporated and whether or not it has limited liability. This information must also appear at its place of business in this country.

The trading profits of the branch will be subject to UK corporation tax.

Contractors and subcontractors

Do you or your company carry on a business that includes construction operations or does your expenditure on construction operations average £250,000 per annum over a three year period? If so you are considered to be a contractor for the purpose of the rules which apply to subcontractors in the construction industry. It means that when paying subcontractors who do not produce an exemption certificate you must deduct basic rate tax. The rate of deduction is 25 per cent. The tax you deduct must be paid to the Inland Revenue. Interest is charged on assessments raised on contractors for under-deductions from the payments to subcontractors.

If you or your company are a subcontractor it is important to obtain an exemption certificate. Without a certificate a contractor must deduct basic rate tax from payments to you. Once you can produce a certificate you can be paid in full. You apply to your local inspector for the certificate and he needs to be satisfied that you:

• work in the UK construction industry;

• are carrying on a trade from a regular place of business;

• have a bank account through which most of your business is conducted;

• keep proper records so that accounts can be prepared;

• were either employed, in business, or in full-time education or training during the last three years, although up to six months' unemployment can be part of the three-year period;

• have made full tax returns for the three years; and

• are up to date with your payments of tax and National Insurance.

If you cannot meet the three-year condition, perhaps because you have recently left school, it is possible to obtain a special certificate which allows payments of up to £150 per week to be received without deduction of tax. Any amounts earned in excess of that limit continue to be paid net of basic rate tax, as described above. If you are refused a certificate you have a right to appeal against the decision.

As a subcontractor you are carrying on a trade and must provide the inspector with details of your income and expenditure on a yearly basis so that your tax liability can be calculated.

3 Understanding the UK Tax System

Introduction

The UK, which consists of England, Wales, Scotland and Northern Ireland, has both direct and indirect taxes. The direct taxes on income and profits are:

- income tax and National Insurance;
- corporation tax; and
- petroleum revenue tax.

There are two taxes on capital:

- capital gains tax;
- inheritance tax.

The indirect taxes are:

- customs and excise duties;
- value added tax;
- stamp duties;
- motor vehicle duties.

It is generally true to say that under our tax system, tax is imposed on:

- income, profits and gains from sources within the UK, wherever the recipient is resident; and
- income, profits and gains wherever they arise of those who are resident in the UK.

Special reliefs are given where a person is not UK-domiciled.

The tax year starts on 6 April. For example, the tax year 1992/93 starts on 6 April 1992 and ends on 5 April 1993. In March each year the Chancellor of the Exchequer produces his Budget for Government expenditure for the next tax year and indicates the extent to which it will be financed from the different taxes. In his Budget speech in the House of Commons he announces any changes that will be made to taxation. Following the Budget it is necessary for the Ways and Means Committee of the House of Commons to pass a resolution to impose, increase or extend the taxes.

The March 1993 Budget will be the last Spring Budget. In his 1992 speech, the Chancellor announced changes to the Budget process which will result in future Budgets being held in December, starting with December 1993.

Residence

You are regarded as resident in the UK for tax purposes if you are present in this country for more than 182 days in any one tax year or for three months on average in a four-year period. Unless you are working full time abroad the availability of accommodation in the UK is sufficient to make you resident here in any year in which you set foot in the UK. Furthermore, courts have decided that residence in the UK extends to residence on a boat in our territorial waters and oil rigs in certain parts of the Continental Shelf.

There is also a concept known as ordinary residence which is concerned with a more continuing presence in the UK. Whether you are ordinarily resident here depends on many factors, such as where you live for most of the time, how frequently you visit this country and whether you have a place of residence here.

A company is treated for tax purposes as being resident in the UK if its central management and control is in the UK, irrespective of where its shareholders are resident. Usually, the board of directors manage and control the company. It therefore follows that the residence of the company is likely to be where they hold their meetings and make their decisions. This would not, however, be the case if it comes to light that either it is not the named directors who manage and control the company or that the board meetings held in this country simply ratify and record decisions made elsewhere.

Since 15 March 1988 (15 March 1993 for the pre-15 March 1988 companies) a company is also treated as resident in the UK if it was incorporated in the UK, regardless of the location of its central management and control.

Domicile

In general, you are domiciled in the country with which you have the closest ties. This may be the country where your father was domiciled when you were born (your domicile of origin) or where you have your permanent home or where you intend to live indefinitely.

If you are not domiciled in the UK you receive favourable treatment under our tax system. For example, any non-UK income and gains are taxed only if remitted here, and you can set up trusts which will escape inheritance tax when the trust property is situated abroad.

The Law Commissions' Report published in 1987 proposed a number of changes to the laws on domicile. Parliament have indicated that these changes will be enacted shortly.

For the purposes of inheritance tax you are deemed to be domiciled in the UK:

- for three years after you cease to be domiciled here; or
- if you have been resident here for 17 out of 20 years at the time you make the gift.

Income tax

Income tax, which is now a permanent feature of our tax system, was first introduced in 1799 by Pitt as a temporary tax to finance the war with France.

Income is classified into various categories known as Schedules, and taxed according to the rules relating to each Schedule: see Appendix 14. Business profits are assessed under Schedule D and the basis is set out in Chapter 9.

Each year your income is taxed after making certain deductions. The position for 1992/93 is as follows.

The first £2,000 of your net income is taxed at 20 per cent (the lower rate) the next £21,700 is taxed at 25 per cent (the basic rate) while any excess over £23,700 is taxed at 40 per cent (the higher rate). To arrive at your net income, you take your total assessable income and deduct certain allowances and reliefs. Everyone is entitled to a tax-free personal allowance (for details see Appendix 5). The other reliefs can be divided into main categories:

- Those which are allowed at your top rate, e.g. interest on loans to purchase shares in a close company (see Chapter 13).
- Those which are allowed at basic rate only, e.g. interest on the first £30,000 of loans to purchase your main home.

Corporation tax

Corporation tax, which was introduced in 1965, is a tax on the income and gains of companies and unincorporated bodies. If your company is resident in the UK it is chargeable to corporation tax in respect of all its profits wherever they arise. On the other hand, if your company is not resident in this country, but carries on a trade here through a branch or agency, it is liable to UK corporation tax on its income and gains from that branch or agency. Corporation tax is considered in detail in Chapter 13.

Capital gains tax

Capital gains tax, also introduced in 1965, taxes gains arising on disposals by individuals and trustees. If you are resident in the UK for the tax year in which you dispose of an asset you are chargeable to capital gains tax on any gains that may arise, wherever that asset is situated. If you are neither resident nor ordinarily resident in this country but trade here through a branch or agency, you are only chargeable on the gains which arise on the disposal of any of the assets used for that branch or agency. The rules are more generous if you are not domiciled in this country, in that some gains from disposals of assets abroad are only chargeable to UK capital gains tax to the extent that the sale proceeds are remitted here. The subject of capital gains tax is dealt with in Chapter 7.

Value added tax

The legislation for value added tax (VAT) was introduced in 1972, prior to Britain joining the European Community on 1 January 1973, and was effective from 1 April 1973. Customs and Excise have the responsibility for administering the tax. For VAT purposes, the Isle of Man is treated as being part of the UK. VAT is an indirect tax charged on supplies of goods and services and it is collected at each stage of the process of production and distribution. Goods and services are either taxable at 17.5 per cent or at a zero rate, or are exempt. If you make taxable supplies above a certain level you must register for VAT and charge your customers and clients with VAT. This subject is dealt with in detail in Chapter 8.

Inheritance tax

Inheritance tax, which was introduced in 1986, is a tax on capital transferred by individuals or trustees either at death or within the seven years before death. It is similar to estate duty, the forerunner of capital transfer tax, in operation from 1974 to 1986. If you are UK domiciled the transfer of your capital is chargeable wherever it is located.

As a general rule, if you have a foreign domicile those assets situated outside the UK are not chargeable to UK inheritance tax. The tax is administered by the Capital Taxes Office of the Inland Revenue. It is considered further in Chapter 32.

Stamp duties

Stamp duty, which was last consolidated in 1891, is a tax on documents. The usual rates are either 0.5 or 1 per cent on the amount or value of the consideration, which is inclusive of any VAT that is payable. If you acquire land for up to £30,000 the stamp duty is nil, but if you pay more than £30,000, duty is payable at 1 per cent on the acquisition price. This limit was £250,000 from 20 December 1991 to 19 August 1992. The current duty of 0.5 per cent when you buy shares and securities and all other stamp duty, except on land and buildings, is scheduled for abolition in May 1993 to coincide with the introduction of TAURUS, a computerised paperless dealing system which the Stock Exchange wishes to introduce in order to enhance London's competitiveness as an international centre for financial services.

If you enter into a transaction which is liable to stamp duty, it should be paid at a stamping office of the Inland Revenue within 30 days of executing the document. The Revenue can charge penalties for stamping the document out of time. Because it is a duty on documents, it follows that if the transaction can be effected without one, for example, by simple delivery of the asset, no liability to stamp duty arises.

Stamp duty reserve tax, introduced in 1986, is charged on agreements to transfer certain securities which are not liable to stamp duty, such as renounceable letters of allotment. This tax will also be abolished when stamp duty on shares is abolished.

You should bear in mind that a document which ought to be stamped but is not cannot be admitted in evidence in civil proceedings.

National Insurance

Lloyd George, who introduced the National Insurance Bill in 1911, described National Insurance as a temporary expedient. The basic idea is that contributions made by all those who have earnings are used to provide pensions, sick pay, industrial injury compensation, unemployment and other similar benefits. However, there are parts of the system, for example, the Class 4 contributions, where there is no link between the amount you contribute and the benefits you receive. The responsibility for National Insurance is with the Secretary of State who is the head of the Department of Social Security (DSS). It has in recent years become the

Government's second largest source of income and most people tend to regard it as a tax. Further details on National Insurance can be found in Chapter 21.

Case law

Apart from reading the tax legislation, an understanding of our tax system requires a knowledge of the way in which the courts have interpreted certain words and phrases. This can be found in published tax case decisions.

Regulations

In addition, the Treasury and the Board of Inland Revenue have issued many regulations. For example, most of the rules on the pay as you earn system, National Insurance and value added tax are in the form of regulations.

Practice and concessions

The legislation, tax case decisions and regulations are further supplemented by the Inland Revenue's published statements of practice, extra-statutory concessions, press releases and the record of the Finance Bill debates that are published in *Hansard*. These last four items are not law but are sometimes helpful in understanding how the Revenue intend to interpret the legislation. For example, it appears from a literal reading of the legislation on capital allowances for short-life assets that for each asset a separate election and a separate capital allowances computation is required. In their statement of practice the Revenue recognise that this approach would be impracticable and make helpful suggestions to make the scheme work (see page 37).

Often the extra-statutory concessions illustrate that the Board of Inland Revenue are human. The general rule is that anything an employee receives from his employer is taxed as remuneration unless there is a specific exemption in the legislation. In this area the Revenue have, by concession, agreed not to tax Christmas parties and long service awards provided they are within certain monetary limits: (see pages 159 and 160).

Press releases are used to update the public, for example by notifying the latest figure for the Retail Prices Index. They may also give advance notice of changes that will be made to the legislation in the next Finance Act.

In addition to all the published material, tax advisers are able to draw on their experience of Revenue attitudes and their knowledge of unpublished concessions. With such a complicated tax system and so many sources of information it is not surprising that there are so many tax advisers in this country.

4 Computing Trading Profits

Trading income

The profits of a UK trade are assessed under Case I of Schedule D. While the profits of a profession carried on in the UK are assessed under Case II, the basis of the computation is, for all practical purposes, the same. In computing trading profits for tax purposes, there is the general principle that only revenue (as opposed to capital) profits are taken into account and only expenses 'wholly and exclusively laid out or expended for the purposes of the trade, profession or vocation' are allowed as deductions from those profits.

The legislation does not state what is meant by the terms 'capital' and 'revenue' so it is necessary to refer to accountancy practice and tax case decisions. In general terms, receipts which relate to the disposal of assets which you purchased to keep and use in the business are likely to be capital receipts: for example, the proceeds you receive from selling a company car or an item of factory machinery. Any profit that you make on these sales is not taxed as a trading profit but in some cases may be taxed as a capital gain.

The sale of goods to your customers and the provision of services to your clients produce trading income and any resulting profit is a trading profit. Normally, net profit is calculated by bringing into account income earned whether received or not. However, for certain professionals such as surgeons and barristers, it is acceptable for tax purposes to calculate profit on a cash basis. Your net profit for accounts purposes will usually have to be adjusted to arrive at the trading profits for tax purposes. For example, the following profits and income need to be excluded:

- Capital receipts and profits, including profit or loss on the sale of fixed assets.
- Dividends and royalties.
- Interest received assessable under Case III of Schedule D.
- Rental income assessable under Schedule A.
- Income assessable under Cases IV, V and VI of Schedule D.

Chapter 6 explains how rent is taxed and the taxation of capital gains is considered in Chapter 7. If you sublet part of your business premises because it is surplus to your requirements, strictly the rental income and a proportion of the related expenses should be extracted and assessed under Schedule A. However, in practice, if this cannot easily be done and the rental income is incidental, the profits are not separated.

Allowable expenses

Whether an expense has been incurred wholly and exclusively for the purposes of the trade or profession may be open to argument, but some items have been the subject of court decisions and others are specifically dealt with in the legislation. The following are examples of allowable expenses:

- *Accountancy fees*. Additional costs relating to in-depth investigations by Inland Revenue are only allowable if they do not result in the reopening of an earlier year.

- *Advertising*.

- *Bad debts*. Doubtful debts are allowed only if specific; round figure provisions are not allowed.

- *Donations to charities* where your business or staff may benefit, e.g. a local hospital. See page 28 for treatment of 'Gift Aid' and payments under deed of covenant.

- *Employees' salaries and wages* including those paid to the proprietor's spouse and children provided the amount paid is appropriate for the duties performed.

- *Film production expenses*. Pre-production expenditure may be written off as it is incurred. Film production costs may be written off evenly over a three year period beginning in the year the film is completed provided it is a film certified under the Films Act 1985 as having the necessary EC content.

- *Gifts to customers* which are a form of advertising; not consisting of food, drink, tobacco or a gift token; and where the cost does not exceed £10 per customer.

- *Hire-purchase charges*.

- *Incidental costs of raising loan finance*.

- *Insurance premiums* for employer's liability, fire, etc.

- *Interest* paid gross on loans for the trade.

- *Lighting, heating and the uniform business rate* but subject to apportionment if the proprietor shares the premises.

- *Legal costs* in connection with disputes with customers, preparation of services agreements, bad debts, defending business rights, and damages arising in the course of the trade.

- *Lease renewals* where the renewal period is less than 50 years.

- *Loss from burglary, theft or an employee's embezzlement* where not covered by insurance.

- *National Insurance contributions* by employers.

- *Patents, trade marks, etc.* The cost of applications for the grant or renewal, whether successful or not.

- *Pension contributions* for employers and employees.

- *Redundancy payments* to employees.

- *Rent paid* including a proportion of any lease premium paid (see page 54).

- *Renewal of shop front and renewals of short life plant and machinery* such as loose tools.

- *Repairs* except for any element of improvement.

- *Scientific research.*

- *Subscriptions* to certain trade associations and professional bodies.

- *Training and Enterprise Council contributions* for a period of five years from 1 April 1990.

- *Travelling expenses.*

- *Waste disposal sites.* Expenditure on preparing or making good landfill sites for waste disposal, provided that capital allowances are not being claimed.

Non-allowable expenses

Your profit and loss account may include certain items which are not allowable expenses for the purposes of calculating trading profits for tax. The following are examples of items that must be added back to the net profit in calculating the profits for tax purposes:

- *Appropriations of profit*, i.e. dividends and partners' salaries.

- *Capital expenditure or capital losses.* Where a farmer elects for his livestock to be treated as fixed assets under the herd basis the initial cost is not deductible as an expense.

- *Depreciation provisions.*
- *Entertaining.*
- *General reserves*, for example, for doubtful debts.
- *Interest and other payments*, such as covenanted payments to charity, where tax must be deducted at source (see 'Charges on income' below).
- *Legal costs* in connection with the purchase of property, or the preparation of a partnership deed.
- *Non-business expenses or losses.*
- *Payment to terminate a lease of trading premises.*
- *Tax appeal expenses*, whatever the outcome of the appeal.

Repairs

Normally, if you repair an asset that has recently been purchased to keep and use in the business the expenditure will be treated as capital and will not be deductible in calculating trading profits. This principle has been modified following a case concerning a company which acquired theatres that were in a poor state of repair: the cost of repairs was allowed as a trading expense and not treated as part of the original capital cost of acquiring the assets to be used in the trade. This was because at the time of acquisition the theatres were already in a commercially viable state and in fact were used for the trade before being repaired. Furthermore, the repairs were carried out over a number of years and were treated as revenue expenditure in the accounts.

Charges on income

This term is commonly applied to payments made net of basic rate income tax. Examples that may be encountered in a business are:

- Annual interest paid by companies.
- Payments (charitable or otherwise) under a deed of covenant.
- Single payments to charity of £400 (£600 before 7 May 1992) or more made under the 'Gift Aid' rules.
- Patent royalties.

Charges on income are always added back in arriving at trading profit for tax purposes. However, they are allowed as a deduction from an individual's (or company's) total income. Charges in the context of companies is discussed further in Chapter 14.

Adjustment of profit

Example

Nigel, who is a retail stationer, prepares the following profit and loss account for his business for the year to 31 March 1993:

	£	£
Gross profit		120,000
UK dividends		2,000
Insurance commission		1,000
Profit on the sale of machinery		800
		123,800
Wages and salaries	58,000	
Depreciation of vehicles	2,200	
Bad debts	500	
Advertising	1,400	
Printing, stationery and telephone	2,300	
Rent and rates	2,400	
Lighting and heating	1,300	
Bank interest	900	
Business travelling	1,100	
Entertaining	1,900	
		72,000
Net profit		£51,800

One third of the rent and rates relates to Nigel's flat over the shop. Included in the figure for wages and salaries are Nigel's drawings of £20,000.

Nigel

Calculation of Trading Profits for Income Tax purposes for the Year to 31 March 1993

	£	£
Net profit per profit and loss account		51,800
Add: Depreciation of vehicles	2,200	
Rent and rates of flat	800	
Proprietor's drawings	20,000	
Entertaining	1,900	24,900
		76,700
Less: UK dividends	2,000	
Insurance commission (assessed under Case VI)	1,000	
Profit on sale of machinery	800	3,800
Trading profit for tax purposes		£72,900

The deductibility of expenses that are only incurred by companies is considered in Chapter 14.

Trading stock

As goods bought or produced in an accounting period are not always sold in the same period, it is necessary for the stock-in-hand at the beginning and at the end of an accounting period to be brought into the calculation of trading profit. Where the stocks are of raw materials and finished goods they must be valued at the lower of cost or realisable value. If your business has stocks of work-in-progress they must be valued on a consistent basis using:

- cost; or
- cost plus overheads; or
- cost plus overheads plus a profit contribution;

or net realisable value if lower.

Unless an election has been made for the herd basis, a farmer's livestock is treated as trading stock and may be valued:

- at 75 per cent (60 per cent for cattle) of market value; or
- at cost provided adequate records are kept.

Where goods are taken from trading stock for the proprietor's personal use or are disposed of other than in the ordinary course of a trade, this is treated as a sale at market value. If you are a trader it is therefore preferable to use your business contacts to make private purchases at a discount rather than take goods from your business stock. Furthermore, it is better to decide at the date of purchase that a certain item will be a fixed asset, rather than take it into stock and make the decision later. The Inland Revenue do not apply this market value rule where services are rendered by the proprietor or where expenditure is incurred on the construction of a fixed asset for use in the trade.

Where a trade is discontinued, or in the case of a partnership is treated as discontinued, the closing stock will be valued:

- at the amount realised if sold for valuable consideration to a UK trader (or intending trader); and
- in any other case, at market value at the date the trade ceases.

An exception is made to this rule if the trade ceases because of the death of the trader.

5 Capital Allowances

Introduction

Although you are not allowed to make a deduction for depreciation in computing net trading profit you can claim allowances, known as capital allowances, for capital expenditure incurred on certain types of assets that are used in your business.

Allowances are generally available in respect of assets owned at the end of an accounting period. This means that a full year's allowances will be available in the year in which an asset is acquired, but not in the year in which it is disposed of. Allowances are restricted where a company's accounting period is less than 12 months.

In the year of disposal a balancing allowance or a balancing charge may arise. The procedure in the year of disposal is discussed later.

Allowances of 100 per cent in the year of expenditure are now only available for buildings in enterprise zones and for scientific research. Annual allowances of 4 per cent or 25 per cent, can be claimed on other assets.

Capital expenditure

In order to claim capital allowances you must first incur capital expenditure. It has been said that expenditure is of a capital nature if it brings into existence an asset for the enduring benefit of the trade. It includes not only the price you pay for the asset but, where relevant, any costs of transportation, construction and installation. It does not include any costs of financing the purchase, such as interest. On several occasions the courts have been asked to decide whether expenditure had resulted in the replacement or improvement of an asset, and was therefore capital, or had merely been used to repair the asset, in which case it was revenue expenditure. It has become the general rule that if the expenditure involves the reconstruction of merely a part of an asset, it is revenue expenditure, but if the reconstruction is of an asset which is in fact a separate entity it is capital expenditure.

Capital contributions

There are occasions when you could receive a contribution (not a loan) from another person towards the cost of purchasing a business asset. One example is a Government grant. Another is where a landlord, in order to attract the right tenant, agrees to make a capital contribution to the tenant's expenditure on plant. There is also the possibility that the tenant could make a capital contribution to the landlord's expenditure on plant. The position regarding capital allowances is as follows:

Contributions made

Capital allowances are available if you make a contribution provided you are not connected with the owner of the asset and either:

- the asset is for the purposes of your trade, profession or vocation; or
- you are a landlord and the asset is used for the purposes of your tenant's trade, profession or vocation.

Contributions received

If you receive a contribution from the Crown, a Government or public or local authority or an exempt body such as a pension fund or a charity, you must deduct it in arriving at the amount on which you claim capital allowances. An exception has been made to this rule for regional development grants. If you receive one of these grants you can claim capital allowances on the full purchase price.

If you receive a contribution from any other person it does not reduce the amount on which you can claim capital allowances provided:

- the amount you receive is insurance or compensation moneys payable in respect of an asset which has been demolished, destroyed or put out of use; or
- the person making the contribution could not obtain capital allowances in respect of the contribution.

Date expenditure is incurred

If you are to claim capital allowances in a particular accounting period it is necessary to ensure that you have at that time incurred the expenditure. The general rule is that you incur expenditure on the date when the obligation to pay becomes unconditional. In most cases this will be the invoice date but, as explained below, there are special rules if you enter into a conditional contract or one which has a long credit period.

Example

Frank, who makes up his accounts to 31 January each year, orders a machine on 22 January 1993, takes delivery on 27 January, receives an invoice dated 30 January on which the terms of payment are 60 days' credit. He pays for the machine on 28 March 1993. Frank can claim capital allowances on this machine in the year ended 31 January 1993 because on 30 January he has an obligation to pay which is unconditional.

Example

John, who also makes up his accounts to 31 January each year, orders a machine on 22 January 1993 and receives an invoice dated 30 January on which the terms of payment are 60 days after date of delivery. The machine is delivered on 2 February and he pays for the machine on 28 March 1993. At 31 January 1993 John's obligation to pay is conditional on the machine being delivered so he is not eligible for allowances in the accounting period ended 31 January 1993. The position would be the same even if John pays for the machine on 31 January.

There are three exceptions to this 'unconditional obligation to pay' rule:

- Where all or part of the expenditure need not be paid in the next four months.

- Where it has been deliberately agreed between the parties that the date on which there is an unconditional obligation to pay will be earlier than is normal for that business so that the purchaser can make an earlier claim for allowances.

  In both these situations the expenditure is deemed to be incurred on the last day of the credit period. The actual date of payment is ignored.

- The third situation relates to long-term contracts such as building contracts, where payments are made on the issue of stage payment certificates and the purchaser becomes the owner of the partly finished asset.

  Capital expenditure during the first month of an accounting period is treated as though it was incurred during the previous accounting period, provided the asset was the purchaser's property at that time.

The above rules determine the date of expenditure for the purpose of deciding what rate of allowance is used when rates change and also the accounting period in which you can make a claim.

There are further rules which relate to specific situations or assets, which deem expenditure to be incurred earlier or later than the actual payment date:

- *Pre-trading.* If you incur capital expenditure before the start of a trade it is deemed to be incurred on the first day of trading. Similarly, if you buy plant which you will be letting to another person the expenditure is deemed to be incurred on the day the letting starts.

  This rule determines the date and thus the accounting period in which you can claim allowances. The actual date the expenditure is due determines the rate of allowances. This is significant when rates change.

- *Hire-purchase.* If you buy plant or machinery on hire-purchase terms it is deemed to belong to you for the purposes of claiming capital allowances and any outstanding payments are deemed to be incurred on the date the asset is brought into use.

Plant and machinery

While it is relatively easy to identify items of machinery that are used in the business, the courts have often had to decide whether a particular asset is plant eligible for capital allowances. They have decided that the following items are eligible:

- A dry dock.
- Movable office partitions.
- A concrete grain silo.
- A building society's window screens.
- Books in a barrister's library.
- A swimming pool at a caravan park.
- Special light fittings and murals in a hotel because they helped to create the hotel's atmosphere.
- Mezzanine floors constructed in a single-storey warehouse.

Assets which have been held not to be plant for capital allowances include:

- A canopy over the petrol pumps in a garage.
- A ship used as a floating restaurant.
- Wallpaper pattern books.
- A football stand.
- False ceilings.
- A glass shop front.

The principle that has emerged from these court decisions is that plant which merely provides a setting for the business does not qualify for capital allowances. The plant must actually be used in carrying out the business activity. In the case of the garage canopy it was held that the canopy did not help to supply petrol but merely provided shelter and make the business of supplying petrol more comfortable.

The legislation specifically includes certain items as plant for the purposes of capital allowances:

- Certain fire safety expenditure incurred by hotels and boarding houses, factories, shops, offices and railways with a minimum of ten employees.

- Thermal insulation of an existing industrial building.

If you lease such premises you can claim capital allowances on contributions made towards your tenant's expenditure:

- Computer software licences or the provision of software by electronic means (expenditure after 9 March 1992).

Pooling expenditure

You are entitled to claim an annual writing-down allowance of 25 per cent when you purchase or improve plant. The plant does not have to be new, it can be second-hand. The allowance is a percentage of cost in the year you incur the expenditure. In subsequent years you apply the percentage to the reducing balance which is the unrelieved part of the expenditure also known as the 'written-down value'. Normally you will add together ('pool') all your expenditure on plant and apply the percentage to the total amount.

Example
Kevin, who runs a garage, buys the following items to use in his business: a recovery transporter for £11,900, welding equipment costing £2,100 and a micro computer for £10,000. His capital allowances are as follows:

		Pool	Capital Allowances
		£	£
Year 1	Expenditure	24,000	
	Writing-down allowance	6,000	6,000
		18,000	
Year 2	Writing-down allowance	4,500	4,500
		13,500	

When you sell plant that has been pooled, you deduct the proceeds received, if less than cost, from the pooled expenditure. If the proceeds are more than cost then it is the cost that you deduct from the pool. When you incur further expenditure on plant in later years you add it to the pool before calculating the allowance.

Example
Continuing the previous example, in year 3 Kevin purchased shelving for the stores costing £2,500 and in year 4 he sold the computer for £2,000 and purchased another one for £12,000.

		Pool	Capital Allowances
		£	£
Balance brought forward		13,500	
Year	Additions	2,500	
		16,000	
	Writing-down allowance	4,000	4,000
		12,000	
Year 4	Additions	12,000	
		24,000	
	Sale proceeds	(2,000)	
		22,000	
	Writing-down allowance	5,500	5,500
		16,500	

If you sell plant that has been pooled and the proceeds (or cost if lower) exceed the written-down value of the pool there is a clawback of allowances equal to the excess. This clawback is referred to as a balancing charge. In the above example, if plant was sold for £17,200 in year 5 there would be a balancing charge of £700.

Expenditure on the following plant is not pooled:

- cars costing over £12,000 (see page 162);
- plant where there is private use by the proprietor (see page 163);
- short life assets where a de-pooling election has been made.

Hire-purchase and leased assets

Where you acquire plant or machinery under a hire-purchase contract, it is treated as though all the capital expenditure has been incurred at the time when it is brought into use for the trade. Capital allowances are available immediately on the full cash cost of the asset and the interest element of the repayments is treated as an allowable deduction for tax purposes.

Where a lease is entered into with an option to buy the asset at the end of the period then capital allowances and relief for interest payments are the same as for hire-purchase contracts. For VAT purposes hire-purchase and lease-purchase are treated as any other purchase.

Where there is no option to purchase the asset at the end of the contract, capital allowances are not available to the lessee. However, the full amounts of the rental payments are allowable for tax purposes and you can normally reclaim all the VAT incurred on the rental.

Short life assets

Using a 25 per cent writing-down allowance, it would take eight years to obtain relief for 90 per cent of the capital expenditure on plant. Furthermore, because this expenditure is usually pooled, when you sell the plant, you would not get relief in the form of a balancing allowance. Any shortfall between proceeds and written-down value would simply be carried forward in the pool.

Accepting that the system of capital allowances was unsuitable for items of plant which have a short life, the Government introduced a de-pooling election. It is available to individuals and companies and for most items of plant but not ships, certain leased plant or cars. When you purchase one or more items of plant which are likely to have a life of less than five years you can elect, in writing within the next two years, for the expenditure to be kept out of the main pool.

Example
In an earlier example Kevin bought a computer for £10,000 and sold it in its fourth year for £2,000. By the time of the disposal he had received the following allowances:

		Pool	Capital Allowances
		£	£
Year 1	Expenditure	10,000	
	Writing-down allowance	2,500	2,500
		7,500	
Year 2	Writing-down allowance	1,875	1,875
		5,625	
Year 3	Writing-down allowance	1,406	1,406
		4,219	£5,781

Year 4	Proceeds	2,000
	Balancing allowance	2,219

Although the computer had decreased in value by £8,000 at the date of disposal, the relief given was only £5,781. If Kevin had elected not to pool the expenditure on the computer the allowances in the first three years would have been the same, but in year 4 he would have received a balancing allowance of £2,219 thereby getting relief during the life of the asset for the loss in value of £8,000.

If you make a de-pooling election and you still own the plant in the fifth year the unrelieved expenditure is transferred to the pool.

If you purchase short life assets in large numbers and identification is either impossible or very difficult, but the asset's life is predictable, the inspector can agree to give you writing-down allowances on the expenditure. Examples of such expenditure might be the purchase of containers, linen, typewriters, technical instruments, amusement machines, calculators and tools.

Example
Mycroft New Trend Hotels Ltd buys linen for £12,000 and elects not to pool the expenditure. The inspector is satisfied that the linen has a life of three years. The allowances would then be as follows:

		Linen
		£
Year 1	Expenditure	12,000
	Writing-down allowance	3,000
		9,000
Year 2	Writing-down allowance	2,250
		6,750
Year 3	Balancing allowance	6,750

Any amount received on the disposal of the linen in year 3 would reduce the balancing allowance. When Mycroft buys linen in future years, each year's expenditure must also be kept separately and a de-pooling election made in respect of it.

Where it is possible but difficult to identify the items purchased, the inspector could agree to allow apportionment of the expenditure based on the quantity purchased.

Example

Barlow Hi-tech Products Ltd bought 100 technical instruments in 1989 for £20,000. In 1991 30 were sold for £675 and in 1992 35 were sold for £653. The capital allowances are as follows:

		£	Technical Instruments £	Capital Allowances £
1989	Expenditure – 100 units		20,000	
	Writing-down allowance		5,000	5,000
			15,000	
1990	Writing-down allowance		3,750	3,750
			11,250	
1991	Proceeds – 30 units	675		
	Unrelieved expenditure 30/100 × £11,250	3,375	3,375	
	Balancing allowance	2,700		2,700
			7,875	
	Writing-down allowance		1,969	1,969
1992	Brought forward		5,906	
	Proceeds – 35 units	653		
	Unrelieved expenditure 35/70 × £5,906	2,953	2,953	
	Balancing allowance	2,300		2,300
			2,953	
	Writing-down allowance		738	738
			2,215	

Plant in let buildings

Under property law, plant which is a fixture in a building belongs to the landlord. Examples are lifts, heating and ventilating plant. In some instances, tenants are required to pay the landlord a capital sum for the use of such plant. There are rules to determine who can claim capital allowances for fixtures. In all cases the person who claims the allowance must have incurred capital expenditure and must have an interest in the property.

Where more than one person meets these requirements the person with the most subordinate interest is given priority to claim. For example, if you are a landlord with an existing tenant and you spend £20,000 on fixtures and your tenant agrees to pay £20,000 for the use of them, it is your tenant who can claim allowances for the £20,000. If, on the grant of a lease, you are the lessee and pay an amount for fixtures you can obtain the capital allowances if you are not connected with the lessor and you make a joint election to that effect. Where you acquire an interest in property and pay a lump sum for fixtures, for which another person has claimed allowances, your claim will be restricted to the disposal value brought into account by the previous claimant which is usually their original expenditure.

Industrial buildings

In some cases you can obtain capital allowances for expenditure on the construction of industrial buildings and structures. The latter includes such items as loading platforms, roads, walkways, walls, embankments, bridges, toll roads, dams and culverts. Whether expenditure on the construction or improvement of a building qualifies for allowances depends on whether the trade carried on by the occupier qualifies. Specifically excluded are retail shops, showrooms, offices and dwelling-houses, although welfare buildings for employees qualify if the owner's trade qualifies and sports pavilions qualify whatever business is carried on.

If there is a non-qualifying part of a building, such as an office, you will get an allowance based on the total cost of the building if the expenditure on that part does not exceed one-quarter of the total cost. If it does exceed one-quarter, the industrial part of the building is treated as a separate building and the expenditure is apportioned and only the industrial part is eligible for allowances.

The annual allowance is 4 per cent of the cost of constructing or improving the building. The cost of the land is not eligible. You can claim the allowance if you have either carried out the construction or have purchased an unused building from a builder. There is no pooling of expenditure and on a disposal within 25 years balancing charges and allowances arise.

Example

Woolley and Archer Plastics Ltd makes up its accounts to 30 June. It bought a factory from a builder on 1 July 1989 for £140,000 and sells it for £170,000 on 3 July 1996. The allowances would be as follows:

	Factory £
Year to 30 June 1990	
Expenditure	140,000
Year to 30 June 1990–96	
Writing down allowances	
4% × £140,000 × 7 years	(39,200)
Unrelieved expenditure	100,800
Lower of proceeds or cost	(140,000)
Balancing charge	£(39,200)

The second or subsequent purchaser of an industrial building can also claim capital allowances. The allowance is calculated by reference to the vendor's unrelieved expenditure, increased by any balancing charge or reduced by a balancing allowance. In most cases the resulting figure is equal to the original cost of the building. This figure is divided by what remains of the period of 25 years which starts with the date the building was first used. In the above example the new owner could claim allowances of £7,778 a year (£140,000 over 18 years).

Hotels

Industrial buildings allowances are given if you incur expenditure on constructing or extending a qualifying hotel. In order to qualify your hotel must:

- be open for at least four months during the period from 1 April to 31 October;
- have at least ten letting bedrooms; and
- the sleeping accommodation must consist wholly or mainly of bedrooms for letting to the public which are normally not in the same occupation for more than one month; and
- the services provided normally include breakfast and an evening meal, the making of beds and the cleaning of rooms.

Buildings in enterprise zones

If you incur expenditure on the construction of a commercial building in an enterprise zone you can obtain a capital allowance in the first year equal to 100 per cent of that expenditure. Commercial buildings include retail shops, offices, hotels and industrial buildings. The cost of the land is not eligible for the allowance. Enterprise zones, which have a life of ten years, are areas in which the Government wishes to stimulate investment and economic activity and a list of these areas is to be found in Appendix 6. If you wish, you can disclaim part of the allowance in the first year. You are then entitled to a writing-down allowance of 25 per cent of cost in subsequent years. The rules regarding balancing allowances and charges, and writing-down allowances for purchasers of second-hand buildings in enterprise zones are the same as for industrial buildings.

Some of the earlier enterprise zones have now expired. If you buy an unused building after the zone has expired you are still entitled to the 100 per cent allowance. Furthermore, you will not be denied the allowance where buildings have been used for up to two years from first being brought into use.

Agricultural buildings

If you have a major interest in agricultural land and incur capital expenditure on buildings or works on that land for the purposes of husbandry or forestry, you are eligible for capital allowances. Buildings include barns, farm cottages and farmhouses but only one-third of the expenditure on farmhouses qualifies. There is no allowance for expenditure on land but works such as fencing, roads and drainage qualify for the allowance. Husbandry includes intensive rearing of livestock or fish to produce food for human consumption.

If you qualify you can obtain an annual writing-down allowance of 4 per cent of cost. When you dispose of your interest before 25 years have elapsed, the new owner normally takes over the annual allowance. This means that in the year of disposal each party only gets the allowance for part of the year. It is possible, however, to elect for a balancing allowance or charge to be made if you dispose of your interest or any buildings or works are destroyed.

Example

Dougal, who is a farmer, prepares his accounts to 31 December each year. On 1 October 1989 he built a barn at a cost of £30,000. He sold the barn to Bob on 1 July 1991 for £28,000. Bob also makes up his accounts to 31 December each year. Assuming no election is made the capital allowances would be as follows:

			Barn	Capital Allowances
		£	£	£
Dougal				
1990/91	Year to 31 December 1989			
	Expenditure		30,000	
	Writing-down allowances			
1990/91	4% × £30,000	1,200		
1991/92	4% × £30,000	1,200		
1992/93	4% × £30,000 × 6/12	600	3,000	3,000
	Unrelieved expenditure		27,000	
Bob				
1992/93	Year to 31 December 1991			
	Writing-down allowances			
	4% × £30,000 × 6/12	600		

Thereafter a writing-down allowance of £1,200 a year is given.

There would be the following changes to the capital allowances if Dougal and Bob had jointly elected for a balancing adjustment to be made. In 1992/93 Dougal would not have received a writing-down allowance of £600 but instead would have suffered a balancing charge of £400. Bob would be entitled to an annual writing-down allowance of £1,217 calculated by reference to Dougal's unrelieved expenditure of £27,600 increased to £28,000 by the balancing charge of £400. The £28,000 would be divided by 23, being the remainder of the 25-year writing-down period.

Whether or not an election is made, the overall effect is to give total net allowances of £30,000 over 25 years.

Patents and know-how

If you have been granted a licence to use a patent you will be able to get a deduction from your profits for the licence fees you pay. If, on the other hand, you purchase patent rights, capital allowances are available. The allowance is similar to that for plant. The expenditure is pooled in a special pool, an annual writing-down allowance of 25 per cent is applied to the reducing balance of expenditure and a balancing charge arises if disposal proceeds exceed the unrelieved expenditure. When the trade is permanently discontinued or when the patent rights come to an end, a balancing allowance equal to the remaining unrelieved expenditure is given.

An allowance, similar to that for patents, is usually available if you incur capital expenditure on acquiring know-how, for example secret industrial information. The exception to the rule is where you purchase know-how with a trade in which case it is treated as part of the goodwill acquired and no capital allowances are available.

Example

Barlow Hi-tech Products Ltd makes up its accounts to 31 July each year. On 5 May 1989 it purchased for £22,000 the world-wide patent rights to manufacture a gas regulator device. On 7 August 1991 it granted a licence to manufacture the product in America for £10,000. The capital allowances would be as follows:

	Patents £	Capital Allowances £
Year to 31 July 1989		
Expenditure	22,000	
Writing-down allowance	5,500	5,500
Year to 31 July 1990	16,500	
Writing-down allowance	4,125	4,125
Year to 31 July 1991	12,375	
Writing-down allowance	3,094	3,094
Year to 31 July 1992	9,281	
Proceeds	10,000	
Balancing charge	719	(719)
		12,000

If the disposal proceeds had been less than £9,281 the unrelieved expenditure would have been available for writing-down allowances in subsequent years. This is because only part of the patent rights have been disposed of.

Scientific research

If you incur capital expenditure on scientific research for your current or future trade you can claim an immediate capital allowance equal to 100 per cent of your expenditure. Scientific research means activities in the fields of natural or applied science for the extension of knowledge. The allowance is given on plant and buildings (but not land) that are used for scientific research.

Timing and use of allowances

Generally, capital allowances reduce the trading profits earned during the period in which you incurred the expenditure and during subsequent periods in which the asset is used. If you are a sole trader or a partner special rules apply during the opening and closing years of business and these are dealt with in Chapter 9. Where your capital allowances exceed trading profits, loss relief is available and further details can be found in Chapters 10 and 14.

No part of the writing-down allowance on industrial buildings may be disclaimed. Apart from this exception, it is possible to claim only part of the allowance or no allowance at all in a particular year. This allows you to claim the allowance at some time in the future when it is more useful to you. It is not possible, however, to claim two years' allowances in one year.

Nothings

Not all capital expenditure is eligible for capital allowances, for example, the cost of shops and offices. Business expenditure which qualifies neither for a revenue deduction nor for capital allowances is sometimes called a 'nothing' and, not surprisingly, is the cause of some dissatisfaction among businessmen and their advisers.

6 Rental Income

Introduction

If your business involves the receipt of income from UK land, such as rents, lease premiums, parking fees and fees for the display of advertisements, your profits from these activities will be taxed under the Schedule A rules. These are less generous than those that apply to your trading profits.

You are taxable on the rental profits to which you are entitled in the current tax year and the tax on those profits is payable on 1 January in that year. The previous year basis used to assess trading profits does not apply. However, because of the practical problems of assessing profits of a tax year that has not yet ended, a provisional assessment is raised based on the profit of the previous year and an adjustment is made when the final figures are known. If you tell the inspector before 1 January in the current year that last year's profits are not appropriate because, for example, you have sold a property, he will usually make an adjustment to last year's figures.

Example

Fred granted a tenancy on a property on 6 June 1992 and informed his local inspector that he expected to receive rent from letting property of £8,333 in 1992/93 and £10,000 in a full year. He estimated his allowable expenses for the current year would be £1,333 and £1,600 in a full year. In fact his allowable expenses for the two years were £2,100 and £3,000.

For the year 1992/93 he will receive a provisional assessment for £7,000, the tax being due on 1 January 1993. After he has submitted his tax return, he will receive a revised assessment for 1992/93 for £6,233 and a provisional assessment for 1993/94 for £8,400.

In order to prevent taxpayers from securing artificial advantages, legislation has been introduced whereby rent received in arrears after 9 March 1992, from a trader who is a 'connected person', is assessed on the basis of when it accrues instead of when it falls due.

Rental profits

Rental profits consist of rental income reduced by allowable expenses. The general principle is that you are taxable on rents, etc. that are due whether you receive them or not. There are two exceptions to this rule:

- Where you have not received payment but you have taken all reasonable steps to enforce payment. Although you would be expected to take proceedings against the tenant, you may be able to show that there is no point in going ahead because the tenant cannot be found or has no means to pay.

- Where you have waived the payment without receiving any other form of consideration from the tenant and your action was reasonable because of the tenant's hardship.

If you obtain a deduction under these rules and at any time later receive the outstanding amount, it will not be treated as income of the year in which it is received. Instead, an adjustment will be made to the assessment of the year to which it relates. If you receive such an amount you are required to let the Inland Revenue know within six months.

Allowable expenses

Having calculated the income that is due, you are allowed to make deductions for the following items in arriving at the assessable profit:

- *Maintenance and repairs*. This includes the expenditure you incur on redecorating inside and outside the premises; roof repairs; repairing and replacing garden fences, walls, paths and drives; and landlord's fixtures such as lavatory basins, sinks, taps, lighting, heating, water and drainage systems. More information on the difference between repairs and improvements is contained in the section on capital expenditure in Chapter 5.

- *Insurance*. Premiums for insuring the building and the landlord's fixtures are allowed and also for insuring against third party risks.

- *Management*. This includes any costs you incur in collecting rents; for periodic inspections to find out if tenants are complying with the terms of their leases; agent's costs for dealing with tenants' complaints; costs of granting, varying and surrendering leases; advertising for properties available for letting; and professional fees for the preparation and submission of accounts for tax purposes. It also includes legal fees in connection with the recovery of rents.

- *Services you provide*. You may, for example, pay wages for a porter, gardener or cleaner or incur costs on central heating or lighting of certain parts of the building.

- *Rates*. This would be both water rates and the uniform business rate if applicable. In general, the community charge is not allowable.

- *Rent payable to a superior landlord.*

- *Certain capital allowances.* You can claim allowances where you have incurred capital expenditure on plant that is let with the building. This includes boilers and pipes for central heating, air conditioning plant and lifts. However, no allowances are available for the provision of plant in a dwelling-house. Where plant relates to several dwellings, such as central heating in a block of flats, allowances are available because the plant is not specifically for one dwelling. You could also carry on a trade of leasing plant and receive leasing payments in addition to rent for the building. Capital allowances are also available for plant that is used for maintenance of your let properties, such as lawnmowers and floor polishers.

If you incur expenditure on constructing a building which you will let and it is either a commercial building in an enterprise zone, an industrial building, an agricultural building, a building used for scientific research or an hotel, you are able to claim capital allowances (see Chapter 5 for details).

Types of lease

Expenditure on maintenance and repairs is only allowed if it is 'incurred by reason of dilapidations attributable to a period falling within the currency of the lease'. To fully understand this phrase one needs to know how leases are classified. There are three types of lease:

- *Lease at a full rent.* A full rent is a rent which is sufficient, taking one year with another, to cover the lessor's costs of fulfilling his obligations under the lease and of meeting any expenses of maintenance, repairs, insurance and management which he must bear under the terms of the lease. For this purpose rent includes any part of a lease premium that is taxed as rent. A lease is therefore 'at a full rent' if it is likely, over the period of the lease, to produce a profit. It does not necessarily have to be a rack rent, i.e. the best market rent which can reasonably be obtained.

- *Tenant's repairing lease.* A tenant's repairing lease imposes on the tenant the responsibility of maintaining and repairing the whole or substantially the whole of the leased premises.

- *Lease not at full rent.* As its name suggests, this is a lease where the rent payable is unlikely to cover the lessor's costs.

To obtain a deduction for maintenance and repairs the dilapidations must have occurred since the landlord acquired the premises and during any of the following periods:

- *during the term of the present lease*; or
- *during previous leases*, provided they were, and the present lease is, at a full rent, whether or not tenant's repairing leases; or
- *during a period when the premises were not let* (a void period) which began either with the termination of a previous lease at full rent or with the acquisition of the premises by the landlord.

Example

On 1 May 1992 Tom entered into a 99-year lease of factory and warehouse premises. Unfortunately, the premises needed to be repaired before they could be let and this work was carried out during June and July. The premises were leased to Woolley and Archer Plastics Ltd on 1 August 1992 for an annual rental of £36,000 payable monthly in advance. The terms of the lease were that Tom should be responsible for repairs. Between 1 May 1992 and 5 April 1993 the following expenses were incurred:

	£
Initial repairs	12,000
Repairs of flood damage which occurred in July	1,000
Repairs from 1 August	3,000
Business rates from 1 August	2,000
Water rates from 1 August	600
Insurance (full year to 30 April 1993)	600
Management of property	4,000
Ground rent (full year to 30 April 1993)	6,000

The Schedule A assessment of rental profits for 1992/93 will be:

		£	£
Rent (9 months)			27,000
Less:	Repairs (£3,000 + £1,000)	4,000	
	Business rates	2,000	
	Water rates	600	
	Insurance	600	
	Management of property	4,000	
	Ground rent	6,000	
			17,200
			£9,800

The initial repairs relate to dilapidations which occurred prior to Tom's acquisition and were necessary to enable the premises to be let. The expenditure is therefore capital expenditure and not allowable. The period falling between 1 May and 1 August is a void period beginning with the acquisition of the premises by Tom. Therefore, the ground rent, insurance and repairs to flood damage relating to that period are allowable against rental income arising from the subsequent lease at full rent. Of course, the repairs would not be allowable if they were covered by insurance receipts.

If rental income in a tax year is insufficient to meet expenses the following reliefs are available:

- Taking each lease by itself there is an indefinite carry forward of the excess expenditure, although for a lease which is not at a full rent the carry forward is limited to the currency of that lease.
- For leases which are at full rent and are not tenant's repairing leases, the losses of current or earlier years can be offset against the profits from similar leases.
- Losses on full rent tenant's repairing leases can be offset against profits from leases at full rent which are not tenant's repairing leases.

A loss from renting property cannot be set against other income or profits such as interest received or trading profits; and it cannot be set against capital gains.

Example

Harry receives rents from four properties:

2 South Gardens which he rents to his aged aunt at £260 per annum.

Unit 371, Fairland Trading Estate which he rents to an engineering company for £12,000 per annum.

Great Oaks, a block of six residential flats where each tenant pays rent of £4,000 per annum.

47 High Road, Nethercrowe which is let as an office to a firm of solicitors for £8,500 per annum.

Harry is responsible for the repairs of the properties with the exception of Unit 371. He has received the following income and incurred the following expenditure:

	South Gardens (lease not at full rent)	Unit 371 (full rent, tenants repairing lease)	Great Oaks (full rent)	47 High Road (full rent)
	£	£	£	£
1990/91				
Rental income	260	12,000	24,000	8,500
Expenses	800	4,000	26,000	4,500
Profit (Loss)	(540)	8,000	(2,000)	4,000
1991/92				
Rental income	260	12,000	24,000	8,500
Expenses	660	7,000	23,000	10,000
Profit (Loss)	(400)	5,000	1,000	(1,500)
1992/93				
Rental income	260	12,000	24,000	8,500
Expenses	500	13,000	14,000	6,000
Profit (Loss)	(240)	(1,000)	10,000	2,500

The rental profits assessed would be as follows:

	(Notes)		£	£
1990/91	(1)	2 South Gardens		Nil
		Unit 371		8,000
		47 High Road	4,000	
	(2)	Great Oaks	(2,000)	2,000
				£10,000
1991/92	(1)	2 South Gardens		Nil
		Unit 371		5,000
		Great Oaks	1,000	
	(2)	47 High Road	(1,000)	Nil
				£5,000
1992/93	(1)	2 South Gardens		Nil
		Great Oaks	10,000	
		47 High Road	2,500	
			12,500	
	(3)	Unit 371	(1,000)	
	(2)	b/fwd 1991/92	(500)	11,000
				£11,000

Notes
1. For a lease which is not at a full rent any loss can only be carried forward against income from that same lease. There is therefore no relief for the South Gardens losses.
2. For leases which are at full rent and are not tenant's repairing leases, the losses of current or earlier years can be offset against the profits from similar leases.
3. Losses on full rent tenant's repairing leases can be offset against profits from leases at full rent which are not tenant's repairing leases.

Interest relief

Interest is not generally a deductible expense in arriving at rental profits. However, you will get relief for interest paid on a loan (without limit) to purchase or improve let property. Examples of improvements are set out in Appendix 7. The property must, in any period of 52 weeks during which the interest is payable, be let at a commercial rent for more than 26 weeks and when it is not being let it must be:

- available for letting at a commercial rent;
- your main residence; or
- unavailable because of construction or repair works.

The period of 52 weeks may fall wholly or partly within a tax year of assessment. The example below illustrates that the rules are sometimes difficult to comply with and it is possible to obtain no relief at all.

Example
On 10 March 1991 Terry used money borrowed from his uncle to buy an industrial property. Terry had plans to use the property for a new business venture but there were planning problems and on 16 September he advertised for a tenant at a commercial rent. The property was first let on 18 September 1991 and the tenant occupied the building until 16 February 1992. Repair work was then carried out and the property was re-let on 15 June 1992. Terry agreed to pay interest on his loan on 1 June, 1 September, 1 December and 1 March.

The interest payable on 1 June 1991 is not eligible for relief as the property is not let for a 26-week period in any 52-week period which includes 1 June 1991. The letting period 18 September 1991 to 16 February 1992 consists of only 22 weeks.

When the interest is due on 1 September 1991 there is a 26-week letting period in the 52 weeks ending 31 August 1992, but the condition is not met for the remaining 26 weeks as there is a period 1 to 18

September 1991 when the property is neither available for letting, nor undergoing construction or repair.

Terry could have obtained full relief on his interest if he had agreed with his uncle that no interest was payable before 1 December 1991.

Relief is given for interest paid by reducing the amount assessed for rental profits in the year in which it is paid. Where the interest paid exceeds the rental profits the excess cannot reduce other income. The excess is carried forward and reduces future rental profits so long as the property meets the conditions for the relief.

Furnished lettings

If you let furnished property the rules that apply are very similar to those for unfurnished property. But because the profit is normally assessed under Schedule D, Case VI, the offset of losses between furnished and unfurnished property is restricted. As explained earlier, unfurnished property is assessed under Schedule A. However, you can elect to divide the profit between the amount attributable to the use of the property and that which is for the use of the furniture. You have to make this election within two years of the end of the year of assessment to which it is to apply. Where you make the election the profit from the use of the furniture continues to be assessed under Case VI.

Example

In 1992/93 Peter received profits of £28,000 from renting a block of furnished flats of which £8,000 relates to use of the furniture. In the same year he made a loss of £13,000 letting a retail shop. All the properties are let at a full rent and Peter is responsible for the repairs.

Without an election Peter would receive an assessment for the furnished letting profits of £28,000. If he makes an election by 5 April 1995 for the part of his furnished letting profits which relates to renting the building to be separately assessed under Schedule A his assessments would be as follows:

		£
1992/93	Rental profits on flats (building only)	20,000
	Less: Loss on shop	13,000
	Schedule A assessment	£7,000
	Schedule D, Case VI	
	Rental profits on flats (furniture only)	£8,000

Rent a room

A new scheme of tax relief for people who let rooms in their homes has been introduced with effect from 1992/93. To qualify for this relief you can be either the owner or tenant of your only or main home, in which you let one or more rooms as furnished accommodation. Gross annual rents from such letting which do not exceed £3,250 are exempt from income tax altogether. If your gross annual rents exceed £3,250 you will be able to choose between:

- paying tax on the amount by which your gross rents exceed £3,250 without any separate tax relief for allowable expenses; or

- calculating your profit from letting (gross rents less actual expenses) and paying tax on that profit in the normal way.

Lease premiums

For tax purposes a distinction is made between short leases of 50 years or less and longer leases. If you grant a short lease at a premium, part of the amount is assessed as rental profits in the year you receive the premium. The amount is calculated by reducing the premium received by one-fiftieth of that amount for each complete period of 12 months during the period of the lease except the first one.

Example
Joe grants Paul a 21-year lease for which he receives a premium of £20,000.

	£
Premium received	20,000
Less: 1/50 × 20 years × £20,000	8,000
Assessed as rental profits	£12,000

Joe will also be treated as having received £8,000, the balance of the premium, as sale proceeds for the disposal of an interest in land for the purposes of capital gains tax. If he had granted a lease for a term exceeding 50 years the whole premium would have been treated as sale proceeds liable to capital gains tax. The above rules would not have applied if Joe had assigned an existing lease to Paul.

Paul can obtain relief for the rental element of the premium he pays but only against rents he receives or trading income. Assuming relief is due, Paul's relief would be calculated as follows:

$$\frac{\text{The part of the premium assessed on Joe}}{\text{Number of years of the lease}}$$

$\dfrac{£12,000}{21 \text{ years}} = \dfrac{£571}{\text{years.}}$ which will be treated as rent paid in each of the next 21 years.

Holiday lets

While income from furnished lettings is taxed as unearned income and assessed under Schedule D, Case VI, income from a boarding house, where services such as meals and cleaning are provided, is taxed as trading income. In 1982 and 1983 two borderline cases were brought to the courts and the taxpayers lost.

Following pressure from the tourist industry the law was changed in 1984 in respect of income from furnished holiday lettings. This income is now assessed under Case VI but enjoys the following tax benefits that are available to traders:

- Trading expenses are allowable including pre-trading expenses and capital allowances.
- It is 'net relevant earnings' for the purposes of tax relief on personal pension plans (see page 241).
- Loss relief is available against other income in the year of the loss and the following year as an alternative to carrying the loss forward.
- Income tax is payable by two instalments, on 1 January in the year of assessment and 1 July in the following year.
- Replacement of business assets relief.
- Retirement relief.

Qualifying lettings

To obtain the above tax benefits you must provide furnished holiday accommodation in the UK. 'Holiday accommodation' is not defined and therefore does not have to be at a holiday resort. The property does not have to be let during the holiday season but must, in a 12-month period:

- be available for letting for 140 days;
- be commercially let for 70 days; and
- not be let to any one person for more than 31 days during seven months of that period.

In a year when letting commences the 12-month period commences with the first day the property is actually let.

Example

Martha started advertising her cottage in Yorkshire in March 1992 as suitable for family holidays. Her records show:

		Days
4 April to 24 April	One holiday let	21
25 April to 9 May	Available but no lettings	15
10 May to 12 July	Nine holiday lets of one week	64
13 July to 20 September	Available but no lettings	70
21 to 30 September	One holiday let	10
1 to 31 October	Available but no lettings	31
		211

According to these records Martha meets the necessary conditions. In the remainder of the 12-month period Martha can leave the property empty, rent it to a tenant for more than 31 days, or use it herself.

If you have several properties normally qualifying as holiday accommodation, but in a 12-month period one particular property is not let for 70 days, you can claim to average the lettings for all your properties if this would produce an average of at least 70 days.

7   Capital Gains

Introduction

So far we have established what is meant by trading profits. If you purchase an asset with the intention of selling it at a profit, then, depending on whether you sell it for more or less than it cost, for tax purposes you have either made a trading profit or a trading loss. In this chapter we look at capital gains and capital losses.

Capital gains tax is payable on chargeable gains which arise on the disposal of assets other than trading stock. Individuals and trustees of settlements are chargeable if, for any part of the tax year, they are resident or ordinarily resident in the UK (see Chapter 3).

There are some persons who are specifically exempt from capital gains tax such as government agencies, charities, pension funds, registered trade unions, unit and investment trusts. Normally if a person is chargeable it does not matter if the asset being disposed of is outside the UK. The exception to this rule is where the individual is not UK domiciled, when gains are only taxed when remitted here.

Capital gains tax was introduced in 1965 to apply to gains arising after 5 April 1965. Where assets had been acquired before that date the gain was either apportioned on a time basis or the market value of the asset at 6 April 1965 was substituted for its cost.

In 1988 the Government announced a fundamental reform of the tax. Generally speaking, for disposals after 5 April 1988, only gains accruing since 31 March 1982 are charged to tax. However, in certain circumstances it is still necessary to refer to the old regime.

Rate of tax

For individuals, the first £5,800 of gains in 1992/93 is exempt from capital gains tax. This annual exemption used to be shared by married couples, but since 6 April 1990 each spouse has had their own.

Any excess over the annual exemption is charged at rates equivalent to the income tax rates that would apply if the amount of the excess was treated as additional income.

The annual exemption for trustees is £2,900 in 1992/93 while any excess gains are charged at 25 per cent, 35 per cent or 40 per cent, depending on the type of trust.

Chargeable gains made by UK resident companies are included with other profits and are subject to corporation tax at the same rate.

Chargeable assets

Most assets are chargeable although some are exempt. Chargeable assets include land and buildings, goodwill, plant, machinery, vehicles, shares, personal possessions and legal rights.

Exempt assets

The following assets are exempt:

- Private motor vehicles.
- Your main residence.
- Woodlands.
- Certain investments such as gilt-edged securities, national savings certificates, premium bonds, and qualifying corporate bonds.
- Decorations for valour, sterling currency, life assurance policies, betting winnings, personal and professional damages, and non-sterling bank accounts of individuals who are not UK domiciled.
- Wasting chattels.

In many cases the legislation has removed assets from the capital gains tax net because they are likely to cost the Revenue more in allowable losses than they would receive from chargeable gains.

Disposals

You have a disposal of an asset when:

- you sell or give it away;
- you receive a capital sum in respect of it;
- you dispose of part of it;
- it ceases to exist;
- you grant an interest in, or rights over it: for example, when you grant a lease.

If you are to plan your disposals so that they fall within a particular month or tax year it is important to know when a disposal occurs. In most cases the date of the disposal is the date of the contract, even if the asset is not transferred, conveyed or delivered until a later date. If, however, the contract is conditional or subject to an option, the disposal occurs when the condition is satisfied or the option is exercised. Where you receive compensation for damage to, or destruction of an asset, the time of the disposal is when you receive the compensation. It may therefore suit you to delay the receipt.

Most disposals are chargeable but there are some exceptions. When an individual dies there is no capital gains tax charge when the personal representatives take over the deceased's assets at market value. Assets transferred between husband and wife and between companies in a 75 per cent group (see page 228) are deemed to be transferred at such a value that no gain or loss arises.

Chattels

Chattels are items of property which are both tangible (touchable) and movable such as jewellery, pictures and antiques. Where chattels are also wasting assets, i.e. having a life of 50 years or less and do not qualify for capital allowances, gains from their disposal are exempt from capital gains tax and losses are not allowable. For chattels with a longer life there is an exemption where the consideration for the disposal does not exceed £6,000. Where the consideration just exceeds £6,000 marginal relief is available. This limits the chargeable gain to five-thirds of the excess of the disposal value over £6,000. There is a similar restriction in respect of allowable losses.

Other reliefs and exemptions

There are many reliefs available which can exempt, reduce or defer your gains. For example, gains arising from the disposal of business interests on retirement can be exempt (see page 248). Gains can be deferred in the following circumstances:

- When business assets are replaced (see page 67).

- When a business incorporates (see Chapter 12).

- When gifts of business and certain other assets are made (see page 252).

- When shares are sold to a qualifying ESOP, provided certain conditions are met (see Chapter 20).

Calculating the gain

Chargeable gains are calculated by reducing the consideration received from the disposal of the asset by certain allowable expenditure and an allowance for inflation known as the indexation allowance, which is explained later in this chapter.

In most cases the consideration received will be the sale proceeds but there are situations where a different amount, such as market value, will be used instead. The allowable expenditure is usually your acquisition cost, costs of improving the asset, and incidental costs of buying or selling the asset such as legal fees, estate agents' fees and stamp duty.

Example

Jack purchased a workshop in August 1982 to use in his plastic components business. The purchase price was £40,000 and Jack paid a further £3,000 in incidental costs relating to the acquisition. In July 1983 improvements were carried out at a cost of £15,000. The workshop was sold on 10 April 1992 for £107,000 and Jack incurred selling costs of £4,000.

	£	£
Sale proceeds		107,000
Less: Acquisition cost	40,000	
Incidental costs of acquisition	3,000	
Improvement cost	15,000	
Incidental costs of sale	4,000	62,000
Gain before indexation allowance		£45,000

Indexation allowance

Over the period that you own an asset the increase in its market value will partly reflect the rate of inflation. The indexation allowance was introduced in 1982, following a period of high inflation. The allowance only gave relief for the effect of inflation after March 1982 even though, until April 1988, gains accruing since 6 April 1965 were fully taxable.

Calculating the allowance

To calculate the allowance you need to know the increase in the Retail Prices Index (RPI), also known as the 'cost of living index'. There are monthly index numbers published by the Government about the middle of the following month which are reported in some newspapers and business magazines (see Appendix 8).

To calculate the increase in the RPI you need two index numbers:

RD   This is the RPI for the month of disposal.

RI   This is the later of:

- the RPI for March 1982; and

- the RPI for the month in which the asset was acquired or expenditure was incurred on improvements.

The increase is calculated as follows:

$$\frac{RD - RI}{RI}$$

and rounded to the nearest third decimal place.

The indexation allowance, which should be given automatically, is the RPI increase multiplied by the relevant expenditure on the acquisition or improvement of the asset.

Example

Continuing the previous example, part of the £45,000 gain is due to the effect of inflation on the expenditure of £43,000 from August 1982 when the RPI was 81.90 to April 1992 when it was 138.8. Part is due to the effect of inflation on the expenditure of £15,000 from July 1983 when the RPI was 85.30. The indexation allowance is calculated as follows:

Increase in RPI August 1982 to April 1992

$$\frac{138.8 - 81.90}{81.90} = 0.6947496$$

Increase in RPI July 1983 to April 1992

$$\frac{138.8 - 85.30}{85.30} = 0.6271981$$

	£	£
Gain before indexation allowance		45,000
Less: Indexation allowance		
RPI increase August 1982 to April 1992		
0.695 × £43,000	29,885	
RPI increase July 1983 to April 1992		
0.627 × £15,000	9,405	39,290
Chargeable gain		£5,710

It is important to keep proper records of when expenditure is incurred in order to calculate correctly the increase in the RPI and thus obtain the maximum indexation allowance. Expenditure on acquiring an asset is assumed to have been incurred when the asset was acquired or provided and other expenditure is assumed to have been incurred when it was due for payment. If your records only show when payment occurred you could be losing out.

Example
Eric bought a warehouse for the storage of antique furniture in March 1982 for £50,000 but the purchase price was not paid until April 1982. He sold the warehouse in May 1991 for £80,000. RPIs are March 1982 79.44; April 1982 81.04; May 1991 133.5.

The indexation allowance should be:

RPI increase March 1982 to May 1991
        0.681 × £50,000 = £34,050

If April was recorded as the month of acquisition the following indexation allowance would be calculated in error:

RPI increase April 1982 to May 1991
        0.647 × £50,000 = £32,350

This would result in an increase of chargeable gains of £1,700 resulting in the payment of additional tax.

Assets owned at 31 March 1982

Since 5 April 1988, if you dispose of an asset that you owned at 31 March 1982 the gain or loss is calculated assuming that the asset was sold on 31 March 1982 and immediately reacquired at its market value. The effect is that the costs you incurred before 31 March 1982 are replaced by the market value of the asset at that date. This is known as re-basing at March 1982.

Example
Paul started a hairdressing business in 1970, which he sold on 15 August 1991. The sale proceeds included £140,000 for the freehold property used as a salon and £60,000 for goodwill. He had purchased the property in August 1970 for £10,000. At 31 March 1982 the value of the property was £80,000 and the goodwill was worth £30,000. RPIs are March 1982 79.44 and August 1991 134.1.

	Property £	Goodwill £
Sale proceeds	140,000	60,000
Less: Deemed acquisition costs		
MV 31 March 1982	80,000	30,000

Unindexed gains	60,000	30,000
Less: Indexation allowance		
RPI increase March 1982 to August 1991		
0.688 × £80,000 and £30,000	55,040	20,640
Chargeable gains	£4,960	£9,360

However, unless you have elected for re-basing to apply to all your disposals (see below) it will also be necessary to compare the gain from re-basing with the gain as calculated using the old rules. The lower gain is then chargeable. In most cases, where assets have been growing steadily in value, re-basing will produce a lower chargeable gain. Losses are also computed using both methods and the lower loss is taken as the allowable loss.

When the two calculations produce a gain on the one hand and a loss on the other, you are treated as having incurred neither a gain nor a loss, as in the following example:

Example
Mr Sugden bought a farm in 1972 for £100,000 and sold it in May 1991 for £630,000. At 31 March 1982 it was valued at £500,000. RPIs are March 1982 79.44 and May 1991 133.5.

	£000	£000
Sale proceeds	630	630
Less: Cost	(100)	
MV 31 March 1982		(500)
Indexation allowance		
RPI increase March 1982 to May 1991		
0.681 × £500,000	(341)	(341)
Gain/(Loss)	£189	£(211)

Neither a gain nor a loss is deemed to have arisen and no tax is payable.

If you do not have acquisition details of assets or you do not want to keep records you can elect to calculate the gains and losses on all your assets using 31 March 1982 values only. The election should be made within two years of the end of the year of assessment (individuals) or accounting period (companies) in which you make the first disposal following the introduction of re-basing.

Part disposals

There will be times when you want to dispose of part of an asset, for example, sell 15 acres of a 40 acre site; or where you decide to create an interest in an asset, say you own a freehold and decide to grant a lease. In both cases, the original acquisition cost and subsequent improvement expenditure relates to both the part of the asset being disposed of and the part retained.

In calculating any gain or loss on the disposal a formula based on the market values of the two parts is used to apportion the costs. This is known as the A over A plus B formula, where A = sale proceeds of part sold, and B = market value of remainder.

Example

Wilton Investments Ltd purchased ten acres of land in April 1983 for £96,000. In February 1990 four acres were sold for £60,000 and the remaining six acres were valued at £120,000. These six acres are sold in June 1991 for £173,388. RPIs are April 1983 84.28; February 1990 120.2; June 1991 134.1.

February 1990 disposal
The following proportion of the acquisition cost is deductible:

$$\frac{\text{Sale proceeds of part sold}}{\text{Sale proceeds plus market value of remainder}}$$

$$\frac{£60,000}{£60,000 + £120,000} = 1/3$$

	£	£
Sale proceeds		60,000
Less: Acquisition cost 1/3 × £96,000	32,000	
Indexation allowance		
RPI increase April 1983 to February 1990		
0.426 × £32,000	13,632	45,632
Chargeable gain		£14,368

June 1991 disposal		
Sale proceeds		173,388
Less: Acquisition cost – balance	64,000	
Indexation allowance		
RPI increase April 1983 to June 1991		
0.591 × £64,000	37,824	101,824
Chargeable gain		£71,564

Leases

When a lease is granted from a freehold or a longer lease, there is a part disposal and the A over A plus B formula is used to apportion costs. If a short lease (with a term of 50 years or less) is granted at a premium, only part of that premium will be treated as consideration for the grant of the lease, the remainder will be treated as rent. For further details of how the consideration is apportioned see page 54.

For capital gains tax purposes a lease is a wasting asset if at the date of disposal it is a short lease. When calculating a gain or loss on the assignment of a short lease or the grant of a sub-lease, acquisition and improvement costs are reduced by reference to a table of depreciation rates. The costs are reduced by the following proportion:

$$\frac{\text{Depreciation rate for remaining term}}{\text{Depreciation rate at acquisition}}$$

If the lease was not a short lease when acquired the denominator is 100. If the lease was acquired before 31 March 1982, the acquisition date is deemed to be 31 March 1982 when calculating the relevant percentage. The depreciation rates are shown in Appendix 9.

Example

Blake was granted a 56 year lease in March 1980 for a premium of £77,800. In March 1992 he assigns the lease for £150,000. The market value of the lease at 31 March 1982 was £80,000. RPIs are March 1982 79.44; March 1992 136.7.

	£	£
Sale proceeds		150,000
Less: Acquisition cost		
£80,000 × $\frac{97.595 \ (44 \ \text{yrs})}{100 \ \ (50 \ \text{yrs}+)}$	78,076	
Indexation allowance		
RPI increase March 1982 to March 1992		
0.721 × £78,076	56,293	134,369
Chargeable gain		£15,631

By concession if certain conditions are met, no capital gains tax is payable where a lessee surrenders an existing lease and is granted a longer lease on the same property at a different rent.

Capital losses

A capital loss arises on a disposal where the allowable expenditure and the
indexation allowance exceed the consideration received. If you sell an
asset, on which you have claimed capital allowances, for less than cost, the
capital loss will be restricted. In the capital gains tax computation the
acquisition cost is reduced by the capital allowances given and not clawed
back. The loss is therefore equal to the indexation allowance.

Example

Alex purchased machinery for use in his garden centre business in May
1982 for £40,000 and sold it in April 1992 for £30,000. He had claimed
capital allowances on the machinery. RPIs are May 1982 81.62; April
1992 138.8.

	£	£
Sale proceeds		30,000
Less: Acquisition cost	40,000	
Less: Capital allowances given and not clawed back (40,000 − 30,000)	10,000	30,000
Unindexed gain		Nil
Less: Indexation allowance RPI increase May 1982 to April 1992 0.701 × £30,000		21,030
Allowable capital loss		£21,030

A disposal can arise if you have an asset which is destroyed. If no
compensation is received this will result in a capital loss. Furthermore, if
you can satisfy the inspector that an asset has become of negligible value
you can claim a capital loss.

Use of losses

Each person's chargeable gains and allowable losses in a tax year (or
accounting period for companies) are set against each other to arrive at a
net chargeable gain or loss.

Before 6 April 1990 the net gains and losses of a married couple were
aggregated unless one of them had a loss and elected for it not to be offset
against the gains of the other. Since 6 April 1990 losses and gains of
married couples are no longer aggregated.

If you have a net chargeable gain for the year this will be reduced by
any allowable losses brought forward from earlier years. However, brought
forward losses do not reduce current gains below the exemption limit.

Example

In 1992/93 Mrs Biffen has gains of £7,500 and losses brought forward of £6,000. Of the £6,000 losses, £1,700 will be set off, thus reducing her gains to £5,800 which is exempt. The remaining losses of £4,300 will be set off against any future gains.

The only occasion when a loss can be carried back is when it occurs in the year of death when it can offset gains of the previous three years. If you make a loss on a disposal to a connected person, for example a sale to your partner, your son or to another company under common control, the loss can only be offset against chargeable gains arising from further disposals to that person.

Trading losses

In certain cases individuals may be able to offset trading losses against their capital gains: see Chapter 10 for further details.

Replacement of business assets

In most cases if you realise a gain on the sale of a business asset and use the proceeds to buy another business asset you will be able to defer the gain until the replacement asset is sold. Provided the conditions are met, you could get the relief again when you sell the replacement asset and thus the gain could be deferred indefinitely. This relief is often referred to as roll-over relief. To obtain full relief, both the old and the new assets must be used for your trade and you must reinvest the sale proceeds during a period which commences one year before and ends three years after the disposal date. The business assets for which this relief is given are:

- Land and buildings occupied and used for the trade.
- Fixed plant and machinery.
- Ships, hovercraft, aircraft, satellites and spacecraft.
- Goodwill.
- Milk and potato quotas.

By concession, sale proceeds can be used to carry out improvements to existing assets and to acquire a further interest in an existing business asset. For example, if you have a leasehold interest in a property you could buy the freehold reversion. It is not possible to obtain roll-over relief on movable machinery such as combine harvesters or earthmoving equipment. There is, however, a less generous version of the roll-over relief available for depreciating assets which is considered below.

The rolled-over or deferred gain is carried forward by reducing the acquisition cost of the replacement asset or assets.

Example

In May 1985 Alexis Designer Productions Ltd sold a warehouse for £200,000, which it had purchased in April 1982 for £150,000. In August 1985 the company purchased offices at a cost of £210,000. Both assets were used in the trade and a claim was made to roll-over the gain. The offices were sold in April 1992 for £350,000. RPIs are April 1982 81.04; May 1985 95.21; August 1985 95.49; April 1992 138.8.

Sale of warehouse	£	£
Sale proceeds		200,000
Less: Acquisition cost	150,000	
Indexation allowance		
RPI increase April 1982 to May 1985		
0.175 × £150,000	26,250	176,250
Chargeable gain – rolled-over		£23,750

Sale of offices	£	£
Sale proceeds		350,000
Less: Acquisition cost	210,000	
Less: Rolled-over gain	23,750	
	186,250	
Indexation allowance		
RPI increase August 1985 to April 1992		
0.454 × £186,250	84,558	270,808
Chargeable gain		£79,192

There are some occasions when a roll-over relief claim is not appropriate. For example, where capital losses are available to offset the gain or, in the case of individuals, where the gain is covered by retirement relief or the annual exemption. If the gain is rolled-over it has the effect of reducing the indexation allowance on the disposal of replacement assets. In the above example, the allowance would have been £95,340 (0.454 × £210,000) if the gain had not been rolled-over.

If only part of the sale proceeds is used to purchase replacement assets, the amount of the chargeable gain that can be rolled-over is reduced by the amount not reinvested. If, in the above example, only £190,000 had been reinvested the chargeable gain rolled-over would have been restricted to £13,750 and £10,000 would have been a chargeable gain in that year. If only £170,000 had been reinvested, the amount not reinvested of £30,000 would have exceeded the chargeable gain of £23,750 and no part of the gain could have been rolled-over.

Assets used partly for the trade
If during your period of ownership only a part of the asset was used for the trade, or the whole asset was used for the trade for part of the time, it will be necessary to agree an apportionment of the gain with the inspector.

Depreciation assets
If you use the sale proceeds to purchase one or more depreciating assets the gain can be held over until the earliest of the following events:

- the depreciating asset is sold;
- it ceases to be used in your trade;
- ten years from the replacement date.

A depreciating asset is one which has, an estimated useful life of 60 years or less.

Example
Phil Archer & Co. sold a piece of land in March 1990 for £30,000 which had been bought in June 1982 for £12,000. In July 1991 fixed plant was purchased for £35,000 which had an estimated useful life of 15 years. Both assets were used for the trade. RPIs are June 1982 81.85; March 1990 121.4.

	£	£
Sale proceeds		30,000
Less: Acquisition cost	12,000	
Indexation allowance		
RPI increase June 1982 to March 1990		
0.483 × £12,000	5,796	17,796
Chargeable gain – held over		£12,204

During the period that the gain on the first asset is being held over, you might purchase a non-depreciating asset. Assuming the conditions are met, you can then claim that this third asset is the replacement for the first in order to obtain roll-over relief.

Gains deferred 1982/88
Where roll-over has been claimed between 1 April 1982 and 5 April 1988 and all or part of the deferred gain has accrued before 1 April 1982, the

deferred gain will be halved. When introducing this relief, the Government admitted that it 'involved a degree of rough justice' but this was the price to be paid for simplicity.

Example
Dennis bought a pub in 1974 for £80,000 which he sold in January 1983 for £145,000. He purchased a wine bar for £148,000 in February 1983 and claimed roll-over relief. Dennis sold the wine bar in August 1991 for £270,000. RPIs are March 1982 79.44; January 1983 82.61; February 1983 82.97; August 1991 134.1.

Sale of pub	£	£
Sale proceeds		145,000
Less: Acquisition cost	80,000	
Indexation allowance		
RPI increase March 1982 to January 1983		
0.040 × £80,000	3,200	83,200
Chargeable gain – rolled-over		£61,800

Sale of wine bar	£	£
Sale proceeds		270,000
Less: Acquisition cost	148,000	
Less: 50% of rolled-over gain	30,900	
	117,100	
Indexation allowance		
RPI increase February 1983 to August 1991		
0.616 × £117,100	72,134	189,234
Chargeable gain		£80,766

Payment of capital gains tax

Whether you are in business, on your own, or are in partnership you must give details of any disposals of business or private chargeable assets on your tax return. The only exception to this requirement is where your chargeable gains do not exceed the annual exemption and the aggregate consideration for all your disposals does not exceed twice this exemption. You should, however, make a statement on your tax return to this effect. Also it is in your interest to disclose allowable net losses whatever their size as they can be set against future gains.

For individuals and trustees capital gains tax is payable by 1 December following the end of the tax year or 30 days after the inspector raises the assessment, if this is later. If the consideration for an asset is payable by instalments more than 18 months after the disposal you can ask to pay the tax by instalments. This is likely to be allowed if the total tax payable is more than 50 per cent of the first or later instalments.

8 Value Added Tax

Introduction

VAT is an indirect tax on supplies of goods and services and on certain importations. It is collected by VAT-registered businesses at each stage of production and distribution. The burden falls on individuals and businesses with no entitlement to claim a refund or credit for VAT incurred by them. Customs and Excise (not the Inland Revenue) are responsible for the administration of the tax.

A VAT-registered business is entitled to a refund or credit of most of the VAT incurred on expenditure which it uses in making taxable supplies – that is to say, supplies taxable at either the standard rate (17.5 per cent from 1 April 1991) or the zero rate.

Sales are called outputs (goods and services 'out' of the business). VAT charged on sales is output tax. Purchases are called inputs (goods and services 'into' the business). VAT incurred on purchases is input tax. The difference between output tax and input tax is normally paid (or claimed) from Customs and Excise on a quarterly or monthly basis.

Some supplies of goods and services are taxed at the standard or zero rates. Some supplies are exempt. Some fall outside the scope of VAT altogether. For example, non-business supplies by charities fall outside the scope of VAT. In certain circumstances, the transfer of the assets of a business as a going concern fall outside the scope of VAT.

Although no VAT is charged on zero-rate and exempt supplies, the difference between them is important. Zero-rating gives the supplier an entitlement to input tax credit; exemption normally does not.

Zero-rate supplies include:

- Most food (but *not* catering which includes meals in restaurants, and hot take-away food and drink).
- Books and newspapers.
- Sales, long leases and construction of new housing and some other new buildings.
- Young children's clothing and footwear.
- Exports of goods.

- Dispensing of prescriptions and the supply of many aids for handicapped persons.
- Mobile homes and houseboats.

Exempt supplies include:

- Most sales, leases and lettings of land and buildings (but *not* lettings of garages, parking spaces or hotel and holiday accommodation).
- Insurance.
- Betting, gaming and lotteries (*not* gaming machine takings, admission to premises, club subscriptions and certain participation charges).
- Most services supplied by financial institutions.
- Stockbrokers services.
- Certain education and training.
- Services of doctors, dentists, opticians, etc. (but some practitioners are *not* exempt, e.g. osteopaths).
- Certain supplies by undertakers.
- Membership benefits provided by trade unions and professional bodies.
- One-off fund-raising events by charities and other qualifying bodies.
- Entry to certain sports competitions.

Most of the items listed in the zero-rated and exempt categories above are subject to exceptions, so you will need to look for further detail if these affect your business. For example, many exempt services such as insurance and finance are zero-rated when supplied to persons belonging outside the European Community.

The VAT implications of buying and leasing business cars and the payment of motoring expenses are considered in Chapter 19.

Land and buildings

Not all land transactions are exempt. Freehold sales of 'new' buildings (excluding those designed as dwellings or certified for use for a relevant residential or charitable purpose) are taxable at 17.5 per cent. 'New', broadly speaking, means less than three years old. Surrenders of leases or other interests in land are also taxable at 17.5 per cent. If you sell or let non-domestic buildings and land, you can elect to charge VAT at 17.5 per cent on supplies that would otherwise be exempt and thereby recover VAT on your costs. You are allowed to elect to charge VAT on one building but not on another, but once made the election will apply to all subsequent sales, lettings or services to existing and future tenants of that building.

You must notify Customs and Excise within 30 days of making the election unless the value of your rental income is less than £20,000 per year. You will find out more about this in the VAT Notices 'Property Development' (742A) and 'Property Ownership' (742B).

Registration

If you are about to start in business you will need to decide whether to register for VAT. In order to make this decision you should ask at your local VAT office for a copy of the booklet 'Should I be registered for VAT?' (700/1/91) and an application form (VAT 1).

If your business only makes supplies that are exempt you cannot register for VAT and therefore cannot recover any VAT on goods and services that you buy for the business. This will be the case if, for example, you are in business renting out properties which you have not constructed, and which you have not opted to tax.

If you make taxable supplies, that is supplies that are standard-rated or zero-rated, you must register at the end of any month if the value of your supplies in the last 12 months has exceeded the annual limit, or at any time, if there are reasonable grounds for believing that the value of your outputs in the next 30 days will exceed this limit. From 11 March 1992 the annual limit is £36,600. You should start charging your customers VAT and keep VAT records as soon as you know you are required to register. But you must not show VAT as a separate item on any invoice until you know your registration number. If in your business you make both taxable and exempt supplies special 'partial exemption' rules apply and these are dealt with below.

Having decided that you need to register, you have to complete a form VAT 1. You must send this to Customs and Excise within 30 days of the date you were required to be registered. If, having returned the VAT 1, you do not get a reply within a couple of weeks, telephone the local VAT office. Speak to the New Registrations section and get the name and extension of the person who is, or will be dealing with the matter.

Should you wish to register a group of companies you should first read the VAT Leaflet 700/3/91 entitled 'Registration for VAT – Corporate Bodies Organised in Divisions'.

VAT returns

Every three months you will receive a VAT return (form VAT 100). The return covers a tax period which ends on a fixed date. Your first return starts with the date of registration and therefore may not be for three months. If you make zero-rated supplies or anticipate having large VAT refunds you should ask to complete your returns on a monthly basis as this will improve your cash flow.

If you are a small business and your taxable (standard rate and zero rate) turnover is below £300,000, you may be eligible to join the Annual Accounting Scheme and/or the Cash Accounting Scheme.

If your annual VAT payments to Customs and Excise exceed £2 million you will normally be required to make payments on account for each of the first two months of every quarter.

Accounting systems

When setting up your system ensure that your records are sufficiently detailed to make the completion of the return as easy as possible. Incidentally, you are not required to attach documents to the return but you must be able to produce them when a VAT officer visits your premises. Customs have the power to require you to keep records and documents for a maximum of six years from the end of your accounting period. You will normally be required to issue a tax invoice when making standard-rated supplies to another VAT-registered business.

Normally, tax invoices for VAT purposes must include the following information:

- A number which identifies the invoice.
- The date of supply.
- Your business name, address and VAT registration number.
- The name and address of the person to whom the goods or services are supplied.
- The type of supply, e.g. sale, hire-purchase, hire, lease, rental.
- A description which identifies the goods or services supplied.
- For each item, the quantity of goods or extent of the services, the rate of tax and the amount payable, excluding tax, expressed in sterling.
- The total amount payable, excluding tax, expressed in sterling.
- The rate of any cash discount offered.
- The amount of tax chargeable at each rate, with the rate to which it relates, expressed in sterling.
- The total amount of tax chargeable, expressed in sterling.

Where the value of your supply is £100 or less you may issue a less detailed invoice.

Retail schemes

Most retailers selling for cash do not issue tax invoices. Special schemes have therefore been designed for retailers to calculate the VAT due on their sales. If you are a retailer ask your local VAT office for details of these special schemes.

Cash accounting

All business with taxable turnover below £300,000 per annum have the option of accounting for VAT on the basis of cash paid and received. If you want to use the scheme you have to apply to your local VAT office and, once approved, you must remain in the scheme for at least two years. As a result you will not have to pay output tax until your customer pays you. This gives you a cash flow benefit where customers are late payers and results in automatic bad debt relief.

Reclaiming VAT

If you are making taxable supplies, the input tax you have paid on any purchases of goods or services for your business should be reclaimable subject to various exceptions. You cannot reclaim VAT on the cost of:

- entertaining;
- purchasing a car; or
- non-business expenditure.

If you incur expenditure which is partly for business and partly for private use, for example, personal telephone calls, the VAT paid must be apportioned. Periodically you will be visited by a VAT officer who will make a point of looking to see if you have reclaimed any of these items.

The VAT you pay on imported goods can be reclaimed if the goods are for resale or are to be used in your business.

Input tax on the purchase of goods and services incurred before you were registered is normally reclaimable on the first VAT return subject to certain conditions.

Bad debt relief

You can recover VAT that you have paid to Customs on goods and service supplies to a customer who was unable to pay for them, if you meet the following conditions:

- the supply concerned must have been made after 1 April 1989;

- the value of the supply must not have exceeded its open-market value;
- ownership, in the case of a supply of goods, must have passed to your customer;
- at least one year must have elapsed since the date of the supply;
- an entry must have been made in a special 'refunds for bad debts' account;
- no claim must have been made under the old (insolvency) bad debt relief scheme;
- you hold a copy tax invoice for the supply in question.

Relief cannot be claimed where you have a right of set-off or enforceable security in relation to the debt. Full or partial recovery of the debt will require you to repay all or part of the relief claimed.

This scheme replaced a scheme covering insolvent customers. The two schemes overlap for supplies made from 1 April 1989 to 25 July 1990 (inclusive). Either (but not both) schemes can be used to claim relief on such supplies. For supplies made before 1 April 1989, only the old scheme can be used.

Partial exemption

There is a complication that needs to be dealt with if you are partly exempt, i.e. you make both taxable (including zero-rated) and exempt supplies. Part of your input tax is not deductible because of the principle that you can only claim credit for input tax that relates to taxable as opposed to exempt supplies. If, however, input tax on exempt supplies is de minimis, it can be deducted. The de minimis limits are explained below. You start to disallow input tax as soon as you incur expenditure which relates to an exempt supply, even if the supply will not take place for some years. The input restriction in a VAT quarterly return is provisional and is subject to adjustment.

The usual method for arriving at the amount of input tax that can be deducted is as follows:

- Determine the amount of input tax directly attributable to taxable supplies and supplies that are exempt or outside the scope of VAT. This is not as easy as it sounds and you may need to spend time analysing the VAT incurred on expenditure.

  The input tax attributable to taxable supplies can be claimed in full. The input tax attributable to exempt supplies or to non-business activities cannot normally be claimed unless it is de minimis.

  There are certain exempt supplies that can be ignored, for example deposit interest, insurance commission or hire-purchase commission, provided you are not in business carrying on financial activities. In effect, any input tax which relates to these items is treated as relating to taxable supplies.

- The input tax on the remaining items of expenditure (overheads) must then be apportioned. The items that remain might include your accountant's fees or equipment such as a photocopier used in connection with all your supplies. You can work out the claimable proportion of overhead VAT by using the ratio of standard rate and zero rate turnover to total turnover.

Example	**£**
Input tax directly attributed to taxable supplies	10,000
Input tax directly attributed to exempt supplies	5,000
Remaining input tax (VAT on overheads)	3,000
Taxable turnover	70,000
Exempt turnover	35,000
Total turnover	105,000

$$\text{Deductible input tax} = £10,000 + \left(3,000 \times \frac{70,000}{105,000}\right) = \quad 12,000$$

When you use this 'standard' method you must exclude from turnover:

(a) supplies of capital goods you have used for the purposes of your business;

(b) incidental real estate transactions;

(c) incidental financial transactions;

(d) self supplies.

If you do not want to use the 'standard' method you can apply to your local VAT office for approval to use a special method. For example, the ratio of directly attributable input tax might produce a fairer claimable proportion of overhead VAT.

- Only when you have carried out the analysis and apportionment described above are you in a position to know whether your exempt input tax is above or below the de minimis limits. If your exempt input tax in any period, excluding input tax on the supplies you are allowed to ignore, is less than £600 a month on average, then you are treated as fully taxable and can recover your input tax in the normal way.

- *Capital Goods Scheme*. On 1 April 1990, a special scheme was introduced for the adjustment of input tax on the purchase of computers and computer equipment of a tax exclusive value of £50,000 or more and land and buildings of a tax exclusive value of £250,000 or more. The scheme applies to capital items purchased on or after 1 April 1990 and affects only those businesses which are partly exempt. The scheme provides for input tax on the items to be adjusted over five years for computers and computer equipment and over ten years for land and buildings.

You can obtain a free booklet, VAT Notice 706, from your local VAT office entitled 'Partial Exemption' and a leaflet explaining the capital goods scheme.

Transfer of a business as a going concern

If you are buying or selling a business there will be a lot of money involved and it is important to establish whether VAT is to be charged. The general rule is that no VAT is chargeable or claimable if:

- the business is transferred as a going concern;
- the new owner uses the assets to carry on the same kind of business; and
- the new owner is either registered for VAT already or will register as a result of the transfer.

The first two requirements are modified to include the situation where only part of a business is transferred provided it is capable of being operated as a separate business. There are special requirements for the transfer of land and buildings which the transferor has opted to tax. In all other cases the transfer of chargeable assets is taxable at the standard rate.

Where a business is transferred as a going concern to a group which is, or will during the next tax year become, partly exempt, the transaction will be treated as a supply to and a supply by the group. This means the group has to account for output tax in full on the assets, and will then recover input tax to the extent that the assets are used to make taxable supplies.

Penalties and enforcement powers

A failure to comply with VAT law or regulations can result in penalties or default interest. Penalties can be imposed for:

- late registration;
- late submission or payment of VAT returns;

- serious misdeclaration;
- persistent misdeclaration;
- tax evasion;
- failure to keep or produce VAT records;
- unauthorised issue of tax invoices;
- breaches of most of the other requirements under VAT law.

Penalties and interest will be notified by assessment or letter and are recoverable from you as if they were VAT. You cannot offset any of these penalties or default interest against your direct tax liability (e.g. income tax).

Customs will pay interest on VAT overpayment resulting from their error. This interest is assessable to income tax.

Late registration
A person who:

(a) fails to register; or

(b) when exempted from registration fails to notify a liability to be registered

is liable to a penalty equal to the greater of £50 and a percentage of the net tax due, depending upon the delay:

(a) up to 9 months, 10 per cent;

(b) over 9 months but up to 18 months, 20 per cent;

(c) more than 18 months, 30 per cent.

Default surcharge
If you are late in submitting or paying two VAT returns in any 12-month period, you will be issued with a 'Surcharge Liability Notice' (SLN) warning you that a further default in the next 12 months will render you liable to a default surcharge.

For example, if you were late in submitting your return for the quarters ending June and December 1990, you would be issued with an SLN making you liable to a surcharge if late with any of your 1991 returns. The surcharge is 5 per cent of the tax due on the late return, or £30 if greater. The surcharge then increases in 5 per cent steps for subsequent defaults to a maximum of 20 per cent.

Serious misdeclaration penalty (SMP)
A person who:

(a) underdeclares the amount of VAT due on a return;

(b) claims a repayment to which he is not entitled;

(c) fails to draw an under-assessment to the attention of Customs and Excise within 30 days

makes a misdeclaration. A misdeclaration is serious if it:

(a) equals or exceeds 30 per cent of the VAT actually due; or

(b) equals or exceeds both 5 per cent of the VAT due and £10,000.

A serious misdeclaration on returns for VAT periods beginning on or after 1 April 1990 will incur a penalty of 15 per cent of the misdeclaration. (For assessments issued before 20 March 1991, the rate of penalty was 30 per cent.)

Persistent misdeclarations penalty (PMP)
Where a person makes misdeclarations on two or more VAT returns with a two-year period, and the misdeclarations exceed either £100 or 1 per cent of the VAT due for the period (whichever is greater), he may be sent a 'Penalty Liability Notice' warning him that a penalty may be imposed if a similar misdeclaration is made in the next two years.

The penalty is 15 per cent of the amount misdeclared. Any errors which incur an SMP are not liable to PMP.

Regulatory offences
A person who fails:

(a) to notify Customs that he or she has ceased making taxable supplies;

(b) to furnish Customs with information or documents;

(c) to keep appropriate records; or

(d) to comply with any of the VAT rules and regulations

is liable to a daily penalty as follows:

(a) £5 per day for the first failure;

(b) £10 per day for the second failure occurring within two years of the first;

(c) £15 per day for a third or subsequent failure occurring within two years of the first

subject to a maximum of 100 days, a minimum of £50 and a written warning in the two years preceding the assessment. Failure to preserve records for six years can incur a penalty of £500.

There is a reserve penalty for use where the default surcharge (see above) proves to be inappropriate or ineffective. Failure to furnish a return or pay VAT by the due date can incur a penalty of the greater of:

(a) the daily penalty mentioned above; and

(b) an amount equal to one-sixth, one-third or one-half of 1 per cent of the tax due.

Reasonable excuse

Any of the above penalties may be withdrawn if you can satisfy Customs and Excise, or a VAT tribunal, that you have a 'reasonable excuse'. If your local VAT office rejects your excuse you can still appeal to the VAT tribunal.

Whether an excuse is accepted as reasonable will depend on the individual merits of each case. It is not enough to claim that you cannot afford to pay the tax due, or that an employee or someone working for you failed to perform a task on your behalf.

Default interest

Where a person:

(a) underdeclares or overclaims VAT on a return;

(b) pays an assessment which is later found to be too low;

(c) voluntarily discloses an underdeclaration or overclaim made on previous returns.

he will be charged default interest. This is not a penalty; it is commercial restitution to compensate the Exchequer for not having received the VAT when it was due. Interest is calculated from the date the VAT falls due to the date of the assessment. For repayment claims, interest runs from seven days after the date Customs and Excise authorise the repayment. If the interest assessment is not paid within 30 days, the interest 'clock' is restarted from the beginning of the 30-day period. You cannot deduct default interest when calculating your direct tax liabilities.

Tax evasion

Most cases of VAT evasion are dealt with under the civil penalty provisions but, for aggravated or serious offences, the matter can be investigated for criminal proceedings. For example, criminal proceedings will normally be taken where the VAT evaded is at least £75,000 in total over the last three years, or there is a conspiracy to evade VAT by people not within the same legal entity.

If you are found to have dishonestly evaded VAT and criminal proceedings are not taken, you may be liable to a penalty equal to the amount of VAT evaded. However, Customs and Excise may reduce this by up to 50 per cent to take account of the extent to which you co-operate with them in their investigations.

Other enforcement powers

You should also be aware that Customs have other legal powers of enforcement, for example:

- to assess tax due when returns are not made or are incomplete or incorrect;
- to require production of evidence in support of input tax credit or repayment;
- to enter business premises at a reasonable time and inspect the premises and goods found there;
- to take samples of goods;
- to have access to and inspect and check the working of a computer which is used to produce tax records and tax invoices;
- with the authority of a Magistrate's warrant to enter and search premises.

9 Basis of Taxing Trading Profits

Preceding year basis

Income tax is normally assessed for a year ending on 5 April. However, if you are in business and make up yearly accounts to another date, then the profits shown by your accounts are taxed as if they were profits for a year ending on 5 April in the following tax year. This is known as assessing profits on the preceding year basis. There are special rules for taxing your profits in the first three years and last three years of business which are considered below.

Whatever your accounting date, income tax and Class 4 National Insurance contributions on your trading profits are payable in two instalments, the first on 1 January in the tax year in which your profits are assessed and the second on the following 1 July. This rule positively encourages taxpayers to improve their cash flow by having an accounting date just after 5 April which is why many businesses have a 30 April year end.

Example

Sidney, who has been running a boarding house for many years, makes up his accounts to 31 October each year. His accounts for the year to 31 October 1991 show a taxable profit of £25,000. This will be treated as his trading profits for the tax year 1992/93, i.e. the year ended 5 April 1993. The tax and Class 4 contributions on these profits are payable in two equal amounts on 1 January 1993 and 1 July 1993.

The Revenue have issued a consultative document proposing changes to the taxation of the self-employed. The intention is to devise a system which will:

- make it simpler and more efficient to administer;
- cut down on work and correspondence;
- open up the way for further reform.

If a new system is introduced, it is likely to replace the preceding year basis with some form of actual or current year basis.

Class 2 and Class 4 National Insurance contributions

If you are over 16 but under retirement age and self-employed you are normally liable to pay Class 2 National Insurance (NI) contributions and if your profits are above a certain level, Class 4 contributions.

The Class 2 contribution is a flat rate per week unless your earnings are less than the exception limit set each year. In 1992/93 the flat rate is £5.35 and the exception limit is £3,030. This contribution entitles you to certain social security benefits such as the basic sickness and invalidity benefits and the basic retirement pension. It does not entitle you to unemployment benefit or the additional earnings-related pension.

The contribution is payable every week including holiday periods and you can be prosecuted for failing to pay your contributions. You can arrange to pay your contribution by:

- direct debit; or by
- stamping a contribution card.

If your profit or gains from self-employment are over a certain limit set each year you are normally liable to pay Class 4 contributions. The lower limit in 1992/93 is £6,120. The contribution is expressed as a percentage of your profits up to a maximum level of profits. For 1992/93 the percentage is 6.3 per cent and the maximum profit level is £21,060. Profits for this purpose are calculated as follows:

- Profits or gains chargeable to income tax.
- Capital allowances arising from the business are deducted and balancing charges added.
- Losses can be deducted provided the loss arises from activities that would be Class 4 earnings.
- There are no deductions for contributions to personal pension plans or for personal reliefs.

If you work as an employee as well as being self-employed you may be liable to pay Class 1, 2 and 4 contributions but there is an upper limit and any excess will be refunded to you. If you expect to be employed and self-employed in a tax year you can contact the DSS before the start of the tax year and ask to postpone payment of Class 2 and Class 4 contributions until the end of the year when your liability will be known.

Class 4 contributions are normally assessed and collected by the Revenue with your income tax on business profits. Half of the final settled amount is tax deductible.

Example

In the previous example, Sidney had assessable profits in 1992/93 of £25,000. His Class 4 contribution for that year would be £941.22 being 6.3 per cent of £14,940, the upper profit limit £21,060 less the lower limit of £6,120. Half of this, i.e. £471, will reduce the profits of £25,000 for the purpose of calculating the income tax payable.

First three years

Before you can start to calculate what business profits will be assessed in the opening years of a business it is necessary to establish the date on which your business started. This is generally the date when you were in a position to offer your goods or services to your potential customers. This is important because the figure for your first 12 months' profits will be used to calculate the tax payable in the first three tax years.

The rules for assessing profits in the opening years are as follows:

- The profits assessed in the first tax year are the profits from the date the business started to the following 5 April. The figure is usually calculated by taking a proportion of the profits of the first accounting period.

- In the second tax year the profits of the first 12 months are assessed.

- The profits assessed in the third tax year are the profits of a 12-month accounting period which ended in the second tax year. If no such accounts have been made up, the first 12 months' profits are usually assessed again. There is an alternative basis for assessing the profits of the second and third year which is explained below.

- In the fourth and subsequent years the profits are assessed on the preceding year basis.

These rules are modified where a new business starts because there is a change in the members of a partnership: details are given in Chapter 11.

For individuals who are unemployed but wish to start a business, an Enterprise Allowance is available to supplement their income during the first year of business (see Chapter 1). The payment is assessed in the year of receipt under Schedule D, Case VI.

Example

Magda started her outside catering business on 6 June 1991 and by 5 June 1992 had a taxable profit of £12,000. Her profits would be assessed as follows:

Tax year	Profit period	Profits assessed to tax
1991/92	6 June 1991 to 5 April 1992	10/12 × £12,000 = £10,000
1992/93	6 June 1991 to 5 June 1992	£12,000
1993/94	12 month period ending in 1992/93	£12,000

Because the profits for the first 12 months will be assessed at least twice, every effort should be made to keep the figure as low as possible. The way to calculate the amount of profit that is taxable is described in Chapter 4. Consider the following ways of keeping your profits to a minimum or even creating a tax loss:

- The hire of machinery and vehicles initially as the rent reduces taxable profits.

- Borrow money to use in the business as the interest is an allowable deduction.

- Delay making employees into full equity partners, as until they are partners, their salaries reduce taxable profits.

- Bring your spouse into the business as an employee and obtain a deduction for the salary paid.

Electing for actual profits

In the second and third tax years the taxpayer can elect to be assessed on the actual profits earned between 6 April and 5 April. You would only make such an election if your profits in the second and third years fell below those of the first 12 months. If an election is made both years will be assessed on an actual basis. It is not possible to elect for one year but not the other.

Example

Barry started in business selling records on 1 August 1991 and prepared accounts to 31 July each year. His profits were:

Year to 31 July 1992	£18,000
Year to 31 July 1993	£6,000
Year to 31 July 1994	£24,000

Tax year	Profit period	Profits to be assessed
1991/92	1 August 1991 to 5 April 1992	8/12 × £18,000 = £12.000

Normal basis of assessment

1992/93	1 August 1991 to 31 July 1992	£18,000
1993/94	1 August 1991 to 31 July 1992	£18,000

Actual profits

1992/93	6 April 1992 to 31 July 1992		
	4/12 × £18,000	= £6,000	
	1 August 1992 to 5 April 1993		
	8/12 × £6,000	= £4,000	£10,000
1993/94	6 April 1993 to 31 July 1993		
	4/12 × £6,000	= £2,000	
	1 August 1993 to 5 April 1994		
	8/12 × £24,000	= £16,000	£18,000

As £28,000 (£10,000 + £18,000) is less than £36,000 (£18,000 + £18,000) Barry would be advised to make the election.

This election must be made in writing to the inspector within seven years of the end of the second year of assessment. In the above example Barry would have to elect by 5 April 2000.

Last three years

The rules for taxing the profits when a business ceases are as follows:

- The assessment for the tax year which includes the date of cessation is based on the actual profits for that year.

- The assessments for the two preceding years are increased if the actual profits of the two years taken together are greater than the total amount assessed on the preceding year basis.

The effect of moving from preceding year basis to an actual basis is that certain profits will fall out of assessment, i.e. they will never be taxed. If you recall, in the opening years the first 12 months' profits formed the basis of assessment for three years. Another feature of the opening and closing year rules is that in the second and third years of a business, when the basis of assessment is moving from actual to previous year, the taxpayer has the option to continue to be assessed on actual profits if this reduces his tax. As a quid pro quo the Revenue has a similar option when a business ceases and the basis moves from previous year to actual.

Example
Ray ceased his retail grocery trade on 31 December 1992. His profits were:

Year to 31 December 1989	£10,000
Year to 31 December 1990	£30,000
Year to 31 December 1991	£32,000
Year to 31 December 1992	£12,000

Had he continued in business his assessments would have been:

1990/91	£10,000
1991/92	£30,000
1992/93	£32,000
1993/94	£12,000

Because of the cessation there is no assessment for 1993/94 and the assessment for 1992/93 would be £9,000 (9/12 of £12,000). The actual profits of the two preceding years are calculated as follows:

		£	£
1990/91	6 April 1990 to 31 December 1990		
	9/12 × £30,000	22,500	
	1 January 1991 to 5 April 1991		
	3/12 × £32,000	8,000	30,500
1991/92	6 April 1991 to 31 December 1991		
	9/12 × £32,000	24,000	
	1 January 1992 to 5 April 1992		
	3/12 × £12,000	3,000	27,000
			£57,500

As the actual profits, £57,500 are greater than the profits using the preceding year basis, £40,000 (£10,000 + £30,000), the assessments will be increased. In this example, the profits for the period 1 January 1989 to 5 April 1990 are never assessed.

On reading these rules it may have occurred to you that there is the opportunity to obtain a significant tax advantage if you can choose the date of cessation so that the greatest amount of profit falls out of assessment. Normally, if profits are rising it is better to postpone the date of cessation to the next tax year, but if they are falling the date should not be postponed. Where profits are fluctuating it is a worthwhile exercise to calculate the amounts that would be assessed for two or more possible cessation dates. There may be other factors that would influence the decision such as capital gains tax or retirement relief if your trade is to cease on your retirement (see page 248); whether or not to elect for a continuation of the trade of a partnership (see page 102); or the relief for losses (see Chapter 10).

Although the date a person ceases to trade is one of fact, by concession the closing year rules need not be applied when a widow or widower takes over the business.

Also by concession, where a person reduces the scope of his business or his hours of work in order to qualify for a state pension, he may treat the change as if it were a cessation of one business and the commencement of another.

Capital allowances

Where capital allowances are claimed, a deduction is given from the assessment of the taxable profits which were earned during the accounting period in which the expenditure was incurred.

Example

Gordon, who has been in business for many years as a cabinet maker, makes up his accounts to 30 April each year. He purchased a saw bench for £600 in July 1990 and claimed a 25 per cent writing-down allowance. July 1990 is in the accounting year to 30 April 1991. When the profits for this period are assessed in 1992/93 the profits will be reduced by the capital allowances of £150.

A problem arises when profits of a period are assessed more than once as occurs in the opening years, and when a period of profits falls out of assessment which happens when a business ceases. In the case where all or part of a profit period is assessed more than once the capital allowance deduction first occurs in the earliest year.

Example

In an earlier example Magda was assessed on profits for the following periods:

1991/92	6 June 1991 to 5 April 1992
1992/93	6 June 1991 to 5 June 1992

If she had bought storage units for £1,000 in March 1992 and claimed capital allowances she would first get relief against her assessment for 1991/92.

Where profits for a period do not form the basis of assessment, capital expenditure in the 'gap' is treated as if it occurred in the next period unless that is the year of cessation, in which case it is treated as having been incurred in the previous period.

Example
In an earlier example Ray was assessed on profits for the following periods:

1989/90	1 January 1988 to 31 December 1988
1990/91	6 April 1990 to 5 April 1991
1991/92	6 April 1991 to 5 April 1992
1992/93	6 April 1992 to 31 December 1992

If he had purchased a refrigerated display cabinet for £1,000 in March 1989 he would get his first deduction for capital allowances in 1990/91.

Averaging farming profits

If you carry on a trade of farming or market gardening in the UK and your profits fluctuate from year to year you may be able to claim to be assessed on the average trading profits of a two-year period. By concession this claim can also be made for trades which consist of the intensive rearing of livestock and fish for human consumption. Two years can only be averaged if the profits of either year do not exceed 70 per cent of the profits for the other year and for this purpose a loss is treated as nil profits.

The profits which are averaged are before any deductions for:

- losses of that year; and
- capital allowances (or additions for balancing charges).

Example
Henry, who has been a sheep farmer for many years, makes up accounts to 30 September each year. His recent trading profits are as follows:

1990 £11,000	1991 £40,000	1992 £20,000

Henry makes claims for averaging his profits for these years.

Year	Profits	Average	Final assessment
1991/92 (original)	£22,000	£31,000	£31,000
1992/93 (original)	£40,000	£31,000	
1992/93 (average)	£31,000	£25,500	£25,500
1993/94 (original)	£20,000	£25,500	£25,500

Where profits of one year exceed 70 per cent of the profits of the other year, but do not exceed 75 per cent, marginal relief is available.

10 Relief for Trading Losses of Individuals

Trading losses

The system of reliefs for corporation tax losses is discussed in Chapter 14.

A trading loss is computed in the same way as a trading profit, and for the purposes of obtaining relief it can usually be increased by capital allowances. There are several ways in which you can get relief for a trading loss:

- You can reduce future profits of the same trade.

- You can reduce your total income for the tax year in which the loss occurred and, if you are still trading, the total income for the following year. Strictly, the set-off is of losses and profits of a tax year, but in practice the profits and losses of accounting years are commonly used.

- For losses incurred in 1991/92 and subsequently you can reduce your net chargeable gains for the tax year in which the loss occurred and, if you are still trading, the net chargeable gains for the year following.

- If the loss occurs in the first four tax years of a new trade you can reduce your total income for the three years immediately preceding the year of the loss. The loss to be relieved is calculated on a strict 6 April to 5 April basis.

- Revenue expenditure incurred during the five years before you start to trade is treated as a trading loss incurred in your first year for the purpose of the above loss reliefs.

- If your trade ceases, a loss in the final 12 months can reduce trading profits of the previous three tax years.

- If you transfer your business to a company, accumulated trading losses at the date of transfer can reduce your director's remuneration and any dividends received from the company (see Chapter 12).

Relief against future trading profits

A loss may be carried forward indefinitely against future profits of the same trade. It must be used against the earliest profits first.

Example
Donald's recent results have been:

Year ended 30 September 1989	Loss	£38,000
Year ended 30 September 1990	Profit	£7,000
Year ended 30 September 1991	Profit	£16,000
Year ended 30 September 1992	Profit	£25,000

The assessments after loss relief would be:

	1990/91 £	1991/92 £	1992/93 £	1993/94 £
Profit	—	7,000	16,000	25,000
Loss set-off	—	7,000	16,000	15,000
	—	—	—	£10,000
Loss carried forward	£38,000	£31,000	£15,000	—

There is no possibility of skipping a year with low profits or making a partial set-off in order to make use of your personal allowance or any other relief.

Relief against total income

Relief against your total income in the tax year in which the loss occurs, and in the following year, is available if you are carrying on a trade, profession or vocation. Occupiers of commercial woodlands who had elected before 15 March 1988 to be assessed under Schedule D may obtain similar loss relief but only until 5 April 1993. The claim for loss relief, which must be made within two years of the end of the tax year in which the loss is to be set off, may include or exclude capital allowances for the same period.

Example
Paul, a bachelor, who is carrying on a trade as a hairdresser has the following results:

Year to 31 December 1990	Profit	£13,000
Year to 31 December 1991	Loss	£22,000

He also receives an annuity of £10,000 a year.

Paul's trading profits are assessed on the preceding year basis.

As Paul made a loss in the tax year 1991/92 he can claim to set it against his total income for that year of £23,000 or against his total income of £10,000 in 1992/93 with the balance of £12,000 carried forward for set-off against future profits. If the loss had been, say, £33,000 he could have made claims for both years. What he cannot do is split the loss and claim relief of say £20,000 in the first year and £2,000 in the second year.

Where a person has more than one class of income and the loss is insufficient to cover the total income, the loss is set against income of the same class before income of another class. In Paul's case, if the loss is relieved in 1991/92 it will be set against his trading income before his annuity income. This rule had more impact in the days when investment income was taxed at a higher rate.

Since the introduction of independent taxation on 6 April 1990, your losses can no longer be set off against the income of your spouse.

In a given year, capital allowances need not be claimed in full nor, indeed, at all. When they are claimed they can either augment a loss to be set off against total income or they can be carried forward against future profits of the same trade separately. Which is best for you as the taxpayer will often depend on factors such as your personal allowance or your marginal rate of tax.

If you have made a loss in a trade of farming or market gardening, and you also incurred losses in each of the previous five years, the loss in the sixth year, together with any related capital allowances, will not be available for relief against your total income. Where, however, you can show that the whole of the activities in the sixth year are of such a nature and carried on in such a way as would have justified a reasonable expectation of future profits, the restriction will not apply. It is necessary to convince the inspector that if the activities had been carried on by a competent farmer or market gardener they would not have expected to have made a profit until after the period in question. In any event, the loss can still be relieved against future profits of the same trade.

Trading losses and capital gains

Since 6 April 1991 you have been able to set trading losses arising in the year against capital gains of the same year and, to the extent that unused trading losses cannot be set against income of the following year, the excess may be set against capital gains of the following year. Any trading losses not set against income or gains of the same or following year are available to be carried forward against future profits of the same trade. This rule brought sole traders in line with companies which could already set trading losses against their capital gains. The new rule is intended to help businesses suffering temporary difficulties where the proprietor may need to sell business assets or investments to provide working capital for the business and where a significant liability to capital gains tax would otherwise arise. You may also be able to shelter a capital gain on the sale of a business asset which could qualify for roll-over relief but where you are unable to reinvest the proceeds into replacement assets (see Chapter 7).

Where a claim is made to set trading losses against capital gains for a year, any capital losses of the same year are first used to reduce the gain. However, relief for trading losses is given in priority to any brought forward capital losses.

Example

The income and capital gains of Edward are as follows:

Trading profits/(losses)		*Capital gains/(losses)*	
Year to			
31 December	£		£
		Brought forward at 6 April 1991	(3,000)
1990	22,000	1991/92	15,000
1991	(70,000)	1992/93	8,000
1992	36,500	1993/94	Nil

Assessments	1991/92	1992/93	1993/94
	£	£	£
Trading profit	22,000	Nil	36,500
Trading loss set-off	22,000	Nil	33,000
Net assessment – income tax	Nil	Nil	£3,500
Capital gain	15,000	8,000	Nil
Trading loss set-off	15,000	Nil	Nil
Capital loss set-off	Nil	3,000	Nil
Net assessment – CGT	Nil	5,000	Nil

The above assessments would probably be covered by the annual capital gains tax exemption and the personal allowance respectively. Edward could have set off £8,000 of his trading loss against his capital gain in 1992/93. However, this would not be recommended as it would waste his CGT exemption and result in an income tax liability for 1993/94.

A claim to offset trading losses against capital gains has to be made within two years of the end of the year of assessment in which the loss is incurred.

Losses in opening years

A special relief is available if a trading loss has occurred during the first four years of your business. The effect of this relief is to reduce your total income for the three years prior to the year of the loss, with the income of the earliest of the three years being reduced first.

This relief is similar to the relief against total income in the following respects:

- A claim has to be made in writing within two years of the end of the year of assessment in which the loss is sustained.
- Capital allowances can be used to increase the amount of the loss.
- If the loss is insufficient to relieve the total income it first reduces income of the same class.

Before 1990/91 the set-off was extended to your spouse's income.

This relief is not available for losses resulting from the occupation of woodlands. Nor can it be used to reduce past capital gains.

Terminal losses

If you sustain a loss in the final 12 months before your business ceases this is referred to as a terminal loss. Relief is given for this loss by setting it against the profits of the trade for the three tax years preceding the last tax year. Relief is given for a later year before an earlier one. The loss is made up of the following items:

- The trading loss for the final tax year, i.e. from 6 April to date of cessation.
- The capital allowances for that tax year.
- The trading loss sustained in the part of the previous tax year commencing with a date 12 months before the business ceased.
- The same fraction of the capital allowances for that year unless relieved.

If one of the above items is a profit it is ignored.

Example

Jeffrey, who had traded for many years and whose profits were assessed on the preceding year basis, had the following results:

Year to 30 June 1989	Profit	£20,000
Year to 30 June 1990	Profit	£12,000
Year to 30 June 1991	Profit	£10,000
Year to 30 June 1992	Loss	£7,200
Period to 30 September 1992	Loss	£4,000

Capital allowances 1990/91 £200; 1991/92 £3,000; 1992/93 £1,000.

He ceased trading on 30 September 1992.

The terminal loss period is from 1 October 1991 to 30 September 1992. The date of cessation falls into the tax year 1992/93 and the three previous years of assessment are 1989/90, 1990/91 and 1991/92.

Calculation of terminal loss

	£	£
(1) 6 April 1992 to 30 September 1992 (tax year 1992/93)		
3/12 × £7,200 (year to 30 June 1992)	1,800	
3 months to 30 September 1992	4,000	
Capital allowances for 1992/93	1,000	6,800
(2) 1 October 1991 to 5 April 1992 (tax year 1991/92)		
6/12 × £7,200 (year to 30 June 1992)	3,600	
6/12 × capital allowances for 1991/92 (but these have all been relieved against the trading profits for the year to 30 June 1990 as shown below)	Nil	3,600
Terminal loss		£10,400

Relief for terminal loss

			£
1991/92	Profits to 30 June 1990		£12,000
	Less: Capital allowances		3,000
			9,000
	Less: Terminal loss relief		9,000
	Assessable profits		Nil
1990/91	Profits to 30 June 1989		£20,000
	Less: Capital allowances		200
			19,800
	Less: Terminal loss relief (balance)		1,400
	Assessable profits		18,400

11 Additional Points for Partnerships

Assessing profits

Although in Scotland a partnership is a legal person, in English law a partnership is not recognised as a legal entity separate from its individual members. However, the tax legislation gives authority for the Inland Revenue to raise assessments on a partnership as if it were a taxable person. Although the income tax on the partnership profits is calculated as one sum, the assessment is divided between the partners according to how they share profits in the year of assessment.

If you are carrying on a business in partnership your trading profits are calculated in the same way as those of a sole trader. The profits assessed are those of a 12-month accounting period which ended in the previous tax year, except in the opening and closing years (see Chapter 9). In the first 12 months of the business, consider employing an intended partner. By obtaining a deduction for his salary and National Insurance, you reduce the profits of the initial period which will be the basis for more than one year of assessment.

Capital allowances are claimed for each tax year. In addition to capital allowances for assets owned by the partnership, which are deducted from total profits, individual partners may be eligible for capital allowances, for example, where they use their own cars for business. These personal capital allowances are deducted from each partner's individual share of the trading profits.

To the extent that a partner's personal allowance is not set against other taxable income, it reduces the tax payable on his share of the partnership assessment, as shown in the following example.

Example

Phil, Tony and Peggy Archer have farmed in partnership for many years as Phil Archer & Co. sharing profits and losses equally after paying Peggy interest on capital at 5 per cent per annum and paying salaries of £12,000 per annum to Phil and Tony. Their adjusted profits for the year ended 31 December 1991 amounted to £80,500; a claim was made for capital allowances of £1,500 and Peggy's capital account stood at £20,000.

Division of Partnership Assessment 1992/93

	Firm £	Phil £	Tony £	Peggy £
Interest on capital	1,000	—	—	1,000
Salaries	24,000	12,000	12,000	—
Balance of profits shared equally	54,000	18,000	18,000	18,000
	79,000	30,000	30,000	19,000
Less: Personal allowances	12,055	3,445	5,165	3,445
Taxable income	66,945	26,555	24,835	15,555
Tax payable (nearest £1)				
First £2,000 at 20%	1,200	400	400	400
Next £21,700 at 25%	14,239	5,425	5,425	3,389
Balance at 40%	1,596	1,142	454	—
	£17,035	£6,967	£6,279	£3,789

One-half of the tax is payable on 1 January 1993 and one-half on 1 July 1993.

Where the partnership profits are less than the amounts payable for interest on capital and salaries the deficit is shared by the partners in the same way as they share profits. In some cases this leaves a partner with a negative allocation which is then divided between the remaining partners in proportion to their allocations at that point.

Example

Simon, Derek and Nell have carried on an advertising agency in partnership for many years sharing profits 4/7, 2/7 and 1/7 after paying interest on capital of £2,000, £500 and £600 respectively. The partnership profits for the accounting period ended 30 September 1991 amounted to £300.

Division of Partnership Assessment 1993/94

	Firm £	Simon £	Derek £	Nell £
Interest on capital	3,100	2,000	500	600
Less: Deficit shared	2,800	1,600	800	400
	300	400	(300)	200
Derek's negative allocation shared		(200)	300	(100)
	£300	£200	Nil	£100

Liability for partnership tax

The partners are charged with their share of the tax bill by debiting their individual current accounts in the firm's books. It is important to know the extent to which each partner is personally liable in case the partnership has insufficient funds to pay the tax. A partnership is like a marriage and it is not uncommon for it to end in disagreement or death. It was confirmed in a tax case in 1954 that the tax on a partnership assessment is a partnership debt and all those who were partners at the time are jointly liable. The Inland Revenue can therefore collect the total partnership tax from anyone who was a partner at the time. It would then be up to that partner to recover amounts due from other partners, if necessary by suing them.

Partnership return

A partnership is asked to complete a tax return (form 1) and the declaration as to the correctness and completeness of the form must be signed by the precedent acting partner. The precedent acting partner is the partner who, being resident in the UK:

- is first named in the partnership agreement; or
- if there is no agreement, is named singly, or with precedence to the other partners in the usual name of the firm; or
- is the precedent acting partner, if the person named with precedence is not an acting partner.

If we look at these rules in connection with the farming partnership, Phil Archer & Co., we note that if there is no partnership agreement the precedent acting partner is Phil because of the name of the partnership, unless either he is not resident in the UK or he is not an active partner, i.e. he is a sleeping partner. Details of how the business profits are allocated must be included in the tax return and each partner must, be described as either an acting partner or a sleeping partner. If you are a sleeping partner your share of the partnership profit is treated as unearned income. Although there is no longer an additional tax rate levied on unearned income the distinction is still relevant. For example, your tax relief for contributions to personal pension plans depends on your having a source of earned income.

Changes to profit shares

If during a tax year you change the way in which the partnership profits are shared, the profits for the year are first apportioned on a time basis. The profits for each part of the year are then allocated on different bases.

Example

Continuing the previous example, it was decided that from 1 November 1993 no interest would be payable on capital and that profits would be shared equally. The profits for the accounting period ended 30 September 1992 were £27,101. Until 31 October 1993, interest on capital continued at the same rate as in 1992/93.

Division of Partnership Assessment 1993/94

	Firm	**Simon**	**Derek**	**Nell**
	£	£	£	£
6 April 1993 to 31 October 1993 (7 months)				
7/12 × £27,101 = £15,809				
Interest on capital × 7/12	1,809	1,167	292	350
Balance of profits shared 4:2:1	14,000	8,000	4,000	2,000
	15,809	9,167	4,292	2,350
1 November 1993 to 5 April 1994 (5 months)				
5/12 × £27,101 = £11,292				
Profits shared equally	11,292	3,764	3,764	3,764
Totals for 1993/94	£27,101	£12,931	£8,056	£6,114

Partnership changes

If there is a change of partners then, strictly, that is the end of one partnership and the start of a new one. The profits which relate to the old partnership's business are assessable, using the closing year rules. The rules for assessing the opening and closing years of a trader were considered in Chapter 9. A modified version of the opening years rules applied to assess the profits of the new partnership. The modified rules are as follows:

- In the year of assessment in which the change occurs and in the following three years actual profits are assessed.
- In years five and six the preceding year basis is used with the taxpayer being able to elect for actual profits.

Example

Howard and Hilda have been in partnership for many years and make up their accounts to 5 April each year. On 6 January 1991 they admitted Martin into the partnership. Assume the adjusted trading profits are as follows:

1988	1989	1990	1991	1992
£28,400	£24,000	£24,480	£36,000	£27,600

1993	1994	1995	1996
£24,960	£26,160	£30,000	£45,000

Tax year	**Profit period**		**Assessments**
	Old firm – Howard and Hilda		
1988/89	Year to 5 April 1988		£28,400
1989/90	Year to 5 April 1989		£24,000
		£	
1988/89	6 April 1988 to 5 April 1989	24,000	
1989/90	6 April 1989 to 5 April 1990	24,480	
		£48,480	

The Revenue would not exercise their option to assess actual profits.

1990/91	6 April 1990 to 5 January 1991		£27,000
	(3/4 × £36,000)		
	New firm – Howard, Hilda and Martin		
1990/91	6 January 1991 to 5 April 1991		£9,000
	(1/4 × £36,000)		
1991/92	6 April 1991 to 5 April 1992		£27,600
1992/93	6 April 1992 to 5 April 1993		£24,960
1993/94	6 April 1993 to 5 April 1994		£26,160
1994/95	Year to 5 April 1994		£26,160
1995/96	Year to 5 April 1995		£30,000
		£	
1994/95	6 April 1994 to 5 April 1995	30,000	
1995/96	6 April 1995 to 5 April 1996	45,000	
		£75,000	

The partners would not elect for assessment of actual profits.

Continuation election

It is possible to avoid these cumbersome rules by making an election for the partnership business to be treated as continuing for tax purposes. This election can be made provided there is at least one person who is a member of both the old and the new partnership. It must be signed by all those who were partners both before and after the change and, if a partner has died, his personal representative signs on his behalf. Whether it is of benefit to make the election will depend on the level of profits. It is therefore necessary to prepare alternative computations of assessable profits before making a decision. In some cases it may be necessary to compensate a disadvantaged partner if he signs the election which is beneficial for the other partners.

If within two years of a continuation election there is a further cessation of the business, the profits of the years preceding the later cessation are assessed as if the previous cessation had not occurred.

Mergers and demergers

A merger of partnerships carrying on different activities will result in a cessation of the old businesses and the commencement of a new business. It will not therefore be possible to make an election for the continuation basis to apply. Where, however, partnership businesses carry on similar activities before and after the merger, the new partnership can be said to succeed to the businesses of the old partnerships. The partners will then be able to choose whether to make an election for the continuation basis.

Similarly, when separate partnerships are created to carry on the business formerly carried on by one partnership, it will be a question of fact whether the former business has ceased.

Capital gains

Partnership assets including goodwill are treated for capital gains tax purposes as if each partner owned a fractional share of each asset. It is therefore important to include in the partnership agreement the interest each partner has in the partnership assets if this differs from the ratio in which they share trading profits. When a partnership asset is sold, a partner's share of the chargeable gain is added to gains arising from the disposal of his personal assets, if any, and is reduced by his annual exemption. Gains arising on partners' interests in business assets are eligible for replacement of business asset roll-over relief and retirement relief in the normal way, provided the other conditions are met.

When profit sharing ratios change, whether or not there is a change in the partners, there is deemed to be an acquisition of a further interest in the partnership assets by those partners whose profit shares increase and a disposal of their interests by partners whose profit share decreases. No gain or loss arises on these disposals as the consideration is deemed to be equal to the current balance sheet values of the assets provided no payments are made.

Partners' annuities

Where members of a partnership make annual payments to a retired partner, the Inland Revenue do not treat it as a disposal of partnership assets provided it is no more than a reasonable recognition of the partner's past contribution of work and effort. Where the partner has been in the partnership for ten years, an annuity is regarded as reasonable if it is no more than two-thirds of his average share of profits in the best three of the last seven years in which he was required to devote substantially the whole of his time to acting as a partner.

Up to a certain limit the annuity is treated as earned income in the hands of the partner receiving it, any excess being treated as unearned income. The limit is 50 per cent of his average share of profits calculated as above. This limit is increased in line with the increase in the retail prices index from the December of the tax year in which the former partner left the partnership to the December preceding the tax year in which the annuity is assessed. The amounts which are ascertained as earned and unearned income for the recipient are also used to determine the extent to which the payment is set against the payers' earned and unearned income.

Interest relief

If you take out a loan to acquire an interest in a partnership or to lend money to the partnership, the interest you pay is likely to be tax deductible against your total income. To be eligible for the deduction you:

- must not be a limited partner; and
- must not have recovered capital from the partnership.

However, these conditions do not prevent you from withdrawing any balance that you may have on current account. If you make such a withdrawal and at the same time borrow a similar sum to loan to the partnership you could obtain relief for the interest on your borrowing while at the same time release funds for your private use.

It is the Inland Revenue's practice to allow interest relief to salaried partners in a professional firm if, in their relations with clients, they are indistinguishable from equity partners.

If the partnership should incorporate before the loan is repaid, the Revenue will, by concession, allow the interest relief to continue. The concession is given where the conditions for obtaining interest relief for an investment in a close company would have been met if the loan had been taken out for that purpose.

You can also get relief for up to three years on the interest on a loan taken out to buy machinery or plant, such as a car, for the use in your partnership. You would get relief on a current year basis, whereas if the partnership had borrowed, relief for the interest would have been given as a trading expense on a preceding year basis.

Corporate partnerships

A corporate partnership exists where one of the partners is a limited company. As there are different rules for computing individuals' and companies' liabilities to tax there are special rules governing corporate partnerships. First, the trading profits are calculated as if the partnership were a company, but making no deductions for capital allowances or charges. The company is allocated profits according to the profit-sharing ratio during its accounting period. If the company's and the partnership's accounting periods do not coincide then the profits are apportioned over the accounting periods. The company may deduct its share of capital allowances and charges for the same accounting period. The profit is then combined with the company's other profits chargeable to corporation tax as if it were a separate trade.

Individual partners are assessed to income tax in the usual way. However, capital allowances and charges are apportioned over the tax years in question on a time basis.

Example

Donald Ltd, Peter and Geoff trade in partnership, sharing profits and losses equally. Recent results are as follows:

	Adjusted profit £	Capital allowances £
Year to 31 December 1990	105,000	24,000
Year to 31 December 1991	120,000	18,000
Year to 31 December 1992	150,000	12,000

Partnership assessments are as follows:

Donald Ltd:

Year to 31 December 1991	£
Profit £120,000 × 1/3	40,000
Less: Capital allowances £18,000 × 1/3	(6,000)
Assessment	£34,000

Year to 31 December 1992	
Profit £150,000 × 1/3	50,000
Less: Capital allowances £18,000 × 1/3	(4,000)
Assessment	£46,000

Peter and Geoff 1991/92:

	£	£
Year to 31 December 1990		
Profit £105,000 × 1/3		35,000
Less: Capital allowances		
9/12 × year to 31 December 1991, £18,000	13,500	
3/12 × year to 31 December 1992, £12,000	3,000	
	16,500 × 1/3	(5,500)
Assessment on both Peter and Geoff		£29,500

12 Incorporating an Existing Business

Introduction

If you have been carrying on your business alone or in partnership, and you have been successful, you may be thinking of incorporating. You should first consider the commercial and professional implications of such a decision; find out about the company law requirements such as the annual audit and calculate what it is going to cost. There will be stamp duty, registration fees and professional fees to pay. You should then weigh up the advantages and disadvantages of incorporating, and the tax implications.

Tax rates

Corporation tax rates are currently 25 per cent on profits up to £250,000 and the full rate on profits over £1,250,000 is 33 per cent. Where profits are between £250,000 and £1,250,000, a formula is used which produces a smooth graduation of tax rates between 25 and 33 per cent (see Chapter 13). The marginal rate of tax for this slice of profits is 35 per cent. This compares with the top rate of 40 per cent payable on profits of an unincorporated business.

Advantages

There are several factors that are considered to be advantages of incorporation:

- Limited liability. If the company cannot pay its creditors or any damages awarded against it, you and other shareholders are only liable to the extent of the amount you have paid, or have agreed to pay for your shares.

- This benefit could be eroded in the early years as you may be required to guarantee the company's borrowings. It is nevertheless an important consideration for certain high risk businesses such as builders and those concerned with high-tech products.

- Raising finance can be easier, e.g. issuing ordinary shares, with or without Business Expansion Scheme relief; issuing preference shares; debentures and other loans where the lender can take a floating charge on the company's assets.

- Flexibility of share structure. If you own shares in a company, rather than, say, an interest in a partnership, it is much easier to make gifts. For example, if you wish to make gifts and use your annual capital gains tax exemption or your annual inheritance tax exemption.

- As a director you will be subject to the benefit-in-kind rules which in many cases are generous (see Chapter 18).

- The company has perpetual succession, i.e. it can go on for ever. This has tax implications; for example, if you dispose of the company, but it does not cease trading, no balancing charges arise and tax losses may be preserved. But if a sole trader dies, or there is a change of partners, the trade is treated as having come to an end for tax purposes.

- Some people, and they may include your customers and suppliers, consider that a business carried on by a limited company has a better commercial image than one carried on by a sole trader or partnership.

- There is no limit to the number of shareholders in a company whereas there is a statutory limit of 20 for most partnerships.

Disadvantages

You should also consider the following disadvantages of incorporation:

- You will pay tax on the profits of the business sooner. Corporation tax is payable nine months after the end of your accounting period, whereas you probably have been used to twice as long to pay your tax as a sole trader or partner. There is also pay as you earn (PAYE) and National Insurance contributions (NIC) to be paid monthly on directors' remuneration.

- As a director, NIC paid by you and the company will be considerably higher than NIC paid by a sole trader or partner.

- Your capital in the company cannot easily be returned to you. It is possible for the company to purchase its own shares and thereby release cash to the shareholder but only where certain conditions are satisfied. This possibility is considered in detail in Chapter 26.

- There are company law restrictions which would prevent you borrowing more than £5,000 from the company and the close company rules could tax such a loan as if you had received a dividend. The close company rules are discussed in Chapter 13.

- The rules for getting a tax deduction for expenses are more generous for the self-employed than for directors and employees (see Chapters 4 and 14).

- Loss relief for companies is not as generous as that for sole traders and partners. For further details see Chapters 10 and 14.

- There is a double charge to capital gains tax, in that tax is payable on a disposal of assets by the company and the value of the company's shares reflects the underlying appreciating assets. This is the reason why business premises are often not transferred to the company but remain in the ownership of the sole trader.

- The capital gains hold-over relief for incorporation (described later in this chapter) is not available should you decide later to disincorporate.

- Business property relief for inheritance tax is less generous for a company. If you have an interest in a partnership, however small, it can qualify for 50 per cent relief. However, if you have shares in a company, you must, at the time of the transfer, have more than 25 per cent of the votes if it is an unquoted company. For quoted companies you need more than 50 per cent of the votes. Details of business property relief can be found in Chapter 32.

Timing

When you transfer the business to a company the trade ceases and the rules for assessing the profits in the closing years will apply. This gives you the opportunity to choose a date for the incorporation which maximises the profits that will fall out of assessment under the closing year rules. Normally, if profits have been increasing each year, incorporation should occur shortly after 6 April. Illustrations of how the rules work can be found in Chapter 9.

Capital allowances and stock

If you transfer to the company assets on which you have claimed capital allowances, e.g. industrial buildings and plant and machinery, a balancing charge could arise (see Chapter 5).

However, where a trade is being transferred between connected persons, they can elect to be treated as if any plant and machinery had not changed ownership for the purposes of capital allowances. For industrial buildings, if the transfer is between connected persons all of whom are UK resident, a similar election can be made. So if you, alone or with your immediate relatives or partners, control the new company, you are able to make these joint elections, by writing to the inspector.

As trading stock will also be transferred, technically market value should apply, but the Revenue do not usually take the point and accept the transfer of trading stock at the lower of cost or net realisable value.

Loss relief

As your trade is ceasing, if you have trading losses terminal loss relief is available. Any trade loss in the last 12 months can be carried back to reduce trading profits of the three previous tax years. Capital allowances for the last 12 months can increase the trading loss (see Chapter 10). If certain conditions are satisfied, unrelieved trading losses can be set against the sole trader's or the partners' future income from the company, such as remuneration and dividends. The conditions are that:

- the consideration for the business consists wholly or mainly of shares;
- the shares are owned by the individuals at the time they are claiming loss relief; and
- the company is carrying on the business transferred.

Capital gains

When you incorporate your business, you will be disposing of your business assets to another person, the new company. Large capital gains could arise, particularly if the business owns land and buildings and has built up substantial goodwill over the years. If you are selling or gifting your business and you meet the conditions for retirement relief, the first £150,000 plus half of the next £450,000 of the gain could be exempt. Retirement relief is discussed in more detail in Chapter 30.

Assuming you, either alone or together with your immediate family or your partners, will control the new company, the transfer of the assets will be between connected persons and the deemed consideration for the assets will be their market value. However, there is a roll-over relief if all the assets of the business (other than cash) are transferred to the company in exchange for shares. In this situation, the net gain arising on the transfer is deferred and reduces the cost of your shares in the company. The deferred gain does not crystallise until there is a future disposal of shares.

Example

Mr Duckworth and Mr Watts, who have been carrying on a business as equal partners for seven years, decide to transfer their business to

Duckworth and Watts Ltd in exchange for 120,000 £1 ordinary shares. The partnership assets, net of liabilities, are as follows:

	Indexed cost £000	Market value £000	Chargeable gain £000
Premises	20	80	60
Goodwill	Nil	20	20
Plant	12	11	—
Other assets net of liabilities	11	9	—
	£43	£120	£80

The gain of £80,000 is rolled-over into the acquisition cost of the shares. Mr Duckworth and Mr Watts each have an acquisition cost for their shares of £20,000, being the market value of the shares, £60,000, less the gain rolled-over of £40,000.

It may be that an exchange of your business wholly for shares does not suit you. You may want some cash immediately or a loan account in the company from which you can draw cash without any tax consequences. One possibility is to withdraw the required capital from the business prior to incorporation.

However, if you were to reintroduce the capital into the business shortly after incorporation, the inspector may contend that it was only for tax reasons that these two transactions occurred and therefore they can be ignored. It could prevent you meeting the condition for the roll-over relief, that the whole of the net assets are transferred for shares. If you decide to take any part of the consideration for the business in another form, the non-share proportion of the gain is immediately chargeable to capital gains tax.

Example

Using the same facts as the previous example except that 105,000 shares are issued and each of the partners have a £7,500 loan account with the new company, there is an immediate chargeable gain of £10,000, being 12.5 per cent of £80,000. Each of the partners has a chargeable gain of £5,000 which is covered by their annual capital gains tax exemption; and each has an acquisition cost for the shares of £17,500.

The roll-over relief described above is appropriate for the incorporation of most existing businesses. Where, however, there are reasons why certain business assets should not be transferred to the company it is of no use. In such cases you should consider gifting individual business assets to a company which is controlled by you or your family. You can make a claim for the chargeable gain to be deferred until there is a further disposal of the asset, and the company then takes over your indexed acquisition cost for the purposes of computing the gain on a future disposal.

Stamp duty

As stamp duty is only chargeable on instruments of transfer, where possible you should transfer assets such as plant and machinery and trading stock by delivery. In certain circumstances no stamp duty is chargeable if the value of the consideration given by the company for dutiable assets does not exceed £30,000. This limit was increased temporarily to £250,000 between 19 December 1991 and 19 August 1992. In other cases, duty of 1 per cent of the value may be payable on:

- land and buildings;
- fixtures and fittings;
- goodwill;
- debtors;
- bank deposit accounts.

The consideration for a business transferred to a company in exchange for shares is the market value of the shares plus any liabilities that the company has taken over. It is important that your sale agreement should apportion the total value of the net assets transferred to the company, particularly if you are going to transfer some items by delivery. The Revenue are likely to challenge your apportionment if they consider it is unreasonable. There are ways of reducing stamp duty by not transferring certain assets, for example debtors, but remember you must transfer *all* your business assets to obtain capital gains roll-over relief. See page 22 regarding the abolition of stamp duty in May 1993 on all assets other than land and buildings.

Value added tax

There will be no VAT chargeable on the transfer of your business as a going concern to the company, provided the company uses the assets for the same kind of business and registers for VAT. You can elect to have your VAT number allocated to the company, which is only appropriate if you will be controlling the company. Your VAT records for the last six years should strictly be transferred to the company but Customs may agree to your holding on to them.

Disincorporation

At present, should the owners of a company wish to disincorporate, they are faced with severe tax penalties because the legislation has not taken the possibility into account. In particular, there are no provisions for carrying forward the company's losses or for deferring the gains that would arise when the company disposes of its fixed assets to the unincorporated business. In response to representations received on this subject over several years, the Revenue published a consultative document in 1987 entitled 'Disincorporation'. The Revenue included among their proposals a deferral of the gain on the company's business assets until they are sold and not replaced with similar assets. It is also considered allowing the company's losses to be carried forward to offset profits of the unincorporated business but only at the corporation tax rates. It also proposed that any new provisions would only apply for small companies with a turnover of less than £2 million, a balance sheet value of less than £975,000 with fewer than 50 employees and paying corporation tax at the small companies rate. However, no progress has been made in implementing these proposals.

13 Corporation Tax

Introduction

A company is a legal person quite separate from its shareholders and directors, and its profits are taxed separately. Corporation tax is a tax on the profits of companies, unincorporated associations such as golf clubs, and authorised unit trusts. 'Profits' is a term used to cover both income and chargeable gains (capital gains made by companies). The detailed calculation of corporation tax profits will be considered in the next chapter. A company which is resident in the UK is chargeable to corporation tax on its profits wherever in the world they arise. By contrast a non-resident company is only subject to corporation tax on profits arising from a branch or agency in the UK. The meaning of residence is discussed in Chapter 3.

A company is chargeable to corporation tax on its profits for an accounting period and not for a tax year, as is the case with sole traders and partnerships. An accounting period for tax purposes is usually the same as the company's actual accounting period. If, however, accounts are drawn up for a period which exceeds 12 months, the profits are apportioned and the first 12 months is treated as one accounting period and the balance of the period is treated as a second accounting period. For tax purposes an accounting period begins:

- when the previous accounting period ends; or
- when the company becomes within the charge to corporation tax, for example, because it becomes UK resident or it acquires a source of income.

An accounting period ends when any of the following first occur:

- the expiration of 12 months from the beginning of the accounting period;
- an accounting date of the company or the end of a period for which no accounts have been made up;
- the company ceases to trade;
- the company ceases to be UK resident;
- the company ceases to be chargeable to corporation tax.

When a resolution is passed for the winding-up of a company the current accounting period is deemed to end and a new accounting period commences.

Rates

Corporation tax rates are fixed for financial years which start on 1 April and end on 31 March. The rate to be applied to profits will therefore depend on the financial years in which the accounting period falls. It will also depend on the size of the profits. The full corporation tax rate only applies if profits exceed a certain figure which is at present £1,250,000. A lower rate, known as the small companies rate, is applied where profits are below a lower limit which is currently £250,000. For profits between these two limits a formula is used to calculate the tax and this is explained below. Profits for this purpose are:

- basic profits, i.e. chargeable income and gains; and
- UK dividends received plus related tax credits.

This last item is sometimes known as franked investment income. Although included for the purpose of determining the level of profits it is not subject to corporation tax, as the dividend is a share of profits on which corporation tax has been paid by the company paying the dividend.

Where an accounting period straddles 31 March the profits are apportioned to each financial year and the appropriate corporation tax rate applied. The rates for the last five years are as follows:

Financial year from 1 April	Full rate	Small companies rate	Lower profit limit	Upper profit limit	Marginal relief fraction
	%	%	£	£	
1988	35	25	100,000	500,000	1/40
1989	35	25	150,000	750,000	1/40
1990	34	25	200,000	1,000,000	9/400
1991	33	25	250,000	1,250,000	1/50
1992	33	25	250,000	1,250,000	1/50

Example
Fowler Garden Produce Ltd makes up its accounts to 31 December each year. Its profit for the calendar year 1991 was £1,320,000. Corporation tax payable on these profits would be as follows:

	£
Period to 31 March 1991 3/12 × £1,320,000 × 34%	112,000
Period to 31 December 1990 9/12 × £1,320,000 × 33%	326,700
	£438,900

Marginal relief

If your company's profits are between the lower limit and the upper limit, your profits are taxed at a rate between 25 per cent and 33 per cent for the 1992 financial year by using the following marginal relief formula:

Basic profits × full corporation tax rate
Less: (upper limit − profits) × $\frac{\text{basic profits}}{\text{profits}}$ × marginal relief fraction

Example

For the year to 31 March 1993 Woolley and Archer Plastics Ltd, which does not have any associated companies, has profits subject to corporation tax of £550,000 consisting solely of trading profits. It has not received any dividends from UK companies.

Calculation of corporation tax payable

	£
£550,000 × 33%	181,500
Less: £1,250,000 − £550,000 = £700,000 × 1/50	(14,000)
	£167,500

The effective rate of tax is 30.45 per cent.

Associated companies

If your company has associated companies, the upper and lower limits used to determine the rate of tax are divided by a number equal to the total number of companies. In general terms, your company is associated with another if one has control of the other or if both are controlled by the same shareholders. When the upper and lower limits change, apportionment may be necessary.

Example

Mycroft New Trend Hotels Ltd, which has three associated companies, had taxable profits for the year to 31 July 1991 of £300,000. Of this total, £200,000 (8 months) will be apportioned to the financial year (FY) 1990 and £100,000 (4 months) to the FY 1991. As the total number of associated companies is four, the upper limits for marginal relief will be:

8 months to 31 March 1991 (FY 1990)

$\dfrac{8}{12} \times £1,000,000 \times \dfrac{1}{4}$ £166,667

4 months to 31 July 1991 (FY 1991)

$\dfrac{4}{12} \times £1,250,000 \times \dfrac{1}{4}$ £104,167

Thus the full corporation tax rate of 34 per cent is payable for the FY 1990 but marginal relief will affect the FY 1991.

Capital gains

The calculation of capital gains is covered in Chapter 7. A company's capital gains are taxed along with its other profits at the company's corporation tax rate.

Advance corporation tax

Advance corporation tax (ACT), as its name suggests, is a payment on account of the total corporation tax payable on the profits of a particular accounting period. It is payable if, during the accounting period, a company pays a dividend or makes other distributions of profits such as transferring assets to shareholders at less than market value. An exception is made where a dividend is paid by a subsidiary company to its parent and an election is made not to pay ACT. The rate of ACT is always linked to the basic rate of income tax, for example in the financial years 1988 to 1992 the rate of ACT was one-third and the basic rate of income tax in the tax years 1988/89 to 1992/93 was one-quarter. The reason for this is that, if the recipient of the dividend is a UK resident individual, he receives a tax credit based on the ACT paid which satisfies his liability to income tax at the basic rate on the dividend income. He may still be liable to pay tax at the higher rate. If he is not liable to pay tax on this income, perhaps because it is covered by personal allowances, he can apply for the tax credit to be refunded as if he had paid income tax. The payment by the company of ACT on the dividend thereby ensures that the Inland Revenue have collected tax from which to make such income tax repayments.

UK companies which receive dividends from other UK companies use the ACT tax credit to offset any ACT that they are due to pay.

Example

Alexis Designer Productions Ltd makes up its accounts to 31 October every year. It paid a dividend of £30,000 on 24 June 1992 and received a dividend from a UK company of £12,000 on 13 May 1992.

		£
ACT payable on dividend	1/3 × £30,000 =	10,000
Tax credit received	1/3 × £12,000 =	4,000
ACT payable		£6,000

A company is required to make a return of ACT due (form CT61) on a quarterly basis and pay over the tax as follows.

Quarter	Payment date
1 January to 31 March	14 April
1 April to 30 June	14 July
1 July to 30 September	14 October
1 October to 31 December	14 January

Interest can arise if payment is not made on the due date.

If the end of the company's accounting period does not coincide with the end of a quarter, a fifth return is required which ends on the last day of the accounting period. Therefore, if the accounts are made up to 31 October, two ACT returns must be submitted for the quarter to 31 December.

For cash flow reasons it is preferable for dividends to be paid just after the start of a quarter. In the previous example, if the dividend had been paid a week later on 1 July 1992, the payment of ACT would have been deferred three months until 14 October 1992.

Special rules apply where there is a change in the ACT rate during an accounting period.

Where the tax credits on dividends received exceed ACT due on dividends paid for a particular quarter, the company can obtain a refund of ACT paid earlier in the accounting period. Where the situation is the same at the end of the accounting period this surplus of franked investment income is carried forward to the subsequent period. It is possible to obtain repayment of the tax credit suffered on this income if the company makes a trading loss.

Advance corporation tax set-off

After the end of the accounting period the total corporation tax profits are ascertained and the corporation tax liability calculated. At this point, and subject to certain restrictions, a deduction is given for any ACT paid in the period which has not been refunded.

ACT can be surrendered by a parent company to a 51 per cent subsidiary. It can also be carried back to previous accounting periods; this is limited to six years and the ACT must be used in later years before earlier ones.

The amount of ACT to be set against a company's final corporation tax liability can consist of ACT paid in the current accounting period by the company or its parent company and unrelieved ACT (known as 'surplus ACT') of a previous or subsequent period. Surplus ACT arises in an accounting period where the ACT paid exceeds the maximum ACT set-off. Currently, the maximum amount of ACT that can be set off is 25 per cent of the basic profits.

Example
Alexis Designer Productions Ltd, for the accounting period to 31 October 1992, had profits assessable to corporation tax of £1,800,000. In that period it received dividends from UK companies of £12,000 and paid a dividend of £30,000.

Corporation tax computation
Year to 31 October 1992

		£
Corporation tax		
£1,800,000 × 5/12 × 33%		594,000
Less: ACT set-off	£	
Dividends paid	30,000	
Dividends received	12,000	
	18,000	
ACT thereon 1/3		6,000
Mainstream corporation tax payable		£588,000

For companies where the directors are not restrained by dividend policies there is the opportunity to improve their cash flow position by paying dividends at the end of their accounting period. The ACT would be payable after 14 days and relief would be given just under nine months later.

Income tax

Companies often receive income such as interest and royalties from which basic rate income tax has been deducted. In addition they may make payments from which they themselves must deduct basic rate tax, known as 'charges' (see Chapter 14). Any income tax that a company deducts should be paid to the Revenue on a quarterly basis, together with any ACT that is due, using the same form (CT61). During the accounting period the company offsets the income tax suffered on income received against income tax it is due to pay to the Revenue, paying only the balance. Where at the end of the accounting period the amount of income tax suffered in the period exceeds the amount deducted from payments, the excess reduces the corporation tax payable.

Overseas taxes

Relief is available where a company receives income which has suffered tax in another country. It is usual for there to be an agreement, or treaty, between the UK and the other country which prevents double taxation. Normally, certain types of income are taxable in only one of the countries. However, where income is taxable in both countries or there is no treaty in force, the overseas tax is usually allowed as a credit against corporation tax. Where the overseas tax is at a higher rate than our own, the set-off is restricted to the amount of corporation tax attributable to that income. The deduction for foreign tax is given before the ACT set-off.

As an alternative to the set-off described above, it is possible to deduct foreign tax from the foreign income before charging it to corporation tax. This may be advantageous if a company has losses.

Payment of corporation tax

Normally, you have to pay corporation tax within nine months of the end of the accounting period or within 30 days of the issue of an assessment, if this is later. Often assessments are raised on estimated figures in the absence of a return of profits by the company by the time the assessment is made (see page 135). In such cases an appeal would be lodged against the assessment and an application made to postpone the tax believed to be overcharged. The tax not in dispute is due for payment nine months following the end of the accounting period or within 30 days of the inspector's agreement to the postponement, if this is later. If any of this tax is paid late, interest will be charged until payment.

If any tax which is postponed is subsequently found to be payable, then, provided that the tax is paid within 15 months from the end of the accounting period or within 30 days of the issue of an amended assessment if earlier, no interest will be charged on the postponed tax.

Pay and file

Partly because of the late submission of accounts resulting in the need for estimated assessments, the Government is to introduce a new administration system to improve the collection of corporation tax. The new system will consist of:

The 'pay' element:

- A company will be required to pay corporation tax on a fixed date nine months after the end of its accounting period, whether or not an assessment has been raised.
- Interest will run from the same fixed payment date on any tax paid late by the company or tax repaid by the Revenue.

The 'file' element:

- A company will be allowed 12 months, from the end of the period to which it makes up its accounts, in which to supply its return and those accounts.
- If it fails to send in the return and accounts within that time the company will, unless it can show a reasonable excuse, incur an automatic flat rate penalty.
- If the return and accounts have not been supplied by 18 months after the end of the period in respect of which the return is due, the company will incur an additional penalty of 10 per cent of the tax due but unpaid at that time; this will increase to 20 per cent if the return is still outstanding two years after the end of the return period.
- These penalties will be chargeable by assessment, with the taxpayer having a right of appeal against the assessment.

The necessary legislation for a new procedure was passed in July 1987 and a 'First Guide to Corporation Tax Pay and File' has been issued by the Revenue. However, the new rules will not come into effect before September 1993 at the earliest.

Close companies

There are further rules for companies which are close companies. A close company is one which is under the control of five or fewer persons, or under the control of its directors. When looking at who controls a company you include persons who have loaned money to the company as well as shareholders. They can be individuals, trustees or other companies, although corporate shareholders which are not themselves close are excluded. Any interests held by a person's associates, such as close relatives or business partners, are aggregated with that person's interest in determining control. The five largest shareholders/loan creditors or the directors are considered to have control if they can exercise control over the company's affairs. This is such an open-ended meaning of control that it is usual to start by considering whether they:

- have more than 50 per cent of the votes;
- own more than 50 per cent of the shares;
- would receive more than 50 per cent of the company's income if it were distributed; or
- would receive more than 50 per cent of the company's assets if they were to be distributed, for example, if the company were to be wound up.

Loans to shareholders

A close company is chargeable to tax if it makes a loan or advances money to an individual who is one of its shareholders or loan creditors. The tax, which is payable 14 days after it is assessed, is calculated as if it were advance corporation tax, but in fact it is not ACT and cannot therefore be franked by dividend income. Interest is charged if the tax is paid late.

When the loan is repaid the tax paid by the company is refunded. The individual who borrows from the company is treated as having received income if the loan is written off. Where a husband and wife are both directors of a close company and one of their current accounts is in debit and the other is in credit, the Revenue consider each person's position separately. Tax is therefore payable by the company on the amount of the debit current account balance. In such a situation one spouse should consider transferring money to the other to clear the current account debit balance.

These provisions do not apply in cases where the company lends money in the ordinary course of its business.

Close investment-holding companies

Close investment-holding companies (CICs) are close companies which do not wholly or mainly carry on the following activities on a commercial basis – trading, property investment, property development, dealing in land or shares, or acting as holding companies where the subsidiaries carry on one or more of these activities. CICs therefore are companies whose main business is the holding of cash and shares as investments.

The main disadvantage of being a CIC is that the full corporation tax rate is charged on the company's profits no matter how small they are.

14 Computing Company Profits

Income and gains

As mentioned in the previous chapter, corporation tax is payable on a company's profits which consist of its income and gains for a particular accounting period. The different types of income are computed according to the rules which apply for each of the Schedules (see Appendix 14). For details of how to compute a company's rental profits see Chapter 6. Similarly, when a company disposes of fixed assets in an accounting period, it computes the capital gain or loss using the normal capital gains tax rules which are explained in Chapter 7.

In deciding when income is assessed, income tax law is applied as if a company's accounting period was the year of assessment. In other words, the income assessed is always that of an accounting period, i.e. the trading and rental profits earned, the interest, dividends from overseas companies and sundry income actually received in that period.

An example of a corporation tax computation is shown on page 126, 'Robinson, Ramsey and Clark Ltd'.

Charges

The total of a company's profits for an accounting period is reduced by any 'charges on income' that have been paid in that period. Examples of charges are interest (normally excluding bank interest) patent royalties and certain donations to charities. The payment is an allowable deduction provided it is:

- borne by the company;
- made for valuable and sufficient consideration, except for donations to charity (see below);
- not deductible in computing trading profits;
- not charged to capital unless it is interest.

When making any of the above payments the company must deduct income tax at the basic rate (currently 25 per cent) and account for it to the Inland Revenue on form CT61 (see Chapter 13).

Amounts which are deductible in arriving at a trading profit or other type of profit (for example Schedule A) cannot be treated as charges. In particular, bank overdraft interest is generally treated as a deduction in arriving at a trading profit and not as a charge on income.

Charges can only be set off against a company's total profits to the extent that they have been paid in the period.

Example

In the accounts of the Superior Company Ltd royalties of £4,700 have been deducted in arriving at the net profit. A closer analysis reveals that this is made up as follows:

	£
Amount outstanding at start of year	—
Paid in year (gross)	3,500
Due but not yet paid at end of year	£1,200
	£4,700

When the corporation tax computation is prepared, the following adjustments are necessary:

	£
Net profit per the accounts (say)	10,000
Add royalties – not a trading expense	4,700
Trading profit	14,700
Less: Charges on income – royalties paid	3,500
Profits chargeable to corporation tax	£11,200

Charitable giving

A company can receive relief in respect of donations to charity under a four year deed of covenant. Since 1 October 1990, they have also been able to obtain relief for single cash donations to charity under 'Gift Aid'. Each payment must be at least £400 (net), but there is no upper limit. Between 1 October 1990 and 6 May 1992 the lower limit was £600 (net). The company deducts basic rate income tax when it makes a payment to a charity and accounts for it to the Inland Revenue on form CT61 (see Chapter 13). The company gives a certificate to the charity so that it can claim the tax back from the Inland Revenue.

The gross amount of the payment is allowed as a deduction against the company's profits for the accounting period in which the payment is made. With a basic income tax rate of 25 per cent, the minimum net payment of £400 is equivalent to a gross payment of £533.

In the case of a non-close company (Chapter 13 explains close companies) relief can also be given for a one-off donation to charity subject to a maximum limit of 3 per cent of the dividends paid by the company on its ordinary share capital. This may be of relevance where the donation is less than the 'Gift Aid' minimum of £400.

Trading profits

The rules for computing trading profits and losses are considered in detail in Chapter 4 but there are additional points to be made in connection with companies. When adjusting the net profit shown in the profit and loss account, you must ensure that the following items have not been deducted. If they have, then they must be added back:

- Company formation costs.
- Costs of raising, reducing or reorganising share capital.
- Legal costs for altering the company's articles of association or a debenture trust deed.
- Dividends paid and payable and other distributions. This is because you are taxed on the profit you make before any of it is distributed.
- Taxation. You are taxed on your net profit before any adjustments are made for taxation.

Allowable trading expenses will include the following items:

- Directors' fees, bonuses and salaries.
- Incidental costs of raising loan finance provided loan stock is not converted into shares within three years.
- Costs of setting up an approved employee share scheme or statutory ESOP trust.

Capital allowances

A company's capital allowances for assets used in its trade are treated as a trading expense for accounting periods starting with the one in which the expenditure is incurred. Similarly, balancing charges are treated as trading receipts for the accounting period in which they arise. Other capital allowances are deducted from the relevant source of income, for example rental income. For details of how capital allowances are calculated you are referred to Chapter 5.

Example

The profit and loss account of Robinson, Ramsey and Clarke Ltd for the 12 months to 31 March 1993 is as follows.

	£	£
Gross trading profit		229,800
Dividends from UK companies		8,700
Interest on Government securities (September 1992) (gross)		3,000
Rental income		12,500
		254,000
Less: Wages and salaries	43,900	
Directors' remuneration	22,000	
Depreciation	16,700	
Debenture interest paid (August 1992) (gross)	11,200	
Expenses re rented properties		
Donation to political party	2,100	
Trade expenses	7,100	
Improvements to warehouse	18,800	
Repair of factory	6,300	
Net profit	9,400	137,500
		£116,500

An analysis of the trade expenses revealed £1,300 had been incurred for entertaining customers. Capital allowances for the accounting period were £42,000. Income tax of £750 had been deducted from the interest on Government securities.

Robinson, Ramsey and Clarke Ltd

**Corporation tax computation for the accounting period
to 31 March 1993**

	Note	£	£
Net profit			116,500
Add: Depreciation	(1)	16,700	
Debenture interest paid	(2)	11,200	
Donation to political party	(3)	7,100	
Expenses re rented properties	(4)	2,100	
Entertaining customers	(5)	1,300	
Improvements to warehouse	(6)	6,300	44,700
			161,200

Less: Dividends from UK companies	(7)	8,700	
Interest on Government securities	(8)	3,000	
Rental income		12,500	
Capital allowances	(9)	42,000	66,200
Adjusted trading profit – Schedule D, Case 1			95,000
Rental income – Schedule A			
Income		12,500	
Expenses		2,100	10,400
			3,000
Interest on Government securities (gross)			108,400
Charges – debenture interest paid (gross)	(2)		(11,200)
Profits chargeable to corporation tax			£97,200

Notes

(1)   No deduction for depreciation is allowed for tax purposes. However, it is possible to claim capital allowances (see Chapter 5).

(2)   Debenture interest paid is a 'charge on income' which is not deductible in arriving at the trading profit for tax purposes. Charges may, however, be set off against a company's total income, as shown above.

(3)   Political donations are not deductible in arriving at a trading profit because they are not 'wholly and exclusively laid out or expended for the purposes of the trade' (see Chapter 4).

(4) Expenses of renting properties may be set off against rental income, which is assessable under Schedule A (see Chapter 6).

(5)   The deduction of expenditure on entertaining customers is specifically disallowed (see Chapter 4).

(6)   Expenditure on improvements, as opposed to repairs, cannot be deducted in arriving at a trading profit for tax purposes. The expenditure may, however, be eligible for capital allowances (see Chapter 5).

(7)   This is investment income, rather than trading. The treatment of franked investment income (FII) is discussed in Chapter 13. FII is never included in profits chargeable to corporation tax.

(8)   This is investment income, rather than trading. The gross income is brought into the corporation tax computation. During the year income tax will have been accounted for as follows:

CT61 return for quarter ended 30 September 1992

Income tax deducted from payments of debenture interest	£2,800
Income tax suffered by deduction from interest received	750
Net payment due to Inland Revenue, 14 October 1992	£2,050

(9) Capital allowances claimed by a trading company are treated as a deduction in arriving at the trading profit.

Relief for trading losses

If your company makes a trading loss there will often be alternative ways of obtaining relief. These include:

- setting the loss against future trading profits of the same trade;
- setting the loss against the total profits of the current accounting period and then against the total profits of the three preceding years;
- where the company is a member of a 75 per cent group of companies, surrendering the loss to another group member for offset against that company's profits of the same period.

Relief against future profits

As with loss relief for individuals (see page 93), the loss must be set against the next available trading profits of the same trade. In certain circumstances, a change of ownership of the company will prevent the carry forward of unrelieved losses.

Relief against total profits

The loss must first be set against the total profits of the same accounting period. Only if these profits are insufficient to cover the loss can the excess loss be carried back, in reverse chronological order, against the total profits of the three previous years. Where there has been a change of accounting date, an apportionment of profit may be necessary.

Example
The recent results of Freshfield Bin Liners Ltd are as follows:

		Trading results £	Other profits £
Year to 30 September 1988	Profit	30,000	6,000
Year to 30 September 1989	Profit	84,000	10,000
Year to 30 September 1990	Profit	25,000	15,000
9 months to 30 June 1991	Profit	18,000	9,000
Year to 30 June 1992	Loss	200,000	10,000

Freshfield Bin Liners Ltd
Loss relief allocation

Year to	30/9/88	30/9/89	30/9/90		30/6/92
9 months to				30/6/91	
	£	£	£	£	£
Trading profits	30,000	84,000	25,000	18,000	—
Other profits	6,000	10,000	15,000	9,000	10,000
	36,000	94,000	40,000	27,000	10,000
Loss relief (order)					
(1)					(10,000)
(2)				(27,000)	
(3)			(40,000)		
(4)		(94,000)			
(5)	(9,000)				
Corporation tax profits	£27,000	Nil	Nil	Nil	Nil

The maximum carry back period is three years from 1 July 1991, i.e. to 1 July 1988. Therefore, three months of the year ended 30 September 1988 may be brought into account for loss relief. Of the total loss of £200,000, £180,000 has now been relieved. The balance of £20,000 may be relieved against the trading profits of the year ended 30 June 1993 and, if these are insufficient, subsequent years.

The rules were different for losses incurred in accounting periods ending before 1 April 1991. Under the old rules the maximum period of carry back was one year or, if less, a period equal to the length of the accounting period in which the loss arose. The only exception was in respect of a loss for the final 12 months prior to cessation of trading. For many years the rules have allowed these losses ('terminal losses') to be carried back for three years.

Before leaving the subject of loss relief against total profits four further points should be noted:

- This relief must be claimed within two years of the end of the accounting period in which the loss occurred.

- Your claim may be against total profits of the current period only. You do not have to carry back any excess loss although it will usually be beneficial to do so.

- The relief is only available if you can show that you are carrying on your trade on a commercial basis and with a view to profit.

- Where there has been a change of ownership of the company there are circumstances in which you cannot carry back a loss incurred after the change against profits earned before the change.

Group relief

Trading losses can be surrendered between group members provided they are all UK resident companies. For this purpose a 'group' consists of a holding company and its 75 per cent subsidiaries. If the companies in the group do not make up accounts to the same date, the loss-making company can surrender its loss only to the extent of the claimant company's taxable profits for the corresponding period. The amount of the loss available for surrender is likewise restricted. The claimant's taxable profits are those remaining after deducting charges on income. There are special rules which apply during periods where companies join or leave the group.

Liquidations

There can be problems where a company making trading losses ceases to trade before it goes into liquidation because both the cessation of trade and the liquidation trigger the end of an accounting period. The difficulties arise where, in the period following the cessation of a trade, assets such as business premises are sold and capital gains are realised. These will be profits chargeable to corporation tax but as the trade ceased they cannot be reduced by trading losses. A possible way round the problem is to exchange contracts for the sale of the assets before the trade ceases so that relief can be obtained for trading losses in the earlier period.

Investment companies

An investment company is one whose business consists wholly or mainly of making investments and receives most of its income from that source; for example, a company that lets properties or one which holds shares in other companies as investments.

Income and gains of an investment company are computed in the normal way and the total profits are reduced by charges on income, management expenses and capital allowances. Where in an accounting period the management expenses, together with capital allowances and any charges paid wholly and exclusively for the purposes of the business, exceed the profits from which they are deductible, the excess can be carried forward and treated as management expenses for the subsequent period.

It is more difficult to obtain a tax allowance for directors' remuneration in an investment company than a trading company. As a rule of thumb, the Inland Revenue will normally allow the amount which, including other management expenses, would have to be paid to an outside agent for managing the same investments.

15   Dealing with the Revenue

Tax inspectors

The Board of Inland Revenue is responsible for the administration of the taxes with the exception of value added tax. It appoints inspectors to assess our taxes and collectors to collect them. If you receive a letter from an inspector of taxes it is important to establish whether he is carrying out routine work or is involved in an investigation. In each district there is a tax office and the inspector in charge is called the district inspector. His staff will consist of other inspectors, Revenue executives, Revenue officers and Revenue assistants. Some tax offices deal only with the pay as you earn (PAYE) scheme and there are other units that do only investigation work:

- the Enquiry Branches which deal mainly with fraud involving trading profits;
- the Investigation Office which investigates fraud in the construction industry, false claims for personal allowances and expenses, offences in connection with repayment claims and suspected irregularities by Revenue staff;
- the Special Offices which handle cases involving trusts, taxpayers with wide ranging activities and apparently wealthy individuals with no permanent place of residence;
- the PAYE Audit Units which investigate the irregular operation of the PAYE scheme;
- the Special Investigations Section which investigates particular areas of tax evasion, avoidance and non-compliance;
- specialists units such as the Rag Trade Investigation Unit and the Foreign Entertainers Unit.

The collectors of taxes are responsible for collecting the tax assessed by inspectors. Where the collector does not receive payment he will liaise with the inspector to ensure that a valid assessment has been issued. For example, it would not be valid if it has been issued outside the statutory time-limits, or there was an error in the taxpayer's name and address.

The tax collection procedure is computerised at two centres at Shipley in Bradford and Cumberland. Where distraint or similar proceedings are invoked, local collection offices will be responsible for the action taken and the recovery of outstanding tax liabilities. Where circumstances warrant it may be referred to the Enforcement Office who may instigate bankruptcy proceedings.

Since 1985 the Revenue have been putting the PAYE and self-employed taxpayer records on computer. This is now complete and each tax office has access to the computerised tax record of 1 million employers and 31 million individuals, the latter being identified by their National Insurance numbers. It is also the intention to replace the current tax collection computer program and to computerise the tax records of companies.

The Revenue have announced that they are testing different ways of bringing the work of tax assessment and collection together.

Revenue procedures

The Revenue staff have to follow certain procedures and it is helpful to know about them.

- *Reply-paid envelopes*
  When the Revenue issue a demand for payment, they will include a reply-paid envelope. They used to issue reply-paid envelopes even when payment was not demanded but this practice was stopped as an economy measure.

- *Blank forms*
  If tax districts cannot supply quantities of blank forms you should ask them whether they will accept photocopies. In most cases they do.

- *Second class post*
  Only repayments in excess of £1 million and tax demands are sent by first class post. In other cases it is usual for the Revenue to send letters and forms by second class post.

- *Tax repayments*
  Revenue staff should give priority to tax repayments. So if a delay occurs, write to the district inspector concerned.

Returns

A return is a statement of income, profits, gains, dividends, other payments, benefits or capital transferred. Usually the Revenue require that the relevant information is entered on an official form. There are various kinds of forms designed for different purposes. For example:

- annual tax returns for individuals or partnerships;
- PAYE returns;
- returns of companies' distributions;
- returns of interest paid by banks and buildings societies;
- returns of chargeable transfers for inheritance tax.

If you are sent such a form you must complete it and send it back in the time specified on the return, to the inspector who sent it.

As an individual you must enter on your annual tax return your income from all sources, whether tax has been deducted at source or not, together with details of capital gains. If you later discover that you have made an incorrect return, perhaps because something has been omitted, you should write to the inspector without delay. In the return, you are asked for details of tax allowable payments, such as interest paid, and there is a section where you can claim allowances.

Individuals who have employment income only often do not receive annual tax returns. If you have taxable income or gains but have not received a tax return you have a duty to tell the Revenue. You must send the inspector a statement of income and gains within 12 months of the end of the year of assessment in which they arose. The maximum penalty for non-compliance since 1988/89 is the tax liability for the unreported income and gains.

In addition interest is payable where there has been substantial delay in notifying the Revenue. Delay is substantial where you notify them more than 30 days after the tax return is issued or, if later, after 31 October following the year of assessment in which the gains or income arose.

Companies normally send the inspector their annual statutory accounts, together with a corporation tax computation showing the amount of tax that is assessable. They also send in a return when they pay interest and dividends.

If you or your company have overpaid tax because of an error in a return you can claim relief up to six years after the tax year in which the assessment was made.

Assessments

Assessments of profits and gains are made by the inspector at various times during the year and notices of assessment are issued. These notices of assessment will always be sent to you, the taxpayer, even if you engage an accountant or tax practitioner to act as your agent. The inspector will send copies of all notices of assessment to your agent if you give him written authority on form 64-8. This authority will remain valid for all future years until withdrawn.

If the inspector discovers that an assessment of income or gains is insufficient he can raise an additional assessment. As a general rule, the inspector has six years from the end of the relevant tax year to make an assessment or an additional assessment. If he does not do so the tax cannot be collected. These rules do not apply where there is fraud or neglect. In cases where the taxpayer has died an assessment cannot be raised more than three years after the end of the tax year in which he died.

Example

Tom sold his holiday home in May 1986 and made a capital gain of £8,000. He gave full details of the sale on his tax return.

If the inspector does not raise an assessment before 6 April 1993 he will be out of time. If Tom died in June 1988 the inspector would have had to raise the assessment by 5 April 1992.

If you do not submit details of your trading income in time the inspector will make an estimated assessment and it will be up to you to show that it is excessive. The inspector will usually raise these assessments between August and November and if, at the time, your accounts are outstanding for one or more earlier years the estimate will be increased to encourage you to produce them. Estimated assessments will also be made where you have not submitted details of interest or other income received.

Detailed accounts are not required from individuals and partnerships with an annual turnover of under £15,000 and landlords whose gross rental income is less than £15,000. They only need to provide three figures – total turnover, total business purchases and expenses, and the resultant net profit.

Appealing against an assessment

You will normally have 30 days to appeal against an assessment, although for stamp duty you have only 21 days. If you have a good excuse the inspector may accept a late appeal. The grounds for the appeal must be stated, for example, that the assessment is estimated and likely to be excessive, it is not in accordance with the accounts of the business, it does not take account of loss relief or capital allowances, etc. A claim against the Revenue for repayment of tax is not grounds for appeal. The fact that an appeal is lodged does not mean that you need not pay the tax at the normal time. You can, however, apply to postpone all or part of the payment of income tax, capital gains tax and corporation tax. The application for postponement of tax is separate from the appeal and must

state the amount of tax you wish to postpone and why you consider you
have been overcharged.

When making appeals and postponement applications you should always
use the official form 64-7 even where you feel it is necessary to accompany
the form with a letter. This is because the forms are distinctive and the
Revenue staff can easily see them in the incoming post and give them
priority treatment.

Appeals to the Commissioners

If you cannot agree your assessment with the inspector the case can be put
before the Appeal Commissioners. Appeals on certain specialised areas
are heard by the Special Commissioners, for example, appeals by taxpayers
who are not domiciled and non-resident in the UK, where tax avoidance
provisions apply, etc. Appeals on more straightforward matters are heard
by the General Commissioners.

On matters of fact the decisions of the Commissioners are final, but if
there is a legal point in dispute an appeal can be made to the High Court
against their decision. If either the Revenue or the taxpayer want to
appeal they must ask the Commissioners for a report on the details of the
case and this 'case stated' is sent to the High Court. Further appeals are
possible from the High Court to the Court of Appeal and in some cases to
the House of Lords, but unless there are large amounts of tax in dispute
the legal costs involved will usually prevent the taxpayer pursuing his case.

Paying tax

The due dates for payment of tax vary and are dealt with in the chapters
dealing with the different taxes. The Revenue have asked that you adopt
the following procedure when paying the accounts office:

- Enclose a separate cheque with each payslip, rather than one cheque
  covering several payslips.
- Put the full assessment reference on the back of the cheque.
- Do not send a covering letter if the cheque and payslip agree.
- If the cheque is for less than the original payslip, make a note on the
  payslip of the amended amount and add the words 'assessment
  amended'.
- If the cheque is for more than the payslip, enclose a letter explaining
  why.
- Any letters should include the full name and address of the taxpayer
  with the tax district, reference number and National Insurance number.

• Do not ask for a receipt unless it is necessary, for example, where you need to claim relief against foreign taxes.

Interest on tax

Interest is payable on overdue tax and is not deductible for tax purposes. The rates effective from 6 October 1991 are:

• Inheritance tax – 8 per cent per annum.

• Other taxes – $9\frac{1}{4}$ per cent per annum.

Interest on late payment of tax is rarely waived, unless it is less than £30, as it is regarded by the Revenue as compensation for the loss of the use of money that the taxpayer should have paid over at an earlier time. The interest is computed from the later of 30 days after the notice of assessment or the normal due date for payment.

If you or your company are UK resident and have overpaid tax you may be entitled to interest at the above rates; this is referred to as a repayment supplement. For individuals the repayment supplement is only paid if the amount of tax is repaid more than 12 months after the tax year to which it relates. There are similar rules for companies. The interest received is not taxable. Further details can be found in the chapters dealing with the various taxes. In practice, if you have a query about how interest on tax is calculated you should write to the collector who issued the demand, not the inspector.

Certificates of tax deposit

Certificates of tax deposit are evidence of deposits made by the taxpayer for tax payable in the future. Individuals, partnerships and companies can purchase the certificates which can be used for the payment of most taxes but not VAT, PAYE or tax deducted from subcontractors. There is a minimum initial deposit of £2,000 but thereafter the deposit can be increased by sums of £500 or more. You do not have to state that the deposit is for a specific tax liability and you can withdraw your deposit at any time.

Interest, which is payable gross on the deposits for up to six years, is taxable in the year of receipt. You will find that the prospectus for each issue quotes two rates of tax for deposits of under £100,000. You will receive a higher rate where your deposit is applied in the payment of tax than if you withdraw your deposits for cash. For deposits of £100,000 or over the higher rates differ according to the number of months for which the deposit is held.

Revenue inefficiency

If you have a complaint about Revenue inefficiency you should first write to the district inspector of the district concerned. Where you feel the matter has not been resolved at district level you can write to the Regional Executive Office. In exceptional cases you might write to the Board of Inland Revenue at Somerset House or to your local member of Parliament. It is for your MP to decide whether to take the matter up with Treasury ministers or the Ombudsman. There is a taxpayer's charter which is reproduced in Appendix 4.

Investigations

If the inspector believes there are profits and income that have not been assessed in past years he will start an investigation into the tax affairs of the taxpayer concerned. The Revenue have considerable information powers, for example, to find out who receives bank interest and who is buying and selling securities and land. They can also check on who receives grants and subsidies, and who holds a licence for a taxi or market stall. In difficult cases or those involving large sums the inspector will refer the case to Head Office. If it appears that the case may involve fraud, Enquiry Branch will probably deal with the investigation. There are many reasons why these investigations may start:

- As a result of unsatisfactory replies to enquiries made by the inspector, e.g. the taxpayer's ex-girlfriend or neighbour may have told the inspector that his £20,000 a year salary which he declares for tax purposes does not pay for his villa in Portugal or his Porsche or provide the funds which he has in his overseas bank accounts.

- As a result of the inspector finding inconsistencies in the taxpayer's business accounts, e.g. his profit margin is much lower than that of others in the same trade, the amount he is drawing from the business is not adequate to maintain his life style, etc.

- Because the taxpayer admits that he has not fully disclosed all his profits or other income.

- When the taxpayer's professional adviser ceases to act for his client, having discovered understated profits which the taxpayer will not voluntarily disclose.

It is not difficult to tell when an investigation has been started. The inspector might send a letter asking for certain information and assurances. For example, he may ask whether proper books of account are kept, what procedure is used for recording cash transactions and the proprietor's drawings; what percentage profit is added to cost on different product ranges and how much of each type of product is sold. The inspector might invite the taxpayer and his adviser to come to his office for a meeting. At the meeting the inspector will suggest that there have been irregularities, without being specific, and will ask the taxpayer to make a full disclosure.

It is important to take great care at these initial stages as any replies, written or oral, will be carefully recorded by the inspector and he will be assessing whether the taxpayer is being co-operative.

At the end of the investigation:

- the accounts and computations submitted may be agreed;
- certain adjustments may be made to the accounts but the underlying records and procedures may be accepted; or
- the underlying records may be unsatisfactory.

Accounts of earlier years (up to six years but longer where fraud is involved) may be reopened if the underlying records are inadequate or there is a substantial understatement of profits in the current accounts for a reason which could equally apply to earlier years.

The inspector will arrive at the amount of lost tax and add interest, calculated from the date the tax was due. He could also impose penalties, e.g. if a taxpayer negligently delivers an incorrect return or accounts to the inspector, he is liable to a penalty not exceeding the total of the additional tax payable as a result of correcting the return or accounts.

The inspector has the power to reduce these penalties. Whether he does so depends on the seriousness of the offence and the degree of co-operation offered by the taxpayer.

16 Taxation of Directors and Employees

Your responsibilities as an employer

When you first employ someone (even your husband or wife) you take on certain responsibilities. As an employer you are required by law to deduct tax and National Insurance from the payments you make to your employees and for this purpose a director is an employee. So if you run your business through a company, tax and National Insurance must be deducted from payments you make to yourself as a director even if you are the company's only employee.

Who to employ

Quite often the first employees of a business are the proprietor's spouse and children. This can be tax efficient because, if the spouse or child has no other income, they can set their personal allowances against their salaries.

Since 6 April 1990 husbands and wives have been taxed separately. In 1992/93, both benefit from a personal allowance of £3,445 and the husband receives a married couples allowance of £1,720 which can be transferred to his wife if he has insufficient income. They are each entitled to receive taxable income of £23,700 before becoming liable to higher rate tax. It is obviously beneficial for both parties to have their own income in order to take full advantage of personal allowances and the 20 per cent and 25 per cent rate bands.

If your spouse and children are to be employed their salaries should be reasonable when compared with the duties they perform.

If you are interested in employing a school leaver, a young person who is unemployed or perhaps someone a little older, you should enquire at your local Training and Enterprise Council (TEC) (see page 8 for further information).

If you employ a person who is past the normal retirement age (65 for men, 60 for women), income tax and employer's National Insurance are still payable although the employee does not have to make a National Insurance contribution.

Employed or self-employed?

You can reduce the paperwork involved in running your business by not having any employees and instead contracting out part of your work to self-employed individuals or companies. You may find that this is not always possible because the nature of the work you have to offer dictates that there is an employer/employee relationship. Beware of artificially creating a situation where a person appears to be self-employed but is in fact an employee; as you could be liable to pay the PAYE and National Insurance that should have been deducted from payments you made to him.

Only by considering all the facts can you decide whether an individual has a contract of employment and is therefore an employee, or has a contract for services and is self-employed. Such contracts need not be in writing, although this is advisable, and will be ignored by the courts if the terms do not reflect the real relationship between the parties. For example, a written contract was set aside in the case of a driver of hired plant who was engaged to supply services. The contract purported to give him freedom to work when he chose and, if he wished to send a suitably qualified person to work in his place. In reality he worked the normal hours of a full-time employee, went to the sites at the times set by the company and behaved in all respects like an employee.

The Inland Revenue issue a leaflet (IR 56) 'Employed or Self-employed' which discusses the situation and states that if you are in doubt you should get in touch with them. If you are in doubt about a person who is already working with you, some of the following features may help to clarify the position.

- It is necessary to consider the control you exercise. Are you able to say, not only what is to be done, but also how, when and where it is to be done? The greater your control and supervision the more likely the person working for you is an employee.

- If the service that the person performs is an integral part of the services for which your business was set up he is likely to be an employee, for example if he is a waiter in your wine bar.

- What are the terms of payment? Employees tend to be paid by the hour, week or month, can earn a higher rate for overtime and may share in a bonus if their group reaches certain targets; they may be provided with benefits such as cars and free medical insurance. By contrast, an independent contractor is more likely to quote a fixed sum for the job although he may charge on a time basis.

- A person is more likely to be self-employed if he:

  (a) supplies his own equipment;

  (b) can delegate his duties to others;

  (c) is not committed to working fixed hours;

  (d) is not paid during illness or holidays;

  (e) takes a financial risk;

  (f) can improve his profitability by his own skill, effort and sound management;

  (g) only works for you from time to time and neither of you are obliged to provide or to accept the work.

A remuneration package

It is quite usual these days to offer employees, particularly senior employees, a remuneration package rather than a straight salary. In addition to a salary you might pay certain expenses either directly or by reimbursement and provide non-cash benefits. Details of the most popular benefits are to be found in Chapters 18 to 20. Generally, when you pay expenses and provide non-cash benefits your employees have to pay tax as if these items were part of their remuneration. However, this does not apply to those whose remuneration, including benefits, totals less than £8,500 per annum. Furthermore, non-cash benefits paid to any employee do not usually give rise to National Insurance contributions (see Chapter 21). It is specifically provided that, if a director's income tax is paid by his employer, he will be treated as having received additional remuneration equal to the tax less any amount that he has made good.

Golden payments

If you make a payment to induce a person to come to work for you, a 'Golden Hello', this will be taxable as remuneration unless it can be demonstrated that it is:

- a capital payment for goodwill, which could occur if you are acquiring the person's business. Such a payment is subject to capital gains tax; or

- entirely ex gratia with no binding obligation on the individual to join you.

If you make a lump sum payment to an employee when his employment ceases, a 'Golden Handshake', the treatment can be very generous. Provided it is ex gratia and not part of the contract of employment, the first £30,000 of a payment is tax-free. However, golden payments must be included in gross pay for National Insurance purposes.

If you want to give an employee more than £30,000 you could top up his pension rights within the limits of your scheme without the payment attracting an income tax charge.

A golden handshake is treated as being received at the date of the termination to which it relates. The 'receipts basis' discussed later in this chapter does not apply to such payments. Therefore, if the employee's income will drop significantly after his contract is terminated it may be sensible to time the termination to fall just after the beginning of the new tax year so that the taxable part of the payment is taxed at the lower tax rate.

A gratuitous payment linked to normal retirement (as opposed to loss of office) or on death, is unlikely to qualify for the £30,000 exemption.

Expenses

A round sum expense allowance paid to an employee is normally taxable as part of his remuneration and the cost of travelling from home to his normal place of work is his liability. However, an expenses allowance is not taxable where the employee's remuneration is less than £8,500 per annum and the inspector has agreed that the allowance is reasonable and is no more than a reimbursement of expenses which are necessary for the employee to perform his duties. Expenses normally falling into this category are:

- additional lodging or outworking expenses incurred by an employee whom you send to work temporarily some distance away from his normal place of work; and

- mileage allowances which do no more than meet the cost of business travel.

Similarly, where you reimburse or otherwise meet the expenses of a director or an employee earning £8,500 or more, the amount is taxable as part of the remuneration. To the extent that the expense was 'wholly, exclusively and necessarily' incurred so that he could perform his duties, for example, travelling and subsistence costs, he can make a claim for his taxable remuneration to be reduced.

In order to avoid the need to apply PAYE to routine expenses you can apply for a dispensation. This involves discussing with the inspector what expenses are paid to your employees and convincing him that no tax would be lost by not assessing them, as any benefit would be offset by an expenses claim. He would need to be satisfied that all payments are properly controlled. Whatever the size of your business, consider making an application. The Revenue are actively encouraging employers to seek dispensations and have produced a leaflet (P7 1991) explaining the procedure.

Although the cost of travelling from home to the place of work is usually not available, by concession, the rule is relaxed in the following cases:

- If you are a director of two or more companies within a group you are allowed the cost of travelling from a specified place to other places of business.

- If you are an unpaid director of a company not managed with a view to profit you will not be assessed on any payment you receive for your travelling expenses.

- If you hold your directorship as part of a professional practice and are not assessed under Schedule E, you will not be assessed on the receipt of travelling expenses provided they are reasonable and they are not deducted in calculating your profits.

- Where an employee is occasionally required to work late and the employer pays the cost of his journey home, he is not taxed on the benefit.

If it is necessary for one of your employees to sell his house and buy another in a different location in order to come to work for you or because he is required in another part of your organisation, you can reimburse certain costs without a tax charge arising. Further details are given in Chapter 27.

Returns of benefits and expenses

A form P11D is used to make a return to the inspector of the benefits and expenses you have provided for your directors and most other employees, their families and dependants. Form P11D is reproduced in Appendix 12. You do not have to give details of any expenses for which you have a dispensation. The form is due to be completed and submitted to the inspector within two months of the end of each tax year. A return (form P9D) is required where lower-paid employees have received benefits and expenses of more than £25 which you have not included as taxable pay.

Receipts basis

Since 6 April 1989 the income of employees and directors has been taxed when actually received.

The change had no impact for the majority of employees because they received their income shortly after it was earned and were already effectively taxed on a receipts basis. However, for the half million or so company directors and others who regularly received income several months after it was earned the change was significant.

The present system is simpler than the previous arrangement for the taxation of directors' earnings because until the tax year 1988/89 some directors had been assessed on the 'earnings basis' while others had elected to be assessed on an 'accounts basis'.

In order to ascertain the date when income is treated as received, the rule is that emoluments are treated as being received at the earliest of the following times:

- the time when payment is made;
- the time when a person becomes entitled to payment;

and in the case of a director:

- the time when amounts are credited in respect of his emoluments in the company's books;
- where the amount of his emoluments for a period is determined before the end of the period, the time when the period ends;
- where the amounts of his emoluments for a period is not determined until after the end of the period, the time when the amount is determined.

It is important to note that the above rules apply even where a director's right to draw the emoluments is restricted. 'Director' includes a person acting in the capacity of director even if he is not actually a member of the board.

From the company's or business's point of view, the rules for deciding when payment is made for the purposes of PAYE are the same as the rules about time of receipt. PAYE is covered in detail in Chapter 17.

17 Pay As You Earn

Introduction

Whether you carry on your business through a company, a partnership or as a sole trader, the law requires you to use the pay as you earn (PAYE) system to deduct income tax from any payments you make to your employees unless their pay does not exceed the PAYE threshold. For 1992/93 the threshold is £66.32 a week or £287 a month. PAYE applies to all your employees, whether full-time or part-time, casuals, directors and pensioners, whether their duties are performed in the UK or abroad. Foreign employers operating from this country are also required to apply PAYE.

The inspector who deals with the taxation of your business profits will not be dealing with your PAYE and in many cases the PAYE inspector and his staff will be in a different location. In the next two chapters references to the tax office and to the inspector will be to the tax office and the inspector who deals with your PAYE.

To obtain the necessary PAYE forms and booklets write to or telephone your tax office. They will send you a new employer's starter pack and the necessary registration forms. The starter pack includes the 'Employer's Basic Guide to PAYE', a set of 11 coloured cards which sets out clearly how you should operate the PAYE system. You will also be allocated a PAYE reference number which must be quoted on all future correspondence. The employer's section of your tax office will deal with your queries as an employer, such as requests for more forms. In addition there will be a tax officer dealing with your employees' personal tax affairs.

Not everyone who does work for you is an employee; they could be self-employed. But it should be emphasised that you cannot just accept that someone is self-employed because they also work for other people or because their previous work was as a self-employed person. It depends on what they will do for you and the terms and conditions of the agreement between you. The factors that determine whether a person is self-employed are considered in Chapter 16.

Earnings

The following are earnings from which income tax is to be deducted under the PAYE system:

- Wages and salaries including bonuses and overtime.
- Pensions, fees, honoraria, commissions, tips and perks.
- Round sum expense allowances and some other expense payments.
- Drawings on account of future remuneration.
- Payments to directors as defined under the 'receipts basis' rules (see Chapter 16).
- Christmas boxes and vouchers that can be exchanged for cash.
- Holiday and sick pay including statutory sick pay (SSP) and statutory maternity pay (SMP).
- Lump sums on termination of employment (see page 143).

To calculate the amount of an employee's pay which is taxable you include the items listed above and reduce the figure by:

- superannuation contributions made by the employees to an approved pension scheme; and
- charitable donations made under an approved payroll giving scheme.

What is involved?

As an employer you are required to keep proper records of your employees' earnings from their employment with you, calculate the income tax and National Insurance contributions due, remit those amounts to the accounts office every month and send in a summary of your records at the end of each year.

More specifically, the following procedure is required each time you pay an employee:

- Record the amount paid on the employee's deductions working sheet form P11. It is not necessary to fill in the official forms manually; a variety of substitute deductions working sheets from commercially marketed payroll systems are acceptable including computerised systems. What is important is that all the information that would be recorded on P11 is recorded.
- Work out how much of the pay is taxable by using the employee's tax code and the tax tables provided by the tax office. The PAYE code is normally a number followed by a letter. The number is the employee's total allowances comprising his personal allowances, and allowable

expenses reduced by other income not taxed at source, with the last digit deleted. For example, if an employee is only entitled to the single person's allowance of £3,445 his code would be 345L. The most frequently used letters are:

L   which indicates the code includes the personal allowance.

H   which indicates the code includes the married couples allowance or that the additional personal allowance has been given in addition to the personal allowance.

P   which indicates the code includes the age allowance for a single person.

V   which indicates the code includes the age allowance for a married couple.

T   is for all other cases and can be used for any employees who do not want anyone to know whether they are single or married.

There are five special codes which are either not related to numbers or the numbers do not represent the employee's allowances:

BR   which means that basic rate tax must be deducted.

DO   which indicates that higher rate tax is to be deducted.

F   which is followed by a number and indicates that tax on a pension is to be deducted from current earnings.

OT   which means there are no allowances and tax is to be deducted according to the rate bands, i.e. £2,000 at 20 per cent, £21,700 at 25 per cent, and 40 per cent on the excess.

NT   which means that no tax needs to be deducted.

- Deduct from the current payment any tax due or add any tax refund.
- Calculate the employer's and the employee's liability for National Insurance contributions (NIC) using the tables supplied by the DSS.
- Deduct from the current payment employee's pension contributions.

The employee's wages reduced by income tax and NIC are referred to as his net pay.

Example
Kevin is employed as a car mechanic at £200 per week and has a code number of 501H. The following is an extract from his tax working sheet showing how the tax is calculated:

Week	Pay this week	Pay to date	Free pay to date (per Table A)	Taxable pay to date	Tax due to date (per Tables B and LR)	Tax for this week
	£	£	£	£	£	£
10	200.00	2,000.00	967.00	1,033.00	239.01	24.07
11	200.00	2,200.00	1,063.70	1,136.30	262.84	23.83
12	200.00	2,400.00	1,160.40	1,239.60	286.67	23.83
13	200.00	2,600.00	1,257.10	1,342.90	310.50	23.83

If you have agreed with employees to make deductions from their wages, for example, weekly savings for holidays or Christmas, these amounts should be deducted from their net pay.

From 6 April 1993 'K' codes will be introduced whereby tax on the excess of benefits over tax allowances will be collected under the PAYE system.

Free of tax payments

If you agree with an employee that all or any of his earnings are to be paid 'free of tax' it will be necessary for you to work out the employee's true gross pay. If the agreement is to pay free of basic rate tax the true gross pay will be the payment grossed up by multiplying by 100/75.

Example

Nelson, who earns a salary of £100 a week, is paid a travelling allowance of £45 per week free of tax. His true gross pay is:

	£
Salary	100
Allowance £45 × 100/75	60
	£160

If you do intend to make free-of-tax payments you can get a special package from the tax office which contains:

- special deductions working sheets (P11 FOT);
- special free-of-tax (FOT) tax tables;
- an explanatory leaflet (FOT1)

Remittance of PAYE

Within 14 days of the end of a tax month you are required to pay the accounts office at either Cumbernauld or Shipley in Bradford, any money due for that month consisting of:

- tax due from employees; and
- NIC due from employees together with the employer's contributions;

reduced by

- tax that you have refunded;
- gross statutory sick pay (SSP) and statutory maternity pay (SMP) paid to employees; and
- an amount to compensate for the employer's NIC paid on SSP and SMP.

The payment should be accompanied by a payslip – P30B – showing details of how the payment has been calculated. As the tax month ends on the fifth of the month payments must be made by the nineteenth of each month. If you fall into arrears with your monthly payments the collector can send you a notice of his estimate of your liability. If you do not pay within seven days the estimate becomes an enforceable debt.

Employers whose average monthly payments of PAYE and NIC are less than 400 in total may account quarterly rather than monthly to the Revenue.

End of year procedure

At the end of the tax year you are required to send to your tax office a return (P14) for each employee for whom you used a deductions working sheet for the year that has just ended. The P14 is a three-part form. You send two copies to the tax office. The third copy is for your employee and is called the employee's certificate of pay and tax deducted (P60). It includes details of the employee's total pay for the year including amounts for SSP or SMP, the total amount of tax deducted are refunded and National Insurance contributions made. With the forms P14 you send a form P35 which is called the Employer's Annual Statement, declaration and certificate. The end of year returns, P14s and P35, should be submitted to the PAYE tax office no later than 19 May following the end of the tax year. However, for 1991/92 no proceedings will be taken for returns that are less than two months overdue, i.e. made by 19 July 1992. This period of grace is being gradually reduced until 1995 when penalties will become automatic for returns not made by 19 May.

For selected cases of serious delay before 1995 the Inland Revenue will take proceedings to the Appeal Commissioners (see Chapter 15). They will be able to impose an initial penalty of up to £1,200 per 50 employees and, if the delay continues, a further penalty of £100 per 50 employees per month.

Before 6 June your tax office needs to have details of your employees' expenses and benefits for the previous tax year on forms P11D or P9D. Further information on benefits-in-kind and expenses can be found in Chapters 16 and 18. The new rules described below do not apply to forms P11D and P9D.

It is important to make end of year returns in good time. If you are having problems you should contact the tax office and explain the delay. Your accountant or tax adviser may also be able to help.

Employers joining and leaving

A new employee who has previously been working or has been signing on as unemployed should give you parts 2 and 3 of form P45, part 3 of which is reproduced in Appendix 13. This form provides you with the details you need to prepare a deductions working sheet for the new employee. You should fill in items 7 to 14 on part 3 of the form and send it to your tax office. Part 2 should be kept for reference for three years.

If a new employee brings a P45 for the last tax year you can use the code given if you take the employee on before 26 April in the current tax year. For employees joining after that date use the emergency code (equal to the single person's allowance) and enter 'nil' on the deductions working sheet for the pay and tax from 6 April to the date of being employed by you.

If a new employee does not have a P45 find out if it is possible to get one from the previous employer or from the unemployment benefit office. In any event, if you are going to employ the person for more than one week and the pay is over £1 a week (£4 a month), you need to prepare a form P46 and send it to your tax office. Where appropriate the employee should sign certificate A or B on the form. Certificate A is a declaration that the individual has not previously had regular employment since leaving full-time education. Certificate B is a statement of whether the new job is his only or main employment. Meanwhile you should issue the employee with a coding claim form (P15); prepare the employee's deductions working sheet and deduct tax using the emergency code on a cumulative basis if certificate A was signed, or on a week 1 or month 1 basis if certificate B was signed.

If a tax refund of £200 or less is due on the employee's first day, or it is for a larger amount and you have received a notice from the Revenue authorising the code to be operated (P6), you can go ahead and make the refund. If this is not the case you must fill in form P47, send it to your tax office and wait for the authority (P48) to make the refund.

If you have been deducting tax from an employee, when he leaves you should complete form P45, give parts 2 and 3 of the form to the employee and send part 1 to your tax office.

PAYE audits

Although there is quite a lot of paperwork involved in the PAYE system it is in your interest to operate PAYE properly. If necessary consider paying someone to maintain the system for you. If the correct tax and National Insurance are not deducted from payments to employees, the Inland Revenue and the DSS have power to obtain the amount unpaid from the employer. In recent years the Revenue have been using more of their resources to carry out PAYE audits. They visit the employer to check on whether the PAYE system is being operated correctly. They are particularly concerned with under deductions of tax for the following reasons:

- where you have made payments to a person on the basis that he is not an employee and the Revenue consider he is or you have made gross payments to part-timers or casuals;
- where directors have withdrawn cash on account of future earnings and no tax has been deducted;
- where employees have been treated as lower-paid when they should be treated as higher-paid for the purpose of taxable benefits (see Chapter 18 for details);
- where the amount of the taxable benefits is incorrect, for example, because of incorrect business mileage;
- where there has been incorrect treatment of business entertainment; and
- where there has been incorrect treatment of termination payments.

If insufficient tax has been deducted the inspector may determine the amount to the best of his judgement and raise an assessment (under Regulation 29) on the employer. He has the power, and it is quite often exercised, to review and raise assessments for the previous six years. Interest on unpaid tax is payable from the fourteenth day after the end of the tax year to which the tax relates (or 19 April 1988, if later).

18 Benefits

Introduction

In this and the following chapters we examine how, by giving employees benefits-in-kind,

- they can be taxed on less than the value they receive, for example, the use of cars in certain cases (see Chapter 19);
- National Insurance contributions on certain benefits are avoided;
- the employer's cost can be less than the benefit they receive, for example, share options (see Chapter 20);
- staff motivation can be increased, for example, by incentive awards or profit sharing;
- you may improve staff loyalty or make it more difficult for them to leave, for example, with a good pension scheme or cheap home loans; and
- opportunities can be provided to improve morale, for example by having conferences and social events.

The attraction of different benefits varies from employee to employee. Some employers operate a 'cafeteria' system whereby employees can select their own benefits package.

The way in which you calculate a taxable benefit depends on how much the employee earns. Most directors, and all employees whose earnings, including any benefits but without a deduction for allowable expenses, are at a rate of £8,500 per annum or more, are subject to special rules.

In the case of directors, there are the following additional requirements if they are not to be included in this category:

- they must not own more than 5 per cent of the company; and
- must be full-time working directors unless the company is only engaged in non-profit making activities, such as a charity.

As a general rule only benefits that can be turned into money are taxable on the lower-paid worker and the value of the benefit is its second-hand value, the provision of living accommodation being the major exception. By contrast most benefits, whether convertible into money or not, are taxable on directors and those who earn £8,500 or more.

The rules for ascertaining the taxable value of benefits vary. In some cases a specific charge or formula is used, in others it is the cost to the employer of the benefit or its market value which is used. Before you include a benefit as part of an employee's taxable remuneration, you should make a deduction for any contribution the employee has made.

Mobile telephones

Where an employee has available for private use a mobile telephone provided by his employer, there is a taxable benefit of £200 per annum. It makes no difference whether the telephone is hand-portable or is fitted to the employer's car or the employee's car.

Accommodation

As a general rule if an employer provides any employees with living accommodation, whatever their earnings, they will be assessed on the benefit. The amount assessed is the greater of the rent paid by the employer or the annual value of the property. In each case the benefit is reduced by any contribution made by the employee. If the property is in the UK its gross rateable value is used, and for overseas properties the value is equal to the rent that could be obtained, assuming the landlord pays for repairs and insurance and the tenant pays rates and taxes.

In Scotland the gross values resulting from the 1985 rating revaluation, which did not affect other parts of the UK, have to be reduced for tax purposes. The reduction is equal to the average increase in rateable values in Scotland between 1978 (the date of the most recent rating revaluation for the rest of the UK) and 1985, i.e. 170 per cent. This means that a gross rating value of £270 will be reduced to £100.

Although domestic rates have been replaced, rateable values will continue to be used, as described above, for tax purposes. For new properties after 1 April 1990, a substitute value will be used which is in line with the old domestic rating values.

If the accommodation is only available to the employee for part of the year, for example, while the employee is on holiday, only the appropriate proportion of the annual value is assessed.

There are some circumstances where employees are not taxed on this benefit. These are:

- where it is necessary for the performance of his duties that the employee should occupy the accommodation, for example, a publican, lighthouse keeper, prison warder, caretaker, etc.;

- where it has been the practice to provide accommodation for employees of a particular class to enable them to perform their duties better, for example, a policeman; or

- where, because of a special threat to an employee's security, accommodation is provided as part of the security arrangements, for example, a Cabinet Minister.

The first two exceptions do not apply in the case of a director unless either he is a full-time working director who does not own more than 5 per cent of the company or the company engages only in non-profit making or charitable activities.

If the employer pays for heating, lighting, cleaning, repairs, maintenance, furniture, etc., employees earning £8,500 or more are assessable on a benefit equal to the cost incurred. If, however, any employees are within one of the three exceptions above, the assessment for the additional services is limited to 10 per cent of their net earnings. If accommodation is provided with a cost of more than £75,000, the assessable benefit is increased. In addition to the annual value, the employee is assessed on a sum equal to the excess of the cost of the accommodation over £75,000 multiplied by the official rate of interest prescribed by the Treasury at the beginning of the tax year. At 6 April 1992 this rate was 10.75 per cent.

Example

Barlow Hi-Tech Products Ltd in 1992/93 provided Ken, the managing director, with living accommodation which had cost £185,000. Ken paid the company rent equal to the gross rateable value.

Ken's taxable benefit is £11,825 which is calculated by multiplying the following:

£110,000 which is the excess over £75,000

10.75 per cent which was the official rate of interest at 6 April 1992.

Assets provided for employees

If an asset is sold to a director or an employee earning £8,500 or more at a price that is less than its market value the employee receives a taxable benefit equal to the difference. What some employers do instead is to put assets such as furniture, computers, vans, expensive suits, etc. at the disposal of their employees. If such assets are provided (other than a car or accommodation) to a director or an employee earning £8,500 or more he will be assessed on 20 per cent of the asset's market value at the time it was first put at his disposal. If instead of being bought the asset is rented by the employer, the amount of rent is assessable. If, having been used, the asset is transferred to the employee, the benefit at that time is based on the greater of:

- the open market value at the time of the transfer; and
- the market value at the time it was first used by the employee less the amounts of the benefits assessed while being used by him.

Example

In 1989/90 Sugden and Turner Leather Products Ltd made available an antique dining room table and chairs to Joe, the managing director, and a painting to Alan, the sales director. The table and chairs were worth £40,000 in 1989/90 and £5,000 when they were sold to Joe in 1992/93 for £1,500. The painting was worth £3,000 in 1989/90 and £1,000 when it was sold to Alan in 1991/92 for £800.

Assessable benefits	Joe		Alan	
	£	£	£	£
1989/90 20% × market value	800			600
1990/91 20% × market value	800			600
1991/92 20% × market value	800			600
1992/93 greater of:				
(a) market value when transferred	4,000	4,000	1,000	
(b) market value when first used by directors	4,000		3,000	
Less: benefits already assessed in 1989/90 to 1991/92	2,400		1,800	
	1,600		1,200	1,200
Less: amounts paid by directors		(1,500)		(800)
		£3,500		£400

Subsidised loans

If an employer makes a loan to a director or a higher-paid employee and either no interest is charged or the interest is at a low rate, there may be a taxable benefit. Making a loan for this purpose includes arranging, guaranteeing or in any way facilitating a loan for the employee or a relative of his. There is no need to calculate the benefit if the interest would in any event have been tax deductible, for example, if it were a loan of up to £30,000 to purchase a main residence and the benefiting employee were not a higher-rate taxpayer. To calculate this benefit you need to know the official rates of interest prescribed by the Treasury which during 1991/92 were:

6 April to 5 May	13.75%
6 May to 5 July	12.75%
6 July to 5 August	12.25%
6 August to 5 October	11.75%
6 October to 5 March	11.25%
6 March to 5 April	10.75%

The benefit is the difference between interest at the official rate and that actually paid by the employee in the year.

There is no charge if the amount calculated is less than £300, which, assuming an interest rate at 10.5 per cent throughout 1992/93, excludes an interest-free loan of £2,857. This is intended to take out of charge most employers' loans for season tickets.

Example

On 6 May 1992 Elizabeth, a basic rate taxpayer, borrowed £40,000 at 3 per cent from her employer to enable her to buy a flat which is her main residence. By 5 April 1992 she had paid the interest but had not repaid any part of the loan. Assuming that the official rate was 10.5 per cent from 6 May to 5 July and 10 per cent from 6 July to 5 April 1993, her taxable benefit for 1992/93 would be calculated as follows:

	£
£10,000 × 7.5 per cent × 2 months	125
£10,000 × 7 per cent × 9 months	525
Taxable benefit	£650

If, after including this benefit, Elizabeth remains a basic rate taxpayer, the tax on this benefit would be £650 at 25 per cent   £162.50

If, however, Elizabeth were a higher-rate taxpayer (before including the benefit) her additional tax would be:

	£
£650 at 40 per cent	260.00
Excess liability on interest relief	
£30,000 × 3 per cent × 11/12 × 15 per cent	123.75
	£383.75

If Elizabeth became a higher-rate taxpayer as a result of the benefit the additional tax would fall between £162.50 and £383.75.

Where the loan fluctuates during the tax year there are two possible methods of calculating the benefit. You can take an average of the amounts outstanding at the beginning and end of the year and apply the official rate to the average. Alternatively, at the option of the employee or the inspector, the official rate can be applied on a day-to-day basis throughout the year.

Pensions

The contribution made by an employer into an approved pension scheme for employees is not taxable as a benefit on them and is tax deductible in computing trading profits. You could therefore make substantial contributions to your employees' pension entitlements which could consist of:

- a tax-free lump sum;
- a pension;
- on the death of the employee, a pension for the spouse;
- on death in service, a tax-free lump sum.

Further details on pensions can be found in Chapter 29.

Medical treatment and insurance

If an employer pays for medical treatment or contributes to an insurance scheme such as BUPA or PPP there will be no taxable benefit for lower-paid employees. Directors and employees earning £8,500 or more are taxable on the costs incurred, for example, a proportion of the total premium paid by the business.

There is not a taxable benefit, however:

- in providing medical treatment outside the UK when the employee is working abroad; or
- in providing insurance for the cost of such treatment.

Medical insurance is usually part of a remuneration package since:

- it does not attract National Insurance contributions; and
- the firm can usually negotiate a lower premium than the individual.

Meals and social functions

Meals provided free of charge or at a low cost in a canteen on the firm's premises or elsewhere are not taxable if they are available to staff generally and are provided on a reasonable scale. No tax is payable on luncheon vouchers provided they do not exceed 15p per day.

A concession applies for the cost of an annual Christmas party for employees, or a similar alternative function such as a dinner dance which is open to staff generally. The Inland Revenue's practice is not to tax expenditure up to £50 per annum per employee, so if the expenditure is less than this there is no need to include the item on form P11D. If the concessional limit is exceeded the employee is taxed on the full cost.

The Revenue do not normally tax the provision of sports facilities either on the firm's premises or where there is corporate membership of an outside club, so long as it is for the employees generally.

Furthermore, employees are not normally taxed on the provision of hospitality and entertainment by persons other than their employer.

Training and scholarships

There are valuable concessions if employees attend courses:

- The Revenue do not tax the employee where he attends an external course necessary for his job or which is expected to improve his performance. For those employees who are under 21, this concession is extended to courses of general education. The course cannot exceed 12 months and there is a further condition that the employee must return to his employment afterwards. The costs covered are the course fees, books, travel and reasonable subsistence.

- If you provide your employees with scholarships to attend full-time courses of further education they will not be taxed on the benefit provided:

  (a) the enrolment is for at least one academic year; and

  (b) the rate of payment does not exceed £5,500 or, if greater, the amount which would have been received from a Research Council or similar public body, this amount being in addition to any course fees payable.

Incentives and prizes

You may wish to give your employees an incentive to achieve certain targets. For example, they could be eligible to participate in an employees' lottery for, say, a video recorder or be given vouchers exchangeable at retail stores. Although there is no National Insurance to pay, the cost you incur in providing these awards is taxable on the employees who receive them. There is, however, a scheme available for collecting basic rate tax on these prizes from the employer. Your tax office can provide you with the details.

You might consider having a staff suggestion scheme in which you ask your employees for ideas on how to improve efficiency or productivity and reward the best ideas with a prize.

By concession, the Inland Revenue will not tax the employees on the prize if the scheme meets certain conditions, the main ones being that:

- the scheme is formally constituted and open to all employees on equal terms;
- the suggestions fall outside the employees' normal duties;
- for payments over £25 the suggestion must have been accepted for implementation; and
- the awards made must be calculated by reference to specified fractions of the expected financial benefit to the business, within an overriding tax-free limit of £5,000.

Gifts

Gifts made to an employee by the employer for personal reasons not connected with the employment are not taxable. For example, if you buy wedding presents for your staff.

By concession, tax is not charged on articles that you may give your staff as testimonials for long service, provided:

- the employee's period of service is at least 20 years;
- the employee has not received a similar award in the last ten years; and
- the cost does not exceed £20 for each year of service.

By concession, certain non-cash gifts costing up to £100, received by an employee from persons other than an employer, are not taxed as benefits.

Nurseries

Since 6 April 1990 the costs attributable to child care facilities has not been taxable as a benefit on an employee earning £8,500 or more, if the employer provides and manages the facilities and these are not in domestic premises.

19 Business Cars

Introduction
Before you decide to purchase or lease cars, either for your own business use or for the use of your employees, you should be aware of the tax implications.

Purchasing cars
Assuming you wish to purchase a car rather than lease one, you have the choice of paying in cash or entering into an agreement for lease-purchase, contract-purchase or hire-purchase. If you buy a car for business using any of these methods of finance and take it into use immediately, you are treated for tax purposes as owning the car at that time and having paid the full cost. The cost for this purpose includes any accessories already fitted, delivery charges and non-recoverable VAT. This means that you can set against your business profits an annual writing-down allowance of 25 per cent and the 'interest' element of the hire-purchase repayments is treated as an allowable deduction for tax purposes.

In the first year the writing-down allowance is 25 per cent of cost, thereafter it is 25 per cent of the unrelieved expenditure. Cars costing £12,000 or less are aggregated in a car capital allowance 'pool'. On a disposal of any of the cars the pool expenditure is reduced by the sale proceeds and the writing-down allowance is available on the reduced amount.

Example
Janistra Products purchased a car for £11,000 cash in year 1 and three cars on hire-purchase in year 2, each car costing £8,000 of which £2,000 is paid on deposit. The first car was sold in year 4 for £5,000.

		Car pool £	Capital allowances £
Year 1	Expenditure	11,000	
	Writing-down allowance	(2,750)	2,750
		8,250	

Year 2	Expenditure	24,000	
		32,250	
	Writing-down allowance	(8,062)	8,062
		24,188	
Year 3	Writing-down allowance	(6,047)	6,047
		18,141	
Year 4	Disposal proceeds	(5,000)	
		13,141	
	Writing-down allowance	(3,285)	3,285
		9,856	

Purchasing expensive cars

For cars which cost more than £12,000 the writing-down allowance cannot exceed £3,000. These limits were £8,000 and £2,000 respectively for expenditure before 11 March 1992. As the expenditure is not pooled, an additional allowance, known as a balancing allowance, can arise if the car is sold for less than the written-down value.

Example

Fowler Garden Produce Ltd purchased two cars for the directors, an Audi 80 2.0E for £15,000 and a Granada Ghia for £19,000. After three and a half years they were sold for £7,000 and £9,000 respectively. The following capital allowances would be available:

		Audi	Granada	Capital allowances
		£	£	£
Year 1	Expenditure	15,000	19,000	
	Writing-down allowance	(3,000)	(3,000)	6,000
		12,0000	16,0000	
Year 2	Writing-down allowance	(3,000)	(3,000)	6,000
		9,000	13,000	
Year 3	Writing-down allowance	(2,250)	(3,000)	5,250
		6,750	10,000	
Year 4	Sale proceeds	7,000	9,000	
	Balancing allowance		1,000	750
	Balancing charge	(250)		

Private use

If a sole trader or partner uses a car owned by the business partly for private use, then it is necessary to keep the expenditure outside the pool and calculate the capital allowances separately. Allowances are restricted to the proportion of business use but the full allowance is deducted from the tax written-down value.

Example

Martin, a self-employed plumber, purchased for £10,000 a car to use in his business. He had agreed with his local inspector that the private use of the car was 15%. Four years later Martin sold the car for £4,000.

		Car (private use 15%) £	Capital allowances £
Year 1	Expenditure	10,000	
	Writing-down allowance	(2,500) × 85%	2,125
		7,500	
Year 2	Writing-down allowance	(1,875) × 85%	1,594
		5,625	
Year 3	Writing-down allowance	(1,406) × 85%	1,195
		4,219	
Year 4	Disposal proceeds	(4,000)	
	Balancing allowance	219 × 85%	186

Leasing cars

If you lease a car you will enter into a contract for a fixed period, say 36 months and pay three months rental in advance. The size of the payments will depend on the type of car you are leasing and any extras you require such as accessories and motor club membership. Payments under 'contract hire' will be higher because the agreement will provide for maintenance and a relief vehicle when the leased car is off the road. Under a 'finance lease' the leasing company takes no responsibility for maintenance.

Under a lease agreement you would not normally be given the right to buy the car at the end of the lease period although you may in fact get the opportunity to buy it. A lease where there is such a right is treated for tax purposes as a hire-purchase and you, rather than the leasing company, could claim the capital allowances (see above).

Most lease payments are deductible in full when calculating the profits of the business. VAT is payable on the rental payments and if you are making taxable supplies the VAT will normally be recoverable.

Leasing expensive cars

If a car costing more than £12,000 is hired or leased, there is a restriction on the allowable proportion of hire charges paid, which is calculated as follows:

$$\text{Hire charges} \times \frac{\tfrac{1}{2}\,(\text{Retail price of car when new less £12,000})}{\text{Retail price of car when new}}$$

Example

Fowler Garden Produce Ltd hires a car with a retail price of £16,000 and pays £2,000 hire charges. The amount of interest not allowable for tax purposes would be as follows:

$$£2,000 \times \frac{\tfrac{1}{2}\,(16{,}000 - 12{,}000)}{16{,}000} = £250$$

£1,750 would be an allowable deduction for tax purposes.

Employee benefits

Of all the fringe benefits the 'company car' is still the most popular. If you are looking for staff at managerial level you may find you have to offer a car as part of the remuneration package. There is no taxable benefit for those employees who use pool cars (see below) or for those whose remuneration is less than £8,500. In other cases, tax is payable according to certain scale charges (see Appendix 10).

Benefits covered by the scale charges

The benefits covered by the car scale charges are those associated with the provision of the car, such as insurance, road tax, repairs and maintenance. The scale charges do not cover the provision of a chauffeur; or the expenses of the driver such as fines, tolls and parking costs. There is a separate set of scale charges where petrol is provided for private travel which is considered below.

In cases where the employer provides a chauffeur or pays for any driver's costs, the employee is taxed on the full cost incurred by the employer less any proportion relating solely to genuine business journeys.

Adjustments to the scale charges

The scale charges are increased by 50 per cent where the annual rate of business mileage is less than 2,500 miles; and also for taxing the provision of each additional car, for example, where cars are provided for an employee's wife or children.

If the car's business mileage reaches an annual rate of 18,000 miles the scale charges are halved. Furthermore, where the car is only provided for part of the tax year or is incapable of being used for a period of at least 30 consecutive days, the scale charges are reduced proportionately.

If, as a condition of the car being available for private use, the employee is required to make a contribution towards costs, the scale charge is reduced on a pound for pound basis. The agreed contribution for use of the car should be treated as inclusive of VAT. The scale charge cannot be reduced by the employee making a voluntary annual contribution or by making a lump sum contribution to the initial cost of the car.

The table of scale charges at Appendix 10, currently depends on the car's age at the end of the tax year, its cylinder capacity, and in some cases, its cost. The car's cost for this purpose is not necessarily the price paid by the employer and it does not include delivery costs or number plates. It is the price, inclusive of VAT and car tax, that it might have been expected to fetch if sold in the UK singly in a retail sale immediately before its first registration. So there is no advantage to your employees if you buy a fleet of cars at a substantial discount. On the other hand, employees can benefit by being taxed on a low scale charge if they are provided with an old car such as a Bentley or Rolls-Royce which has a high current value but a low original cost. Because the age of the car is relevant for the scale charge there is an advantage for the employee if a car is registered just before rather than just after 5 April.

It has been decided to change the way in which car benefits are taxed by using a scale charge based entirely on the car's price. Further details are expected in the next few months.

Whether company cars are tax efficient

One of the attractions of having a car provided by the employer can be the tax treatment. However, following the recent steep rises in the car scale charges, a tax saving can no longer be guaranteed and many company cars may now actually be over-taxed.

Example

Company A offers Jonathan a leased car costing £3,660 a year (equivalent to a monthly lease rental of £305 per month). For a mid-range company car with average business mileage, Jonathan would be assessed on a scale benefit of £2,770.

If, on the other hand, he was offered a car allowance of £3,660, Jonathan would be assessed on the whole £3,660 but would be able to claim a deduction in respect of the business element. If his business mileage were more than 25 per cent and his car costs were equivalent to the allowance, his net assessable income would be below the scale charge of £2,770.

Example
Company B offers Colin a prestige car for which the annual lease rental is £7,000. The car scale benefit is £5,750 but as Colin does only 10 per cent business mileage (under 2,500 miles) the scale charge is increased by one-half to £8,625.

If, on the other hand, Colin is offered a car allowance of £7,000, which is equivalent to his car costs, he will be assessed to tax on £5,400 (90 per cent of costs). Thus in this example, Colin would be much better off in tax terms even if he did no business mileage whatsoever.

Although significant tax savings can be achieved, in practice it is necessary to also take into account any variation in the employer's and the employee's costs of providing the car for business use such as car insurance.

Pool cars

Employees will not have a taxable benefit if they drive pool cars which are cars that meet all the following conditions:

- The car is available to, and is actually used by, more than one employee during the tax year.

- It is not ordinarily used by any one employee to the exclusion of the others.

- Any private use of the car is merely incidental to business use. An example would be where the employee had to take the car home one evening because it was necessary to set off early the next day on a business trip.

- The car is not normally kept overnight at or near the home of any of the employees.

If these conditions are not met, all employees earning £8,500 or more and directors who use their employer's cars for private use are taxable using the scale charges. A chauffeur, however, required to garage the company limousine at home for example is subject to special concessionary treatment if his private use is purely incidental for his business journeys.

An employee is not taxed on the benefit if his employer provides or bears the cost of car parking at or near his place of work.

Carfuel

If an employee is also provided with petrol (or other fuel) for private motoring he will be taxed on this benefit by reference to another scale of charges similar to those used to tax the provision of the car (see Appendix 10). Some of the rules for the car scale charge apply for the fuel charge. For example, the charges are halved if the employee's business mileage is at an annual rate of at least 18,000 miles and are reduced proportionately if the car is not available for part of the year. No fuel charge arises where employees use pool cars.

However, there are some differences between the two scales. The fuel charge is not increased if the car's business mileage is less than 2,500 miles and is not reduced where cars are over four years old or where the employee is required to make a contribution to the cost of fuel. The only way employees can avoid the fuel scale charge is if they pay for all the fuel used for private motoring and records are kept to show that this is the position.

Example

During 1992/93 Ross Gifford & Simpson Ltd provided its directors with the following cars and paid for all petrol:

Managing director Eric: a Jaguar XJS which cost £35,000 in March 1990. Business use 2,600 miles. Sales director Hamish; a Granada 2.0 Ghia which cost £16,000 in March 1989. Business use 22,000 miles.

Their taxable benefits for 1992/93 would be:

	Eric £	Hamish £
Car scale charges	9,300	2,770
Less: 50% for high business mileage		(1,385)
Petrol scale charges	940	630
Less: 50% for high business mileage		(315)
	£10,240	£1,700

In deciding whether it is beneficial for the employer to pay for fuel for private motoring it is necessary to consider:

- the amount of the scale charge;
- the number of private miles travelled;
- the car's fuel consumption;
- the price of fuel;
- the employee's income tax rate.

National Insurance

Employer's Class 1A National Insurance (NI) contributions are chargeable on both the car and the car fuel benefit scale charges and detailed records of each employee's business mileage need to be kept. The contributions are assessed annually and collected in arrears. The first payments, i.e. for 1991/92, were due on 19 June 1992 and should have been submitted with the PAYE payment for the tax month 6 May to 5 June. You should enter the actual contributions due in respect of 1991/92 on the 1992/93 end of year documents. The contribution payable in respect of cars will usually be based on the scale charges shown on the employee's form P11D. However, the highest car scale charge, i.e. one and a half times the normal scale charge, must be used unless your records show that the employee's annual business mileage exceeded 2,500 miles. If your records show the employee's business mileage exceeded 18,000 miles a 50 per cent deduction may be claimed.

The full fuel scale charge must also be applied if you provide fuel for your employees. A 50 per cent reduction is only available when your records show that the employee's business mileage exceeded 18,000 miles.

Employees are not liable to employee's NI contributions on the car and fuel scale charges.

Mileage allowances

Employees who use their own cars for work can either receive a business mileage allowance or reimbursement for the expenses they incur when using the car for business. In some cases an employee borrows to buy the car and some employers provide cheap or interest-free loans for this purpose.

Where mileage allowances are given, the normal rule is that these are taxable subject to the employee making an expenses claim for business use. An exception is where employers pay tax-free mileage allowances under the Fixed Profit Car Scheme (FPCS). These allowances are set at a level to reflect the tax allowable costs of using a private car for business purposes. In March 1992 the Revenue revised the FPCS allowance rates, considerably enhancing their value to high business mileage drivers. The new rates still do not make any provision for the interest costs of funding the car, the business proportion of which can be claimed separately.

The FPCS is open to all employers and the Revenue may review current dispensations (see page 143) to ensure that employees do not receive excessive mileage allowances.

The tax-free mileage rates for 1992/93 are as follows:

	Up to 4,000 miles	Over 4,000 miles
Cars up to 1,000cc	25p	14p
Cars 1,001cc to 1,500cc	30p	17p
Cars 1,501cc to 2,000cc	38p	21p
Cars over 2,000cc	51p	27p

Employers wishing to simplify their administration can offer the average of the two middle rates, i.e. 34p and 19p.

Capital allowances for employees

For some time it has been possible for an employee to claim capital allowances on the business use of plant and machinery which is necessarily provided for use in the performance of his duties. Since 6 April 1990 this 'necessity' test has been removed in respect of cars used in an individual's employment. The capital allowances are restricted on the amount of business travel. See page 163 for details of restrictions to capital allowances for private use. For these purposes business mileage does not include travel from home to work, but see page 144 for exceptions.

An employee may not claim capital allowances if he receives a mileage allowance under the FPCS. This is because the FPCS allowances include an element for depreciation.

Capital gains

When a business or an individual disposes of a car any gain is tax-free and any loss is not allowable.

Value added tax

The VAT element of the price of a car is not normally recoverable. Exceptions are made where you intend to sell the car or use it for research and development, or where the car is to be converted into another type of vehicle. From 1 August 1992 taxis, driving schools and car hire firms will be allowed to reclaim VAT on the cost of their cars.

Where you have not been entitled to reclaim VAT on the purchase you do not need to account for VAT when you dispose of a car that you have used for business unless the selling price exceeds the purchase price, in which case you account for VAT on the excess. The purchase price includes any accessories fitted at the time of purchase on which VAT was not reclaimable and the manufacturer's delivery. The excess is treated as including VAT, for example if the excess was £235 the VAT is not £41 (£235 × 17.5 per cent) but £35 (£235 × 7/47).

There have been attempts to charge VAT in certain instances where employers have offered their employee a choice of either cash or a car. Since 1 April 1992 you have been able to offer your employee such a choice without it attracting VAT.

Car fuel

If you are registered for VAT you can claim as input tax the VAT you pay when you buy petrol or diesel in the same way that you account for input VAT on other business purchases. However, if some of the fuel is used for private journeys you have to pay an additional amount of output VAT to compensate for this. The figure for output VAT is calculated by reference to monthly and quarterly scale charges which are different for petrol and diesel. These scale charges are reproduced in Appendix 11. The charges are halved if business mileage exceeds 4,500 miles a quarter.

Example

Vera is provided with a 1.2 Vauxhall Nova as a company car until 31 July 1992 when it is replaced with a 1.6 Cavalier. Her business mileage is as follows:

	Business mileage
Quarter to:	
30 June 1992	3,000
30 September 1992	4,000
31 December 1992	4,800

			Output tax liability
Quarter to:			
30 June 1992	Table A Low business mileage		18.62
30 September 1992	Table A 1 month at £6.26	6.26	
	2 months at £7.89	15.78	22.04
31 December 1992	Table B High business mileage		
	1 quarter at £11.77		11.77

As an alternative to paying VAT on the scale charge, a business may opt not to deduct *any* VAT on the purchase of road fuel.

If you pay mileage allowances to your employees you work out your input tax by multiplying the fuel element by 7/47. You must agree an acceptable fuel element rate with your local VAT office. This will depend on the current price of road fuel and on the engine capacity. For example, 8.38p would normally be acceptable for cars of 1,501–2,200cc with fuel at £2 a gallon. Allowances must be based on actual mileage done.

20 Profit Sharing and Shares for Employees

Introduction

In previous chapters we considered how directors and other employees can best be remunerated with cash and non-cash benefits. We now examine the schemes that can result in your employees feeling more involved in the success of your business. This may be achieved either by letting them participate in a share of the profits in the form of cash or shares or by granting them an option to acquire shares. As an important part of the philosophy of this Government is to encourage employee participation and share ownership, the approved schemes are sweetened with tax reliefs. You may wish to consider one or more of the following approved schemes:

- Profit-related pay schemes where employees share in the profits and each employee can receive up to 20 per cent of his pay tax-free.

- Profit sharing schemes where employees are given shares tax-free provided the shares are held in trust for five years.

- Savings-related share option schemes where employees who enter a savings scheme are granted options at a fixed price and are not subject to income tax charges in connection with the options acquired.

- Executive share option schemes which have the same tax benefits as savings-related schemes but there is no requirement to save and the company need only grant options to selected employees.

- Employee share ownership plans (commonly known as ESOPs) where corporation tax relief is available for payments by a company to an ESOP trust, set up to acquire and distribute shares to its employees.

The department which deals with the approval of profit-related pay schemes is different from the one dealing with approved share schemes. Both addresses can be found in Appendix 17.

For the purpose of calculating National Insurance contributions, all profit-related pay is included as earnings but shares and share options are not.

Profit-related pay

In July 1987 the Government introduced legislation for approved profit-related pay (PRP) schemes whereby employees can receive part of their remuneration tax-free. The schemes are designed to give the work-force a more direct personal interest in the success of their employer's business and to provide a greater degree of pay flexibility in the face of changing market conditions. Since its introduction the Government have introduced a number of improvements to PRP which have maintained and perhaps increased the interest of employers. The main features of the scheme are as follows:

- Each PRP scheme must be registered and approved by the Inland Revenue. An independent auditor's report must accompany an application for registration to confirm that the scheme meets the statutory requirements.

- Existing schemes can qualify if they meet the criteria and are registered.

- The scheme must last for at least one year.

- The scheme must cover at least 80 per cent of the employees in an employment unit, although new recruits may be excluded from the scheme for up to three years and part-timers may be excluded.

- Directors or employees with a greater than 25 per cent interest in the employer company must be excluded.

- The scheme must establish a clear relationship between the PRP of the specified employment unit and the audited accounts that it generates, but see next point.

- If you register one or more conventional schemes you may now register a separate scheme or schemes for general or central units (for example Head Office or Research and Development departments) with PRP based on the profits of the whole undertaking. The number of employees covered by such schemes must not exceed 33 per cent of the numbers covered by the conventional schemes.

- Since the abolition of the original requirement that PRP in the first profit period must amount to at least 5 per cent of payroll if profits remain the same, a PRP scheme can be set up on a much smaller scale than was originally the case. Consequently, companies may now convert their annual Christmas bonus to all staff to a PRP scheme thus obtaining an element of tax relief for employees.

- The PRP must be determined and paid at least once a year but it can be calculated more frequently, for example, monthly or weekly.

- For profit periods beginning after 31 March 1991, the whole of PRP is eligible for tax relief up to the point where PRP is the lower of:
  - (a) 20 per cent of the employee's total remuneration for the year excluding pension contributions and benefits-in-kind; or
  - (b) £4,000.

Example

To the year ended 31 March 1993, Elizabeth has a basic salary of £18,000 and receives a further £7,000 from her firm's PRP scheme. The exempt amount is the lowest of:

£7,000	£7,000
£25,000 × 20%	£5,000
Monetary maximum	£4,000

Elizabeth will not be taxed on £4,000.

- For profit periods beginning after 31 March 1989 and before 1 April 1991, only half of eligible PRP was tax-free.
- The employer is responsible for:
  - (a) ensuring that the scheme complies with the statutory requirements;
  - (b) calculating PRP profits and the amounts of PRP payable to each employee;
  - (c) giving the tax relief due to each employee as part of the normal operation of PAYE.
- The employer's auditor is required to make a return at the end of each PRP period to confirm that the scheme and the tax relief have been operated properly.

Is employee share ownership worthwhile?

The following advantages are to be gained from allowing your employees to own shares in your company:

- For some executives, shares or a share option is an essential part of a remuneration package.
- Family companies can attract and motivate new staff from outside the family.
- It is particularly attractive if the company plans to go public in the foreseeable future.
- It enables employees to share in the success of the company.
- It is a way of providing employees with an incentive to work harder.

- It can give employees a greater sense of participation and improve loyalty to the company and encourage them to stay longer.
- If an approved scheme is used the employee can enjoy tax advantages.
- If shares are to be acquired by subscription your company will receive an injection of funds.
- Although capital in nature, costs incurred after 31 March 1991 in setting up an approved scheme are deductible in arriving at taxable profits. (Previously they had been disallowable.)

There are the following disadvantages:

- The equity held by you and any other shareholders is likely to be diluted. In practice, it is usual for only a small percentage of the equity to be available for employee shares.
- If your company is unquoted there will be the need to agree share valuations.
- There is no market for employees who wish to sell unquoted shares, although the establishment of an ESOP trust may resolve this problem.
- If shares are not acquired through an approved scheme the employee is likely to suffer income tax charges.
- Your employees may not believe that their efforts can influence the price of the company's shares.

Unapproved share acquisitions

If you give your employees the opportunity to acquire shares other than under an approved scheme they should be made aware that the following income tax charges could arise:

- Where shares are given to employees their value is taxed as remuneration.
- Where shares are issued or sold to employees at an undervalue, the undervalue is taxed as remuneration.
- Where shares are acquired by employees earning more than £8,500 and payment for them is wholly or partly deferred, tax is charged as if the employee had received an interest-free loan equal to the amount unpaid.
- Where shares acquired by employees (other than the lower-paid) are disposed of for more than market value the excess is subject to income tax.
- Where a share option is granted, the value of the option is only

subject to income tax if it is capable of being exercised more than seven years after it is granted.

- Where a share option is exercised an income tax charge arises on the difference between the price paid for the shares and the market value at the date of exercise. The tax is payable even though the employee has not realised any cash. Often this means he has to sell some of the shares to pay the tax. The gain charged to income tax is treated as part of the acquisition cost in computing the capital gain on a disposal of the shares.

- Where their shares increase in value because restrictions are imposed, varied or lifted on those shares or other shares, the resulting increase in value is taxed as remuneration.

- Where a benefit is received which is not received by other shareholders its value is taxed as remuneration.

- Where shares are acquired in a subsidiary that does not carry on a business independent of its group, the employer can be assessed to income tax on the growth in value of the shares from the time they were acquired until the seventh anniversary or an earlier disposal.

Approved share schemes

Certain features are common to all schemes:

- The schemes must be approved by the Revenue.
- The shares must be fully paid ordinary shares of:

  (a) the company operating the scheme; or

  (b) its holding company;

which are not redeemable or subject to restrictions.

- The shares must also be either:

  (a) shares in a company not under the control of another company; or

  (b) shares quoted on a recognised stock exchange; or

  (c) shares in a company under the control of a quoted company unless that company is a close company (see Chapter 13).

Shares dealt in the Unlisted Securities Market are not regarded as quoted for this purpose.

- If the conditions are met employees only pay capital gains tax when they dispose of their shares. No income tax is chargeable:

(a) when an option is granted or exercised;

(b) when the shares are acquired without payment or at less than their market value at that time; or

(c) on any growth in value of the shares.

Profit-sharing schemes

With an approved profit-sharing scheme a company allocates profits to trustees who then use the funds to purchase shares for each employee who is participating in the scheme. Tax is paid in the normal way on any dividends paid to the participants.

The main additional features of these schemes are as follows:

- All UK directors and employees with five years' service, who work at least 25 hours a week, must be eligible to participate.

- An individual is not eligible if:

   (a) in the same year he participates under another approved profit sharing scheme; or

   (b) he owns, with his associates, more than 25 per cent of the ordinary shares of a close company, which is the company operating the scheme or its holding company, at any time in the previous year.

- The shares must be held by the trustees for at least two years.

- No income tax is payable provided the shares remain with the trustees for a further three years.

- The maximum value of shares that may be allocated to an employee in any year is 10 per cent of the employee's remuneration, excluding pension contributions and benefits-in-kind, for the current or previous year, subject to the following lower and upper limits.

	Lower £	Upper £
Prior to 6 April 1989	1,250	5,000
6 April 1989 – 5 April 1991	2,000	6,000
After 5 April 1991	3,000	8,000

Example

On 1 February 1987 Joanna was allocated 500 50p ordinary shares in her employer company Simpson Malt Whiskies plc at which time they were worth £500. The shares were allocated under an approved profit-sharing scheme. She sells the shares on 10 February 1992 for £6,000. RPIs are February 1987 100.4; February 1992 136.3.

As it is an approved scheme no income tax charge arises when Joanna is allocated the shares worth £500 or when the trustees transfer them to her on 31 January 1992. When she sells them her chargeable gain is as follows:

	£	£
Sale proceeds		6,000
Less: Acquisition cost	500	
Indexation allowance		
RPI increase February 1987		
to February 1992		
0.358 × £500	179	679
Chargeable gain		£5,321

This gain is below the £5,800 annual exemption (see Chapter 7).

Save as You Earn share option schemes (SAYE)

Under this scheme employees are granted options provided they save regularly for at least five years through a bank, National Savings or building society Save as You Earn Scheme (SAYE).

The main additional features of the scheme are as follows:

- All UK directors and employees with five years' service, who work for at least 25 hours a week, must be eligible to participate.

- An individual is not eligible if, with his associates, he owns more than 25 per cent of the ordinary shares of a close company which is the company operating the scheme or its holding company at any time in the previous year.

- The time for exercising the option must be decided at the time of the grant and can be either five or seven years later.

- The option to acquire shares must be at a price equal to, or not less than, 80 per cent of the market value of the shares at the date of the grant.

- The value of the shares that could be acquired is limited to the amount the employee will receive from the SAYE scheme.

- The employee's savings in the scheme must not be:

  (a) less than £10 a month; or

  (b) more than £250 a month.

- Options are normally exercisable after five years but in, certain circumstances they may be exercised earlier, in which case an income tax charge may arise.

- After five years the savings scheme will attract a bonus of 15 months' contributions or after seven years a bonus of 30 months' contributions.

- The employer must deduct the employee's savings from his pay each month.

Example

On 1 October 1990 Hamish was given an option to purchase 10p ordinary shares in his employer company, Ross Gifford and Simpson Ltd, at a price of 80p per share under an approved savings-related share option scheme. On that date the shares were valued at £1 per share and Hamish entered into a five-year savings contract, saving £100 a month. The contract matures on 30 September 1995 and Hamish acquires his shares on 5 November 1995 at which time the shares have a value of 240p each.

The total Hamish should receive from the savings contract is:

Contributions to saving contract	£1,200 × 5	£6,000
Five-year bonus	£100 × 15	1,500
		£7,500

He can therefore acquire $7,500 \times \dfrac{100}{80} = 9,375$ shares.

There is no income tax charged on the value of the option when it is granted in 1990 nor on the growth in value of £15,000 up to the date he exercises his option. However, his acquisition cost is 80p a share so when he disposes of the shares the gain of £15,000 will be subject to capital gains tax. By disposing of the shares over three or more tax years, it may be possible to cover the gains by his annual exemptions.

Executive share option schemes

With these schemes the employer may, and usually does, restrict entry to key employees.

The main additional features are as follows:

- To be included the person must:
  (a) be a UK full-time director, i.e. working at least 25 hours a week; or
  (b) be a UK employee who works at least 20 hours a week; and

    (c) cannot be a person who owned, or had the option to acquire, more than 10 per cent of the ordinary shares of a close company which is the company operating the scheme or its holding company at any time in the year preceding the grant or the exercise of the option.

- To attract favourable tax treatment, the shares must be acquired:

    (a) within ten years of the option being granted;

    (b) but not earlier than three years; and

    (c) not within three years of exercising another option that attracted favourable tax treatment under an approved scheme.

- The price at which the shares can be acquired must be fixed at the time the option is granted and must not be manifestly less than the market value of shares of the same class at that time (but see below).

- The limit to the value of shares over which an employee may hold unexercised options is the greater of:

    (a) £100,000; and

    (b) four times the employee's remuneration, excluding pension contributions and benefits-in-kind, for the current or previous tax year.

Example

On 1 June 1990 Roy, a marketing executive at Lambert and Grice plc, was granted an option to acquire 15,000 £1 ordinary shares in the company, at a price of £1.25 a share under an approved share option scheme. At that date the shares were quoted at £1.25. He exercises the option after four years, paying £18,750 for shares which are then worth £45,000.

    As it is an approved share option scheme the only liability is to capital gains tax when he disposes of the shares.

Executive options at discount

A significant measure designed to promote widespread employee share ownership was introduced in the 1991 Finance Act. Under the new rules an executive share option may be granted at a discount of up to 15 per cent of market value provided an all-employee scheme is in place and its existence has been notified to the employees within 12 months prior to the date of the grant of the option. As the example below illustrates, this new 15 per cent discount could be most substantial.

Example
Simon and Michael are senior executives who have both been promised options to their maximum entitlement of four times salary.

	Simon £	Michael £
Salary	50,000	75,000
Market value of option shares (four times salary)	200,000	300,000
Price of option shares (after 15% discount)	170,000	255,000
Immediate 'paper' profit	£30,000	£45,000

The very substantial immediate 'paper' profits available to Simon and Michael may considerably focus their minds on the benefit of wide-spread employee share ownership generally.

If you are interested in this scheme, you can obtain from the Revenue their guidance notes 'Executive Approved Share Option Schemes' which includes a set of specimen scheme rules.

Employee Share Ownership Plans (ESOPs)

Although ESOPs have been established in the UK for some time the Government have introduced tax reliefs in order to stimulate their development.

First, payments by a company to an employee share ownership trust, set up to acquire and distribute shares to its employees, qualify for corporation tax relief provided certain conditions are met. The main requirements are:

- The functions of the trust must be to acquire and distribute shares in the founding company and the trust deed must reflect this.

- There must be at least three trustees, most of whom must be employees selected as trustees by the work-force, who do not have and have never had a 'material interest' in the company (more than 5 per cent of the ordinary share capital). One of the trustees must be a trust corporation, a solicitor or a member of an appropriate professional body.

- The beneficiaries must include all employees of the company and its subsidiaries who have been employed for five years or more and who work 20 or more hours a week. The company concerned must not itself be controlled by another company or by a consortium.

- Ex-employees and ex-directors (within 18 months of their departure) and those working 20 hours or more for at least one year may also be included.

- Anyone who at the time of a distribution has, or has had written the last 12 months, a 'material interest' in the company (more than 5 per cent of the ordinary share capital) cannot be a beneficiary.

- Sums received by the trust from the company must be used within nine months after the end of the company's accounting period in the acquisition of ordinary shares of the founding company, in the servicing and repayment of borrowings, in the payment of benefits or in the payment of expenses.

- Shares must be distributed within seven years of their acquisition.

- Shares must be distributed on an all-beneficiary, 'similar terms' basis, for example by reference to level of salary or length of service.

In order to obtain the corporation tax relief the company must make a claim within two years of the end of the accounting period in which it made the payment. The amount is then treated as a deduction in computing the company's taxable profits for the period. If, after corporation tax relief has been given to a company, the trust breaches the conditions mentioned above there will be a charge to tax on the trust of 35 per cent of the payments concerned.

Secondly, for schemes established after 20 March 1990, gains on disposals of shares may be deferred if the following conditions are met:

- The sale is to trustees of a qualifying ESOP.

- The shares are shares in a trading company or holding company of a trading group.

- The ESOP must at some time within 12 months have a 10 per cent interest in the company.

- The proceeds of disposal must be invested in chargeable assets within six months of sale, or of meeting the 10 per cent requirement, if later.

21   National Insurance

Introduction

There are four classes of National Insurance contributions (NIC). Class 1 contributions are payable on the earnings of employees over the age of 16 years. If the amount you pay an employee in a week is equal to or exceeds the current lower earnings limit, which for the tax year 1992/93 is £54.00, both you and the employee are required to pay NIC. The equivalent monthly figure is £234. The employee's contribution is referred to as the primary contribution and the employer's as the secondary contribution.

If an employee's gross earnings are more than £405 a week (or £1,755 a month) no further primary contributions are due, although secondary contributions must still be paid.

For this purpose an employee is a person whose earnings are subject to income tax under Schedule E either:

- under a contract of service; or

- as an office holder, such as a director; or

- is treated as an employee under the Social Security (Categorisation of Earners) Regulations. These include:

  (a) office cleaners;

  (b) agency workers;

  (c) certain lecturers, instructors and ministers of religion;

  (d) the proprietor's spouse.

If you treat a person as self-employed when they are in fact an employee you are liable to pay both primary and secondary contributions for that employee. Furthermore, the DSS can go back for more than six years to recover contributions. In practice it will go back no further than 6 April 1975.

If you operate an occupational pension scheme which provides a certain level of benefits for your employees you can apply to be 'contracted out' of the state earnings-related pension scheme (SERPS). Alternatively, your employee may have a contracted out personal pension. Being contracted out has the effect of reducing the NIC payable.

Gross pay for National Insurance purposes

The 'Employer's Manual on National Insurance Contributions' (NI 269) for use from April 1991 devotes seven full pages to the consideration of what is and is not included in gross pay. Although the law has not changed in this area, the existing rules are now being more strictly interpreted, in particular as regards gifts and rewards to employees and business expenses and allowances.

The rule regarding gifts and rewards (for example on an anniversary or in recognition of long service) is that there is a liability for National Insurance contributions if:

- the payment is part of the employee's contract of service; or
- there is an organised scheme for making such payments; or
- there is the expectation that such a payment will be received, for example, if it is an acknowledged practice within the company to make these payments.

There is no need to include in gross pay payments made to employees to cover proper business expenses. However, it is important that expenses are properly accounted for and evidenced, otherwise the whole amount must be included in gross pay. Normally expenses will be evidenced by a receipt and if receipts are available for only part of the expenses you pay to an employee, any remaining amounts must be included in gross pay. In some circumstances it is not possible to obtain a receipt, in which case you can still exclude expenses from gross pay if a record is kept of individual items of expenditure. An example of this type of expense would be car parking fees or business telephone calls made by an employee from his private telephone.

If you make payments to employees for certain types of expenses based on an *estimate* of costs likely to be incurred you need not include the payments in gross pay provided you can prove that the scheme you operate complies with these requirements:

- There should be no overall element of profit (the aim is to reimburse employees for bona fide business expenses only, not to give additional remuneration).
- You should carry out an accurate survey of the costs involved and base any payments on that.
- The scheme should be designed to accommodate movements in prices.

- The payments you make should be reasonable with regard to the particular employment concerned.

- Employees should submit a proper claim for each item of expense.

- The details of the scheme should be documented in writing and be available for inspection. If there is no written evidence or if the scheme is not considered sound, NIC will be charged on all payments made under the scheme.

The lists below give a guide to the treatment of some common items for NI purposes. The 'Employer's Manual' mentioned above contains further examples and your local DSS office or your accountant or tax adviser can also help with specific queries.

Earnings

Your employees' earnings for NIC purposes are their gross earnings, i.e. before any deduction for superannuation contributions or for charitable gifts under an approved payroll giving scheme. The following are treated as earnings:

- Wages and salaries, overtime and bonuses.

- Commissions, tips and gratuities where the customer pays the employer who decides how the money is shared.

- Round sum expenses allowances and payments in respect of expenses for which there is no adequate evidence.

- Money gifts such as wedding presents unless made as a personal and totally unexpected gift.

- Gilts or other securities and units in a unit trust received by employees.

- Amounts written off loans made to your employees.

- Your employees' income tax if you bear the cost.

- Sick pay, including statutory sick pay (SSP), and statutory maternity pay (SMP).

- Holiday pay unless you contribute to an independently managed central holiday pay fund such as exists in the construction industry.

- Amounts you deduct from your employees as savings which they will receive at Christmas or at holiday time.

- The payment of your employees' private bills such as telephone, electricity, credit cards, etc.

- Payments made under the Employment Protection (Consolidation)

Act 1978, for example, where there is no work for the employee or he
is suspended from working on medical grounds.

- Payments-in-kind which can be turned into cash by surrender, e.g.
Premium Bonds.

- Payment of road fund licence, insurance, car servicing and AA/RAC
memberships on behalf of an employee.

- Part of wages held back for payment later where the employee can get
back the part withheld at any time.

- Payment of a subscription to a club of which your employee is a
member unless you contract directly with the club to provide services
to your employee(s).

- Inducement payments made to recruit, or retain employees, or to
acknowledge their past services.

- Payment by you of a premium or part of a premium for private
medical cover arranged by the employee.

- The full amount of profit-related pay, even though it may be wholly
or partly exempt from income tax.

Earnings do not include the following forms of remuneration:

- Payments-in-kind which cannot be turned into cash by surrender, e.g.
meal vouchers, company car, goods, holidays.

- Reimbursed expenses incurred in carrying out employment duties but
excluding any expenses of travelling to and from work, provided the
expenses are adequately evidenced, as described above.

- Use of your credit card by an employee to pay for actual business
expenses. Any use for private purposes must be reimbursed to you by
the employee, or else the amount is included in gross pay.

- Part of wages held back for payment later where the employee cannot
get the part held back until you decide to pay it. Include in gross pay
when paid.

- Free board and lodging.

- Mileage allowance which is restricted to the mileage rate as calculated
by the AA or the RAC.

- Tips and gratuities paid by customers direct to your employees.

- Payments under certain training schemes.

- Sick pay or maternity pay from a trust or from an insurance policy
where your employee meets the full cost.

- Payment to an employee's approved personal pension if the payment is excluded for income tax under Schedule E.
- Payments from shares in an approved profit-sharing scheme.
- Payment of bills where you have entered into a contract on your employee's behalf with the supplier of the goods or service. The rule applies whether you make payments direct to the supplier or via the employee. For example, you may contract with a private school for the education of your employees' children, contract with a club to provide them with services or contract with an insurance company to provide them with a pension or medical cover.
- Ex gratia payments, for example, for the release from a service contract.
- Payments for unfair dismissal.
- Payments in lieu of notice or redundancy pay.

Scale of Class 1 contributions 1992/93

The rate of contributions payable is expressed as a percentage of the employee's earnings and there are various rates for different bands of earnings. The interval at which earnings are paid, for example, weekly or monthly, is called 'an earnings period'. You work out the NIC either:

- by using the contribution table supplied by the DSS; or
- by applying the appropriate percentage to the gross pay for the earnings period.

You must use only one method for a particular employee in a tax year. It is necessary for the employer to record earnings on which contributions are payable on the deductions working sheet P11 so that the DSS can work out how much to pay an employee if he needs to claim state benefit.

The scale of employee's and employers' contributions are as follows for 1992/93:

Employee (primary)

Weekly earnings	*Standard*	*Contracted out*
£54.00–£405.00	2% on earnings up to £54 *plus*	2% on earnings up to £54 *plus*
	9% on earnings between £54 and £405	7% on earnings between £54 and £405
Over £405.00	no additional liability	
Maximum weekly contribution	£32.67	£25.65

Employer (secondary)

Weekly earnings	Standard	Contracted out	
	On all earnings	First £54	Excess
£54.00–£89.99	4.6%	4.6%	0.8%
£90.00–£134.99	6.6%	6.6%	2.8%
£135.00–£189.99	8.6%	8.6%	4.8%
£190.00 and over	10.4%	10.4%	*6.6%

* Over £405 – 6.6% up £405: 10.4% on excess over £405.

Example

Baldwin Finest Fashions Ltd employs Vera as a machinist at a weekly wage of £100 and Peter as works manager on a monthly salary of £1,800. The company does not have a pension scheme. The NIC payable would be:

		Employee's contribution	Employer's contribution
Vera	*per week*		
	£54 × 2%		
	£46 × 9%	£5.22	
	£100 × 6.6%		£6.60
Peter	*per month*		
	£234 × 2%		
	£1,521 × 9%	£141.57	
	£1,800 × 10.4%		£187.20

If you normally employ part-timers you can save NIC by employing more workers and thus reducing the amount paid per week to each employee.

Example

Magda has an outside catering business and has three part-time employees who work six evenings a week at £22.50 per evening, a total of £405.

James owns a pub and has six part-time employees who work three evenings a week at £22.50 per evening, also a total of £405.

Employer's NIC		Magda *per week*	James *per week*
£135 per week × 8.6%			
× 3 employees	= £11.61	£34.83	
£67.50 per week × 4.6%			
× 6 employees	= £3.10		£18.60

You must pay over the NIC on earnings paid in any income tax month which ends on the fifth of the following month, to the accounts office, together with PAYE, 14 days after the end of the month. For example, contributions for the month of June (6 June to 5 July) are due on 19 July. At the end of each income tax year you are required to send a summary of the figures for employees' and employers' contributions to the inspector of taxes on the annual P35 statement which also records the PAYE deducted.

Special circumstances

If an employee produces a form RD950 it is because he has more than one job and it is likely the maximum NIC will be paid on the other earnings. The certificate has been obtained from the DSS and you do not need to deduct NIC. However, you must still pay the secondary contribution.

When you employ a person under 16 years of age no NIC are payable, but make a note of the date of the sixteenth birthday as a reminder that the first time you pay them after that date NIC are payable.

If you employ individuals of retirement age (65 for men and 60 for women) they do not have to make a contribution but you still have to pay the secondary contribution. They should obtain certificates of exemptions (form CF 384) from their local DSS office as evidence that they do not have to contribute.

Some married women and widows have the right to pay NIC at a reduced rate because of an election they made before 6 April 1977. Before you can apply the reduced rate they need to produce for you a form CF 383. Standard contributions must be deducted until you have seen this form. If they did make the election and are still eligible, but do not have the correct certificate, they can obtain one from the DSS. Once again you pay the full secondary contribution.

Company directors

There are special rules for company directors. If you are a director and are appointed on or before the start of the tax year you will have an annual earnings period. If, on the other hand, you are appointed during the tax year your earnings period for that year is the period starting with the week of your appointment and ending at the end of the tax year. As a director your earnings include:

- salary, wages, fees, bonuses, etc. as described above for other employees;
- payments in advance of fees or bonuses being voted;
- earnings paid by the company after the date you are appointed in respect of previous employment by the company;

- earnings paid by the company in the tax year in which you leave the post; and

- earnings in respect of the directorship paid in a tax year after you leave the post.

Fees and bonuses are added to your other earnings when they are voted. If you have paid contributions on payments in advance, you are due to pay further contributions at the time of voting, on the difference between the amounts paid and the amounts voted. If you have a current account with the company, your contributions are due when fees are credited to this account. Therefore no contributions need be paid when you draw money out of the account, so long as the account stays in credit. As with employees, contributions can be calculated exactly or by referring to the DSS tables. Because directors are treated as having an annual earnings period the weekly limits mentioned in earlier examples are multiplied by 52, as in the following example.

Example
Eric is a director in Pollard and Merrick Antiques Ltd and draws £1,000 a month. He is voted a bonus of £15,000 in October 1992. The company does not have a pension scheme.

		Eric £	Company £
April/May 1992 No contributions as £2,000 is less than the annual lower earnings level of £2,808		Nil	Nil
June 1991	2% × £2,808 *plus* 9% × £192 4.6% × £3,000	73.44	138.00
July 1991	2% × £2,808 *plus* 9% × £1,192 4.6% × £4,000 *Less*: Paid to date Payable	163.44 73.44 90.00	184.00 138.00 46.00
Aug. 1991	2% × £2,808 *plus* 9% × £2,192 6.6% × £5,000 *Less*: Paid to date Payable	253.44 163.44 90.00	330.00 184.00 146.00

Sept. 1991	2% × £2,808 *plus*		
	9% × £3,192	343.44	
	6.6% × £6,000		396.00
	Less: Paid to date	253.44	330.00
	Payable	90.00	66.00
Oct. 1991	2% × £2,808 *plus*		
	9% × £18,252 max	1,698.84	
	10.4% × £22,000		2,288.00
	Less: Paid to date	343.44	396.00
	Payable	1,355.40	1,892.00

From November 1991 to March 1992 Eric will pay no further contributions and the company will pay 10.4 per cent of his total earnings, less amounts already paid.

Individuals entering and leaving the country

Where a UK national employed by a UK company goes abroad to work, both Class 1 contributions are payable for 52 weeks. After that time it is for the individual to decide whether to pay Class 3 contributions (see below).

A foreign national who is employed by a non-resident employer is not normally required to make any primary Class 1 contributions during the first 52 weeks that he works in this country. There is only a liability for secondary contributions if the employer has a place of business, residence or physical presence here.

Other National Insurance contributions

There are four other classes of NIC:

- *Class 1A contributions*. These are due in respect of cars and fuel provided to employees by their employee. See page 168 for further details.

- *Class 2 contributions*. These are paid by those who are self-employed at a flat weekly rate which in 1992/93 is £5.35. If annual earnings are expected to be below £3,030 it is possible to claim exemption from this liability.

- *Class 3 contributions*. These are voluntary payments of a flat weekly rate which in 1992/93 is £5.25. They are usually paid by those who are neither employed nor self-employed but want to maintain their contributions in order to be entitled to sickness and pension benefits, for example, a person working overseas.

- *Class 4 contributions*. These are paid by the self-employed in addition to the Class 2 contributions. The amount payable is calculated as a percentage of the trading profits between lower and upper earnings limits. For 1992/93 the rate is 6.3 per cent and the lower limit is £6,120 and the upper limit is £21,060. Half of the amount paid in Class 4 contributions is allowable for tax purposes. See Chapter 9 for further details.

Statutory sick pay

As an employer you are required to pay statutory sick pay (SSP) to your employees for certain qualifying days up to 28 weeks. Qualifying days will usually be your employee's normal working days, but they do not have to be. Both part-time and full-time employees are entitled to SSP. There is no SSP payable for the first three qualifying days during a period of sickness. You start to pay the employee SSP on the fourth day. After 28 weeks the employee can claim state sickness benefit.

You need to keep records of sickness and decide how your employees will notify you when they are sick. You can insist on written evidence of sickness, for example a self-certificate for periods between three and seven days, and a doctor's certificate if an employee is away for more than seven days. If an employee is one or two days late notifying you of sickness and you consider there was no good reason for the lateness, you can withhold SSP for the same number of qualifying days.

SSP is treated as if it were wages, in that income tax and primary National Insurance contributions are deducted at source. You are also liable for the secondary Class 1 contribution on the SSP.

When you pay the collector the total National Insurance contributions for the month you can deduct the gross amount of any SSP you have paid. You can also deduct an extra amount to compensate for the employer's contributions paid on the SSP.

The minimum weekly rates of SSP for 1992/93 are as follows:

Average earnings per week	Rate
Below £52.00	Nil
£52.00 to £184.99	£43.50
£185 or more	£52.50

Excluded employees

All employees are entitled to SSP unless they are within one of the following categories:

- those who have reached the minimum state pension age on the first day of sickness;

- any employee whose contract is for three months or less;

- an employee whose average weekly earnings are below the lower limit for National Insurance contributions (£54.00 for 1992/93);

- new employees who have not yet started work;

- any person who is absent due to sickness within eight weeks of a previous claim for certain state benefits;

- a pregnant employee who is off sick in the 'disqualifying period' of 18 weeks spanning the week in which the baby is expected to be born. The date on which the 'disqualifying period' begins depends on various factors, including whether the employee is entitled to statutory maternity pay;

- any employee who is sick while involved in a stoppage in work due to a trade dispute;

- those who have already been due 28 weeks' SSP in one spell of sickness;

- an employee who is sick while abroad outside the European Community;

- any employee who at any time, on the first day of sickness, is in legal custody.

You can get further details on SSP from the 'Employer's Manual on Statutory Sick Pay' (NI 270) which is available free on request from your local DSS office.

Statutory maternity pay

Employers are under an obligation to pay statutory maternity pay (SMP) to employees who meet certain conditions. SMP is similar to SSP in that it is paid as if it were wages and you can deduct the amount that you pay from the NIC you pay to the collector of taxes. You can also deduct an extra amount to compensate for the employer's contributions paid on the SMP.

Qualifying employees
To qualify for SMP an employee must:

- have been continuously employed by you for at least 26 weeks continuing into the fifteenth week before the baby is due; and

- have, in that week, average weekly earnings of not less than the NIC lower earnings limit (1992/93 £54.00 per week); and

- still be pregnant at the eleventh week before the expected week of confinement or have been confined at that time; and

- have stopped working for you.

Rates of SMP
There are two rates of SMP. The higher rate is nine-tenths of her average weekly earnings and is payable for the first six weeks. For the remainder of the period SMP is paid at a lower rate, which in 1992/93 is £44.50 per week. To qualify for the higher rate she must have been employed by you for one of the following periods which ends with the fifteenth week before the baby is due:

- for a continuous period of two years if she has normally worked for at least 16 hours a week; or

- for a continuous period of five years if she has normally worked for at least eight hours but less than 16 hours a week.

Calculating SMP
To work out if SMP is payable you will need evidence of the date the baby is due. Your employee should produce a maternity certificate (form Mat B1) but you may accept other medical evidence. An employee must give you at least 21 days' notice of the date when she intends to be absent.

SMP is payable for a maximum of 18 weeks but in some circumstances it may be paid for a shorter period. There is a core period of 13 weeks starting with the sixth week before the expected week of confinement. The remaining five weeks may be taken before or after the 13-week period depending on when your employee stops work. The payment period cannot start earlier than the eleventh week before the expected week of confinement.

More details about SMP can be found in the DSS free booklet NI 257 'Employer's Guide to Statutory Maternity Pay' which is available from your local DSS office.

22   Raising Finance

Types of finance

Whether you have a new or an existing business your choice of finance falls broadly into the following categories:

- grants;
- equity finance;
- overdrafts, loans and other forms of credit such as hire-purchase, leasing, sale and leaseback; and debt factoring.

Assuming you have a choice there are certain aspects of obtaining finance that you should bear in mind:

- whether your ownership of the business will be diluted;
- whether your personal commitment is required;
- the cost of servicing the finance, such as the interest and dividends that will be payable; and
- the tax implications of different sources of finance.

Grants

Grants are available from the Government, some local authorities and other bodies. Your local development agencies and Department of Trade and Industry offices can give advice on what is available. The main Government initiatives are described below.

The receipt of a grant does not affect the ownership of the business and you will not be required to put up a fixed amount of capital or to give any personal guarantees. If a grant is in substitution for profits; represents a Government subsidy to increase profits; or reduces revenue expenditure, then it will be taxed as if it were profits. Included in this category are 'interest relief grants' and 'temporary employment subsidies'. Most grants for plant and machinery reduce the amount on which capital allowances can be claimed and are therefore effectively taxable. This is explained in more detail in the section on capital contributions in Chapter 5.

Enterprise Initiative

This scheme is administered by the Department of Trade and Industry (DTI).

Consultancy Initiative

In the first year of operation of the Enterprise Initiative some 16,000 businesses applied for consultancy help. Consultants are available in six key areas:

Marketing
Business planning
Financial and information systems
Quality control and improvement
Design
Manufacturing systems

The assistance is aimed at independent business with a payroll of fewer than 500. The scheme provides free or low-cost advisory services which can be called upon at any time and also subsidises the cost of using outside consultants to perform in-depth investigations of a one-off kind.

Regional enterprise grants

New and existing businesses employing fewer than 25 in one of the Development Areas or the intermediate areas of Derbyshire and South Yorkshire can receive grants to help finance certain projects. To encourage investment, the DTI will pay 15 per cent of the cost of plant and equipment and other fixed assets up to a maximum grant of £15,000. To encourage innovation, the DTI will pay 50 per cent of the costs of improving existing products and processes and developing new ones. The maximum grant is £25,000.

Regional selective assistance

Grants are available for projects undertaken by firms of all sizes in assisted areas. The amount of the grant will vary according to the needs of the project, which must be 'commercially viable, create or safeguard employment, demonstrate a need for assistance and offer a distinct regional and national benefit'.

Other services

You can also obtain advice on exporting, education, the environment, research and technology and the Single European Market (effective from the end of 1992).

Equity finance

Equity is money that will be used in the business indefinitely and is available to pay the creditors of the business. If you intended to be in business as a sole trader but have been unable to obtain grants or loans, you may have to consider taking on a partner who would make an equity investment. If there are several equity investors interested, you might consider forming a company and issuing them with shares. You may find your local enterprise agency knows of large companies that are interested in having a minority interest in smaller companies. There are also many venture capital organisations that make investments in small companies. The disadvantage of all these courses of action is that you would only own part of the business.

If you want other people to make an equity investment in your business you may find that they will not do so until they are sure of your commitment to the business. This may mean a time commitment, for example, agreeing to work full-time in business, and it may also mean a financial commitment. If you are involved in running the business an outside investor will want to be sure that your capital is also at risk.

The cost of servicing equity is usually much less than loan capital. In most partnerships it is agreed that the profits will be shared among the partners according to a predetermined ratio. Where, however, one of the partners has invested a much larger amount compared with the others, it may be agreed that the first slice of profits should be used to pay 'interest on capital' at a certain rate. In the case of companies, the return on capital is a dividend. If preference shares are issued these will usually carry a fixed rate of dividend.

There are several differences in the taxation of equity and loans:

- The equity investor may be able to get income tax relief on the amount subscribed for shares in an unquoted UK company under the Business Expansion Scheme (see Chapter 23). There is no similar relief for loans.

- Income tax relief could be available where a loss arises on shares of an unquoted UK trading company if the shareholder had subscribed for them, rather than purchased them from another shareholder. When a loan is not repaid there is no income tax relief but a capital loss may be available.

- Interest paid is either an allowable deduction in arriving at trading profits or a charge against profits. The payment of a dividend does not reduce taxable profits.

Loans

It is usual to raise part of the finance for your business through some form of loan. Some of the alternatives are:

- *Bank overdrafts*. These are only suitable for your day-to-day working capital requirements.

- *Loans from banks and finance houses for a fixed term*, for example, a five year loan to buy machinery. You will almost certainly have to provide security for a bank loan, such as the deeds of your property of a life assurance policy. You may also be asked to guarantee a loan to your company.

- *Local authority loans*. Your local authority may have a loan scheme to help local businesses.

- *Loans for businesses* in certain areas, from such bodies as the Welsh and Scottish Development Agencies, the Industrial Development Board of Northern Ireland and the Rural Development Commission incorporating CoSIRA (the Council for Small Industries in Rural Areas); British Steel (Industry) Ltd and the British Coal Enterprise. Addresses are listed in Appendix 17.

- *The Government's Loan Guarantee Scheme*. This is intended to provide finance for new and existing businesses with fewer than 200 employees which would not qualify for a normal bank loan because they lack an established track record or have insufficient security to offer. Loans up to £100,000 are available over a two to seven-year period, with the Employment Department guaranteeing 70 per cent of the loan in return for a premium payment of 2.5 per cent of the guaranteed amount or 1.75 per cent of the overall cost of borrowing. In Inner City Task Force areas 85 per cent is guaranteed in return for a premium of 2 per cent. Loans cannot be used to purchase shares, to buy out members of a partnership or to replace facilities already provided by a financial institution. They can, however, form part of a larger package of finance. Certain activities are not eligible for the loan, for example many that are concerned with land, finance and entertainment. As with most loans, before you approach a bank you will need a business plan to show that you have a viable proposition. The lender will require quarterly financial reports on the state of the business. Details of the scheme can be obtained from your local bank or from the Loan Guarantee Scheme booklet which can be obtained from the Employment Department Loan Guarantee Unit.

- *Debentures, qualifying corporate bonds and deep discount loans.* Companies can issue debentures or bonds to persons in exchange for a loan. These documents set out the amount of the loan, when and how much interest is payable and how the loan will be repaid.

  A qualifying corporate bond is loan stock where:

  (a) the stock is expressed in and redeemable in sterling;

  (b) it is not convertible into another security, except one of a similar kind;

  (c) the interest is not linked to the performance of the company and does not exceed a normal commercial return; and

  (d) the amount repayable does not exceed the amount lent by more than that for similar quoted stocks.

  Deep discounted stock which can, but need not, be secured is stock issued by a company where the issue price stands at a discount to the redemption price and that discount represents a deep gain in that it is:

  (a) greater than 15 per cent; or

  (b) exceeds 0.5 per cent for each of the complete years between the issue date and the redemption date.

  Deep gain securities are redeemable securities where the amount payable on redemption might constitute a deep gain.

Taking out a business loan does not dilute your ownership of the business but it may involve some risk. A serious failure to pay interest or to make repayments could lead to a forced sale of your business assets which may be sufficient to lead to the business closing and the loss of your investment.

For tax purposes interest on a bank loan can be treated as an annual payment and be charged against profits. Alternatively, if the interest is for a business loan it can be treated as an expense in computing trading profits and losses. This alternative is only available if the lender is a bank. The tax relief for interest contrasts with the payment of a dividend which is not deductible either as a charge or an expense. The incidental cost of obtaining loan finance is treated as a trading expense of an expense of management of an investment company. These incidental costs include commissions, advertising and printing costs which, if incurred in connection with raising share capital, would not be allowable.

There is no tax benefit to the company that issues a qualifying corporate bond. For the lender any gain on the sale of the bond is tax-free but any loss is not allowable to offset other gains.

For deep discount stock the yield to maturity is calculated and the borrower obtains tax relief for the discount year by year as it accrues. The lender is not taxed on the discount as it accrues but the discount is taxed as income when the stock is sold or redeemed.

The difference between the amount received on a sale or on redemption of a deep gain security and the consideration paid is taxed as income.

Factoring

Factoring is the facility whereby a person known as a factor purchases all your business's trade debts as they arise. You then have cash available for your day-to-day needs, you can take advantage of suppliers' cash discounts, you are relieved of the task of administering a debtors ledger and you have no bad debts. The factor is likely to pay up to 80 per cent of the value of each invoice raised, with the balance paid being after deducting charges, when the invoice is settled. The fees charged vary but are usually between 1 and 2.5 per cent of the gross invoice values. The facility may reduce your profits but does not affect your interest in the business or have any tax implications.

Leasing and hire-purchase

It may be worth considering leasing plant or purchasing it on hire-purchase rather than buying it outright. There is the advantage that you can use the asset to earn revenue while your working capital can be used for another purpose. The leasing rent or the hire-purchase charges are allowable deductions from trading profits. Where the agreement provides that, at the end of the leasing period, you could or will be the owner of the asset, and when you start to use the asset in your trade, it qualifies for capital allowances, you can claim these allowances. If you sell an asset to a person and then lease it back the amount of the rental charge that is deductible cannot exceed a market rent. An example of a sale and leaseback transaction is given in Chapter 28.

Interest relief

Interest relief is normally available where an individual borrows to provide capital or to lend to his business. For the interest on the loan to be eligible you must have used the money to:

- acquire shares in, or lend money to, a close controlled company which mainly carries on a trade, or lets property to unconnected third parties on a commercial basis, or is a member of a trading group, provided that either:

(a) you are a shareholder and work full-time in the management of the company; or

(b) you, together with your associates own more than 5 per cent of the company's issued share capital.

For shares issued after 13 March 1989 this relief is not available if the individual also claims BES relief on the investment.

- purchase shares in a company which is controlled by its employees and you or your spouse work full-time for the company or a subsidiary;
- purchase shares or make a loan to a co-operative and you work full-time for the co-operative or a subsidiary;
- purchase a share of, or make a loan to a partnership and you are a partner.

The borrowings must be by way of loan and not by overdraft.

23 The Business Expansion Scheme

Introduction

The Business Expansion Scheme (BES) is a tax-efficient way of investing in unquoted UK companies but it will only be available for shares issued up to the end of 1993. There is no requirement that the company should be newly set up. If your company is eligible to issue shares under the BES it will have to meet certain conditions for a period which may be three or four years, otherwise the investors lose their tax relief. There are no tax breaks for the company under the BES, only for individuals who subscribe for ordinary shares and are not otherwise connected with the company. However, many companies have found it easier to attract equity since the BES was introduced and there is usually no pressure on the directors to declare a dividend during the five-year investment period. There is a £750,000 limit on the amount a company can raise under the BES in any tax year and in any six-month period. This limit is increased to £5 million where the company intends to let residential property on assured tenancies or be engaged in ship chartering.

The proceeds you receive from issuing BES shares must be used for one of the following activities:

- to provide and maintain property to be let on assured tenancies;
- to start, expand or purchase a qualifying trade;
- to commence research and development which will lead to a trade;
- to explore for oil.

The BES company cannot use the proceeds to buy shares but they can be used to repay the company's borrowings.

Assuming your company is eligible and you can find individuals to subscribe for shares, they should get income tax relief at their highest rate on the amount of their subscription (which includes any share premium). Relief is normally given in the tax year in which the shares are issued although there are two exceptions which are explained below. There are annual subscription limits for each individual – a minimum of £500 per company and an overall maximum of £40,000.

Example

In May 1992 Martin subscribed £40,000 for ordinary shares in Rhonda Valley Valve Company Ltd. The company met the BES conditions and Martin obtained income tax relief on the investment as follows:

Martin's taxable income for 1992/93

	Before BES relief £	After BES relief £
Trading profits	56,770	56,770
Rental income	18,000	18,000
Bank interest	2,500	2,500
Total income	77,270	77,270
Less: Personal allowance	3,445	3,445
Married couples allowance	1,720	1,720
Taxable income	72,105	72,105
Less: BES subscription	—	40,000
Taxable income	£72,105	£32,105
Tax payable		
First £2,000 × 20%	400	400
Next £21,700 × 25%	5,425	5,425
£48,405 × 40%	19,362	
£8,405 × 40%		3,362
	£25,187	£9,187

By investing £40,000 under the BES Martin has reduced his tax bill by £16,000.

An additional benefit which attaches to BES shares is that they can be sold or gifted at any time after five years with no tax to pay on any capital gains that are realised.

The investor can claim for part of his relief to be set against his total income of the tax year before the share issue. The relief carried back:

- must be in respect of shares issued between 6 April and 5 October;
- cannot exceed 50 per cent of the amount subscribed for those shares;
- cannot exceed £5,000 per anum;

- cannot result in the £40,000 limit being exceeded; and
- must be claimed and the claim cannot be revoked.

Qualifying companies

To qualify, a company must be incorporated in the UK and meet certain conditions for a fixed period ('the relevant period').

For a trading company this period starts from the date of the BES share issue and ends either three years after that date or three years after the company started to trade, if later. For a company letting properties on assured tenancies it is a four-year period starting with the date of the BES share issue. The conditions are as follows:

- The company must be UK resident.
- Its share capital must be fully paid.
- It must not be quoted on the Stock Exchange or the Unlisted Securities Market.
- It must not be controlled by another company or control another company other than a qualifying subsidiary.
- The following activities cannot be carried on to any substantial extent:
    (a) dealing in commodities, shares, securities, land or futures;
    (b) dealing in goods otherwise than in the course of an ordinary trade of wholesale or retail distribution;
    (c) banking, insurance and other financial activities;
    (d) oil extraction;
    (e) leasing or hiring assets although some ship chartering is allowed;
    (f) receiving licence fees or royalties unless attributable to research and development or film production;
    (g) legal or accountancy services.

Activities which produce more than 20 per cent of turnover are considered to be substantial.

The following additional conditions apply for a BES company, where either it or its subsidiary is carrying on a trading activity:

- It must either carry on a qualifying trade, or hold shares in qualifying subsidiaries, or do both. To qualify, subsidiaries need only be 90 per cent owned by the BES company, need not be incorporated or resident in the UK, can be carrying on a qualifying trade, be dormant or exist to hold and manage the group's property.
- More than 50 per cent of its trade must be carried on in the UK. If

there is a group of companies this test is applied to the group as a whole.

- The market value of its interest in land, reduced by certain liabilities, must not exceed half of the market value of its net assets. This condition, which is known as the property test, does not apply to the first £50,000 raised in a 12-month period. The value of plant fixed to land and buildings is excluded.

Companies letting on assured tenancies

Shares in companies intending to let and maintain property on assured tenancies are eligible for BES relief provided they meet the conditions of the scheme with the exception of the property test.

Under this new type of assured tenancy, introduced by the Housing Act 1988, you are free to agree a market rent with the tenant and to include a mechanism for rent increases. Your tenant's security of tenure is similar to that of business tenants. If a tenancy for a fixed term ends and you have not been able to agree another one, your tenant can remain in possession on the same terms, under a statutory periodic tenancy. Once there is a periodic tenancy either you or the tenant can ask a rent assessment committee to decide on what is a market rent. As landlord you can apply to the county court to obtain possession of your property on certain grounds. A list of the grounds for possession can be found in Appendix 15.

At the time the BES company purchases property (freehold or leasehold) it must be empty and there can be no arrangement for letting. However, for shares issued after 9 March 1992 a BES company can arrange for the former owner of the property to become the tenant. A BES company can also buy land and build. The dwelling to be let can be a house or a flat, with or without land, furnished or unfurnished. Your tenants must be individuals who are occupying the dwelling as their principal homes. To qualify under the BES the company must not accept lease premiums from its tenants and it cannot give the tenants options to buy the dwellings. The following tenancies cannot be assured tenancies:

- A dwelling where the rent exceeds £25,000 a year.

- Where the rent is less than £1,000 a year in Greater London or £250 a year elsewhere.

- Protected tenancies, secured tenancies and housing association tenancies.

- Holiday lettings and certain student lettings.

Qualifying individuals

The BES investor must be an individual, not a company or a trustee, who is resident and ordinarily resident in the UK at the time the shares are issued. The individual, together with his associates, must not be part of a group of persons who control the BES company and at the same time be part of a group who control a similar trade. There is no similar restriction where an individual invests in more than one company that is letting on assured tenancies.

As an investor you cannot dispose of your shares for five years and must meet the following conditions throughout a period which commences with the incorporation of the company or two years before the share issue, if this is later; and ends five years after the share issue.

You and your associates cannot:

- be employees or paid directors;
- be entitled to more than 30 per cent of:
  (a) the ordinary shares;
  (b) the total of share and loan capital;
  (c) the votes; or
  (d) the assets if the company were to be wound up; or
  - otherwise control the company; or
  - control a trade which is acquired by the BES company; or
  - receive value from the company; or
  - be one of the BES company's tenants.

Yours associates include business partners, certain trustees of your family settlements, and your immediate relatives. However, you are not an associate of your fellow directors, your brothers and sisters, your in-laws, cousins, uncles and aunts.

By concession, you would not be denied relief because you once held one of the company's two subscriber shares.

Finding Business Expansion Scheme investors

The alternatives open to you are as follows:

- if your company is a public limited company (plc) it can offer shares to the public by means of a prospectus. This will involve substantial costs and is usually not cost effective unless you are likely to raise at least £750,000;
- you could approach the managers of a BES scheme or BES fund;

- you could produce a prospectus for distribution to persons who have expressed an interest in making an investment in your company;
- your bank, the local chamber of commerce or local enterprise agency might know of potential investors;
- you could ask your friends, relatives and acquaintances.

Business Expansion Scheme funds and schemes

The managers of a BES scheme or fund collect varying amounts of money from members of the public who wish to invest in shares under the BES. The managers select four or more qualifying companies for their participants to invest in and monitor the investments over the five-year period. In some cases a fund manager will be appointed a director of the BES company in order to look after the interests of the BES shareholders. There are very few BES schemes and funds available for investment in trading companies and the managers are very choosy about the companies they select. For administrative reasons they tend only to invest amounts in excess of £200,000. They take arrangement and management fees and options to subscribe for shares at a fixed price at a later time. Obtaining BES investors through a scheme or fund is therefore much more expensive than finding your own investors from local businessmen, relatives and associates.

Where an individual invests through an approved BES fund, relief is given by reference to the date on which the fund closed, provided 90 per cent of the fund is used to subscribe for BES shares during the next six months.

Business Expansion Scheme exit routes

If outside shareholders do help to finance your business, at some time they may want to realise their investment and you may want the opportunity to increase your control over the business. It is therefore worth considering at the outset how this can be achieved. The BES shareholders are not allowed to have options to sell their shares. However, the Revenue have stated that BES relief will not be withdrawn where investors grant options to potential purchasers provided:

- the option is granted after the end of the company's relevant period;
- no consideration was received for the grant; and
- the price to be paid for the shares is the market value at the date of exercise or represents a fair price for the shares on an arm's length basis.

Some of the exit routes that are available after five years are as follows:

- you, or other directors or shareholders could buy the BES shares;
- a venture capital organisation could buy all the BES shares;
- a trading company could purchase its own shares from reserves or even reduce its capital if this was for the benefit of the trade;
- the company could be sold for cash and/or shares;
- the company could become quoted on the Stock Exchange or the Unlisted Securities Market thus creating a market for shareholders who wish to sell;
- the company could be liquidated.

24 Franchising

Introduction

Franchising is the term given to the situation where the originator of a proven concept (the franchisor) allows others (the franchisees) to open and operate businesses identical in format, in return for initial and ongoing fees.

There are many companies in the UK who are already heavily committed to franchising such as McDonald's, Kentucky Fried Chicken, Body Shop, Budget Rent a Car, Tie Rack, Athena and many others. The value of all sales by franchised units has grown to over £5 billion and is expected to reach £10 billion by 1994.

The franchisor agrees to provide a range of business support services, for example, operating systems, training and marketing for the duration of the franchise agreement in order to maximise the potential success and profitability of the franchised outlet.

Franchising has been used by a wide cross-section of businesses as a successful method of expansion. In particular, service orientated industries and retail businesses have used it to very good effect.

Franchising provides a number of advantages over traditional methods of expansion:

- If offers a method of off-balance sheet financing, a large proportion of the capital being provided by the franchisees.

- A large network of outlets can be operated and controlled by a small central management team. Franchisees are also particularly self-motivated because they take complete management responsibility for day-by-day control and unit profitability.

- It enables more outlets to be opened more quickly, leading to increased brand awareness.

- It enables a business to expand into unknown markets multi-nationally as well as domestically when franchisees with local knowledge are used.

However, there can also be potential disadvantages:

- Successful franchisees may develop a feeling of independence. Consequently the franchisor may fear that his effort in training the franchisee will lead to future competition.
- The franchisor has to ensure that standards of quality, services and goods are maintained throughout the franchised chain. At the same time he must remember that the franchisee owns his own business.
- There may be difficulties in the recruitment of persons who are suitable as franchisees for the particular business.

The franchisor

There are no specific provisions in the legislation applicable to franchising. There are however certain tax implications of running a franchise operation, and this will depend on the franchise agreement.

The franchisor will generally receive an initial fee and ongoing fees derived either from profits on the supply of goods and services to the franchisee or from ongoing management services fees.

The initial fee is generally structured as a contribution towards initial management services covering items such as general business advice, staff recruitment, training and marketing. The initial fee is usually relatively modest and is little more than a contribution by the franchisee to the overheads of the franchisor. If the franchising agreement fee is correctly structured the initial fee will be treated as a trading receipt in the hands of the franchisor.

The ongoing fee for management services will generally be regarded as trading income in the hands of the franchisor. The franchising agreement should specify the services to be provided such as supervision, promotional help and managerial assistance. The franchisor may also be supplying goods to the franchisee, and this income will also be treated as trading income in the hands of the franchisor.

The franchisee

The franchisee will usually want the initial payment to be treated as a trading expense. In practice the Inland Revenue will accept that the initial fee is a trading deduction in the franchisee's hands if it has been treated as a trading receipt in the hands of the franchisor.

In some cases, however, the Inland Revenue may argue that the payment is a capital set-up cost, and the expenses are not deductible.

The franchisee will purchase property separately and the expenses of refitting the premises will follow the general rules (see Chapter 4).

The ongoing management services fee should always be treated as an allowable trading expense in the accounts of the franchisee.

Incorporation

Whether a franchisee should set up his business as a sole trader or a company follows the normal rules for any business (see Chapter 12). If the franchisee is a sole trader he is protected under the Consumer Credit Act on loans up to £15,000; however, a limited company is not protected against the lender of funds.

Business Expansion Scheme

Because a franchisor company receives income from granting licences there can be difficulties in obtaining Business Expansion Scheme (BES) relief for investors in the company (see Chapter 23). In order to qualify under the BES, the company will need to provide active management services to the franchisee. The franchisee company is in the same position as any other company as regards obtaining BES relief for its investors.

Value added tax

The franchisee's business is a separate entity from the franchisor's business. The business will therefore be required to register for VAT under the normal rules (see Chapter 8). Both initial fees and ongoing management fees will be subject to VAT at the standard rate, currently 17.5 per cent. The franchisee will be liable to VAT in the same way as any other business organisation.

25 Going Public

Introduction
In this chapter we consider why you might wish to have your company's shares quoted on the Stock Exchange or on the Unlisted Securities Market, and the need for the company and the shareholders to plan ahead.

There are several ways in which a company's shares may be bought and sold:

- On the Stock Exchange.

- On the Unlisted Securities Market (USM).

- Under Rule 535.2 where occasional dealings of unquoted shares are permitted on a matched-bargain basis; also known as the Over The Counter Market (OTC).

- By private agreement.

The Stock Exchange and the Unlisted Securities Market
The Stock Exchange, in addition to providing a market place where capital can be raised and securities sold, is also a regulatory body, setting the rules under which securities trading is carried on. It operates a two-tier system: the Official List known as a listing, and the USM. The USM is similar to a listing but is intended to be a less regulated market for the shares of young and/or small companies. The level of disclosure of information to shareholders is similar for both listed companies and USM companies. There are, however, the following differences:

- Companies whose shares are dealt in the USM generally need only have a two-year trading record, as compared with the three-year record for companies seeking a listing.

- Only 10 per cent of a USM company's shares need be in public hands, compared with 25 per cent for a listed company.

- USM companies have fewer advertising requirements for publishing details of the issue of shares.

- The audit report should not be materially qualified for the last three years for a listed company, two years for a USM company.
- Most sponsors stipulate that a USM company must have achieved pre-tax profits of £500,000 or more while the normal threshold for a listing is £1 million or more.

Advantages and disadvantages

The principal advantages of going public are:

- The status of the company is enhanced, which is likely to result in an improved credit rating and a higher profile for the company in the press which can be a motivating factor for staff.
- The market value of the company's shares can be established and the value will increase because they are marketable.
- New shares can be issued to the public to raise additional capital for acquisitions or to reduce borrowings.
- Employee share schemes become more attractive.
- The existing shareholders should be able to realise part of their investment if they wish.

The principal disadvantages are:

- The company is accountable to the public and therefore has to publish detailed accounts.
- The directors are likely to be subjected to increased pressure to improve the company's profits and dividends.
- The costs involved both in obtaining the quotation and in meeting the reporting requirements are high.
- The company can be more vulnerable to an unwelcome take-over bid. The degree of vulnerability will depend on the percentage of shares held by the public.
- The increase in the market value of the shares is likely to increase the shareholders' capital gains and inheritance tax liabilities.

Parties involved

There are certain advisers who are always involved in a flotation:

- The sponsor. This will usually be a stockbroker or a merchant bank. If the sponsor is not a stockbroker it will be necessary to appoint one to deal with the Stock Exchange.

- The company's auditors.

- The reporting accountants. The company's auditors may act as reporting accountants although it would normally be under the control of a different partner who is experienced in flotation matters.

- The company's solicitors.

- The solicitors to the flotation.

- Other advisers might include public relations advisers and property valuers.

Methods of going public

There are three ways in which a company can go public:

- *An introduction*. This is appropriate where no new shares are being offered for sale and there are at least 100 outside shareholders, i.e. shareholders not connected with the company's directors and major shareholders, to ensure there is a market for the shares.

- *A placing*. The stockbroker or issuing house sells to their clients up to 75 per cent of the shares being marketed at a price which has been agreed with the company. The remaining 25 per cent have to go to the market makers for sale to other members of the public. A placing is popular with both USM companies and fully listed companies.

- *An offer for sale*. All the shares being made available are advertised directly to the public. There may be a fixed price or tenders may be invited. The fixed price is as agreed between the sponsor and the company.

Although it is usual for the costs of flotation to be met from the proceeds of a new issue of shares, it is important to have some idea of the amounts involved. There are many factors which determine the costs and these include the proportion of shares being marketed, the complexity of the business and the method of flotation.

	Typical costs	
	USM	**Full listing**
	£000	£000
An introduction	200–450	250–750
A placing	250–500	400–1,000
An offer for sale	300–750	500–1,250

Preparing the company

At an early stage, say a year before the proposed flotation, you need to look at your company to see whether the public would see it is as an attractive investment.The following are examples of questions which arise:

- Are all the assets and trades of value to the company?
- Should any assets and trades owned by the shareholders be transferred to the company or vice versa?
- Is it clear who currently owns the shares if shareholders include other companies and overseas trusts?
- Before the value of the shares increases, should associated companies merge, or group companies demerge?

Rationalising and reorganising the company may well have tax consequences both for the company and the shareholders, so take professional advice and weigh up the tax cost before taking action.

This might be a good time to make changes to the management or to the company's accounting and internal control systems. It might also be appropriate to introduce an executive share option scheme if one does not exist already. The options will provide an incentive for your executives to meet projected profit targets. Bear in mind that the sponsor will require an in-depth report of the company (a long form report) to be prepared by the reporting accountants.

Last six months

Six months before the flotation the directors, with the help of their advisers, need to prepare a document which:

- describes the company's current structure and activities;
- includes industrial statistics;
- sets out the company's financial history;
- gives background details of the management;
- lists the key shareholders;
- describes the company's future plans; and
- includes financial forecasts.

The document is a selling and information document that can be given to the sponsor and to other professional advisers. The preparation of the document is also a useful self-assessment exercise.

The next step is to approach a sponsor and appoint professional advisers. The reporting accountants will then visit the company in order to carry out their investigation and produce a long form report for the sponsor. As part of the investigation the reporting accountants will review the auditor's files on the company for at least the last three years.

The long form report will contain and confirm much of the information given in the document prepared by the company. It will comment on the company's strengths and weaknesses and its relationships with suppliers and customers. The report will form the basis of the company's prospectus. The prospectus will contain a short form report which is a summary of the audited accounts.

Four months before flotation the parties will start to meet regularly to draft the prospectus; they will prepare a draft of the Extel card and submit it with a draft prospectus to the Stock Exchange for comment.

In the last month you will submit final documentation to the Stock Exchange for approval; reach agreement on the participation of employees and directors and the terms of any new service agreements; confirm the company's indebtedness and the sufficiency of the company's financial resources; and decide on the number of shares to be sold and the price.

If your company is a private company it will need to re-register as a public company or create a new group holding company with plc status.

Tax clearances

It is also necessary for your company to apply for the following tax clearances, allowing 30 days for the Inland Revenue to reply:

- A clearance that in the Inland Revenue's opinion all the transactions proposed are being carried out for bona fide commercial reasons and are not transactions in securities, the main purpose of which is to secure a tax advantage for the shareholders (see page 230).

- If there is to be a share exchange a clearance is required that because the exchange is for bona fide commercial reasons the capital gain on the disposal of the shares will not crystallise (see page 229).

Quoted for tax purposes

Shares are always treated as quoted for tax purposes where the company has a full listing on the London Stock Exchange or on other recognised stock exchanges. The tax treatment of the USM companies' shares has changed over the years and much of the inconsistency has now gone. In most parts of the tax legislation a share dealt in on the USM is not a quoted share with the result that:

- a USM company can be a close company even when more than 35 per cent of its shares are held by the public;

- income tax relief is available where a person who subscribed for shares in a USM trading company suffers a capital loss;

- a USM trading company can purchase its own shares and not be treated as having made a distribution;

- for inheritance tax 100 per cent business property relief on holdings above 25 per cent is available;

- capital gains tax relief for gifts of shares in a family trading company is available (see Chapter 31); and

- the shares are valued for capital gains tax and inheritance tax purposes as unquoted shares.

A company's shares are treated as quoted if they are quoted on the USM for the purposes of the Business Expansion Scheme.

Shareholders' capital gains

As mentioned above the flotation will increase the market value of your company's shares which potentially increases your future capital gains tax liabilities. It is advisable to plan well ahead and consider gifting or selling shares to the next generation before the shares increase in value. A word of warning here. If you would be eligible for capital gains tax retirement relief in the next ten years, do not jeopardise your relief, for example by reducing your shareholding below 25 per cent in a situation where the family as a whole are unlikely to hold more than 50 per cent. An outline of the conditions for retirement relief can be found in Chapter 30.

For capital gains tax purposes the deemed consideration for a gift of shares or a sale to a connected person is usually the market value of the shares transferred. In the case of a minority holding in an unquoted company this would be a low value based on dividends paid or the profits earned by the company. An exception is made in cases where the disposal of a shareholding is made to connected persons by a series of transfers. An appropriate proportion of the market value of all the shares transferred would then be used as the deemed consideration. Even where you give away a majority holding, if the transfer occurs when there is no market for the shares the value could still be quite low. Furthermore, where capital gains arise on a gift of a business asset to a UK resident individual or trustee you can claim to defer the gain (see Chapter 30). Finally, if the gains are small, they could be covered by your annual exemption, which in 1992/93 is £5,800. If your spouse does not own any of the shares consider transferring some to him or her so that on a future disposal you can both use your annual exemptions.

Alternatives to going public

If you do not consider that flotation is suitable for your company either in the short term or at any time, what are the alternatives? This must depend on which of the benefits are of most interest to you.

If shareholders wish to realise all or part of their holdings there are the following alternatives:

- A sale of the whole company or a controlling interest.
- A sale of shares by the individuals to an employee trust (see Chapter 20).
- A purchase by the company of its own shares (see Chapter 26).

If your company requires a further injection of funds consider the following:

- Bank or other loan finance (see Chapter 22).
- A rights issue.
- An institutional placing of shares.
- Investment by a venture capital organisation.
- An issue of shares under the Business Expansion Scheme (see Chapter 23).

26 Purchase by a Company of its Own Shares

Introduction

Several references have been made in this book to a company purchasing its own shares. For example, it is one of the exit routes that is available to an outside investor in your company. At the time you retire you may want a lump sum and your company may be in a position to purchase your shares, thus avoiding the need to find a purchaser. It is also a useful possibility to buy out an awkward or uninterested shareholder who perhaps has inherited the shares but has no interest in the business. In this chapter we first consider, very briefly, the company law requirements before looking at the ways in which the amount received from the company is taxed.

Company law

In 1981 there were changes to company law to enable both private and public companies to redeem or purchase their own shares. Before a company can redeem or purchase any of its own shares there are certain conditions to be met and certain procedures have to be followed:

- The company's articles of association must contain a specific power to enable the company to purchase its shares.
- The shares must be fully paid.
- The terms of purchase or redemption must be determined.
- A public company must find the purchase consideration either from distributable profits which are transferred to a capital redemption reserve or out of the proceeds of a fresh issue of shares. In this way the company maintains the same level of capital.
- Market purchases require the sanction of an ordinary resolution and there are Stock Exchange requirements.
- Off-market purchases must be sanctioned by special resolution.

- A private company can, if the distributable profits are insufficient, reduce its capital. In such a case a set procedure must be followed which includes the directors making a statutory declaration of solvency.

- Where shares are purchased they must be cancelled.

- After the purchase there must be at least one member of the company holding non-redeemable shares.

Distributions of income

Normally, if as a shareholder you receive cash from your company you are taxed on that amount as if it were a dividend. Furthermore, the company has to pay advance corporation tax (ACT) on the amount it pays you. Even if a company's share purchase is treated as a dividend there is still a disposal of the shares for capital gains tax. But because the amount received is treated as income the proceeds for capital gains purposes would be nil, leaving you with a capital loss equal to the indexed subscription cost.

Where the shareholder is a company, known as a corporate shareholder, the situation is slightly different. As before, the paying company is treated as if it were paying a dividend. In the hands of the corporate shareholder this would normally be treated as franked investment income (FII) on which no further tax would be due. However, the Revenue treat such payments as proceeds in the calculation of a chargeable gain (or allowable loss) made by the corporate shareholder on the disposal of the shares.

Advantages of a distribution

A distribution can be advantageous for the payer where the ACT paid by the company making the distribution can be used to offset its mainstream corporation tax liability. Any surplus ACT can be carried back against the corporation tax liability of the six previous years and this could result in the repayment to the company of corporation tax paid in earlier years plus interest which, depending on the amounts involved, could be substantial.

As an individual shareholder you will receive in return for your shares a distribution from which basic rate tax has been paid. Only if you are a higher-rate taxpayer will you pay further tax equal to the difference between the higher and the basic rate. Using current rates, the maximum income tax due would be 15 per cent of the gross dividend received (cash plus related tax credit). Capital gains, on the other hand, are taxed at your highest marginal rate of tax of up to 40 per cent.

Treatment as a capital receipt

If the shareholder and the company meet certain conditions, the amount that the shareholder receives from the company for his shares is not taxed as a dividend but as a capital receipt. As noted above, this treatment may not always be beneficial. It should be emphasised that the payment will always be treated as a capital payment, if the conditions are met, so if a distribution would be beneficial you must fail to meet one or more of the following conditions.

Qualifying companies

To qualify as a capital receipt, the company making the purchase must be unquoted and either a trading company or the holding company of a trading group. For this purpose, your company is unquoted if none of its shares are in the official list of a Stock Exchange and it is not a 51 per cent subsidiary of a quoted company. So your shares are considered to be unquoted if they are dealt in on the Unlisted Securities Market.

If your company is dealing in shares, securities, land or futures it is not considered to be trading for this purpose. If your shares are in a holding company its business, disregarding any trade it has, must consist wholly or mainly of holding investments in its 75 per cent subsidiaries and the group as a whole must carry on trading activities.

Reasons for purchase

In addition to your company qualifying, there must be one of the following reasons for the share purchase, if the receipt is to be treated as capital:

- All or almost all of the cash after tax will be used to pay inheritance tax within two years of the death of a shareholder and either there are no other assets available or their realisation would cause hardship.

- The purchase benefits the company's trade or the trade of one of its 75 per cent subsidiaries. However, this reason is not acceptable if one of the main purposes is to:

  (a) enable the shareholder to participate in the company's profit without receiving a dividend; or

  (b) to avoid tax.

There must be a substantial reduction in the shareholder's interest in the company and there are further conditions regarding residence and the period of ownership of the shares, which are discussed later in this chapter.

For the benefit of the trade
It may be thought that an outflow of capital could never benefit a company's trade but the Revenue are prepared to accept that it does in the following situations:

- Where there is a disagreement over the management of the company and the dissenting shareholder is being bought out.
- Where the shareholder is giving up his interest in the company to make way for new management.
- Where an outside investor who has provided equity finance wishes to realise his investment.
- Where on death of a shareholder either the personal representative or the beneficiaries do not wish to retain the shares.

Residence and length of ownership

Both the shareholder and any nominee must be resident and ordinarily resident in the UK in the tax year in which the company purchases the shares.

The shares must have been owned by the shareholder for five years prior to the company's purchase unless they were acquired on the previous owner's death, in which case the period is reduced to three years. Where the shares have been transferred between husband and wife their periods of ownership are added together.

Substantial reduction

If the company does not intend to purchase all the shares held by the shareholder he, together with his associates, must be left with a substantially reduced interest in the company. Associates for this purpose include the shareholder's spouse, if they are living together, and their children who are under 18, but do not include parents, or brothers and sisters.

A shareholder's investment is only substantially reduced if it meets both of the following tests:

- The nominal value of the shares held by him and his associates immediately after the purchase expressed as a fraction of the total nominal value of the shares issued must not exceed 75 per cent of the corresponding fraction before the purchase.
- If the company were to pay out all of its distributable profits after the purchase he and his associates would not be entitled to more than 75 per cent of the amount they would have received had such a distribution been made before the purchase.

Example

Gilroy Leisure Ltd has issued 1,000 £1 ordinary shares and 9,000 £1
8 per cent preference shares, of which Alec and his associates own
500 ordinary shares and 3,500 preference shares. It has been agreed that
the company should buy shares from Alec.

After the sale Alec must not own more than 30 per cent (75 per cent
of 40 per cent) of the total nominal value of the issued capital. This can
be achieved if he sells 1,430 shares.

	Nominal value of shares		
	Before	**After**	
	£	£	
Alec and associates			
Ordinary	500		
Preference	3,500	4,000	2,570 (29.9%)
Others			
Ordinary	500		
Preference	5,500	6,000	6,000 (70.1%)
	£10,000	£8,570	

For this purpose of the second test a company's distributable profits consist
of:

- its accumulated realised profits less realised losses;
- £100; and
- the profit required to pay all fixed rate distributions for a year.

Example

Continuing the previous example, assume the company has distributable
profits of £12,622 and that Alec, who must sell 1,430 shares, decides to
sell 200 ordinary shares and 1,230 preference shares.

Share of profits

	Before			**After**		
	Total	**Alec**	**Others**	**Total**	**Alec**	**Others**
	£	£	£	£	£	£
Preference	720	280	440	662	182	440
Ordinary	11,902	5,951	5,951	12,000	4,500	7,500
	£12,622	£6,231	£6,391	£12,622	£4,682	£7,940

Alec's percentage of profits

£6,231/£12,622	49.37%
£4,682/£12,622	37.09%

Alec does not meet the second test. His percentage of the profit after the sale is 37.09%, which exceeds 37.03%, i.e. 75% of 49.37%, the percentage he would have received before the sale. Because his share of the profits would be too high, he needs to sell more ordinary shares.

The substantial reduction tests are modified where the company is a member of a 51 per cent group and after the purchase the shareholder still owns shares in the group.

Connected with the company

Immediately after the company's purchase the shareholder must not be connected with the company or group. This means he and his associates must not:

- have control of the company;
- own or be entitled to own more than 30 per cent of:
  - (a) the issued ordinary share capital
  - (b) the loan capital and issued share capital
  - (c) the votes; or
  - (d) the assets available for distribution to equity holders in a winding up

Clearance and returns

If your company is planning to purchase its own shares you can put the facts in writing to the Revenue before the event and ask them whether the payment by the company will be capital or income. The Revenue have issued guidelines on the information they would expect to see in such application, which includes a set of recent accounts for the company. The application for clearance and any enclosures should be sent to: Inland Revenue, Technical Division (Company Taxation) Room 28, New Wing, Somerset House, London WC2R 1LB. You can send an additional copy of the application and enclosures if you wish to obtain clearance that the purchase does not give rise to tax advantages from a transaction in securities. Within 30 days of receiving your application the Revenue must either:

- notify the company of its decision, giving reasons for a refusal; or

- request further particulars.

If you have not fully or accurately disclosed information which is material to the decision, the clearance is void.

If a company treats a payment for the purchase of shares as not being a distribution of income, it must make a return to the inspector within 60 days of making the payment.

Other tax matters

If, at the time of the company's purchase, you are not eligible for capital gains tax retirement relief because you are under age 55 and healthy, you will be taxable on the gain arising from the disposal of the shares, subject to relief for your annual exemption. Consider whether by delaying the purchase to a later year you would be eligible for retirement relief. Conditions for this relief are to be found in Chapter 30.

If the reason for obtaining cash from the company for your shares is to give it away or put it into trust, you should first consider the capital gains tax and inheritance tax implications. Assuming your capital gain is not covered by retirement relief, consider gifting the shares rather than the cash (see page 252). Furthermore, if the shares are not quoted on the USM and you have more than 25 per cent of the votes before the purchase, their value is reduced by 50 per cent business property relief for inheritance tax purposes.

Stamp duty of 0.5 per cent of the consideration is payable by the company when it makes a return of the shares purchased (form 169) to the Registrar of Companies. However, stamp duty in respect of shares is to be abolished with effect from May 1993 to coincide with the introduction of TAURUS, a computerised paperless dealing system.

27 Buying and Selling a Business

Introduction

This chapter deals with the tax consequences of buying and selling businesses.

If you wish to buy a business there are basically two options. You can buy the business assets with or without the trade from a sole trader, a partnership or a company. Alternatively, in the case of a company's business, you can buy the company's shares from its existing shareholders.

Buying trading assets

By buying assets rather than shares you obtain the following advantages:

- You can pick and choose the assets you want.
- Capital allowances are available on eligible assets.
- Depending on what is taken over you may be able to argue that you have not acquired a separate trade.
- No automatic take-over of tax skeletons in the target company's cupboard.

When drawing up a contract for the purchase of a business it is advisable to apportion the consideration over the various assets acquired. The purchaser would usually prefer to pay more of the total price for certain assets, such as trading stock, to minimise the trading profit on which income tax or corporation tax will be payable. For the same reason the vendor would prefer a lower figure unless there are unused trading losses. This conflict of interest can only be resolved by negotiation. An apportionment in the contract will carry weight with the Revenue provided it is not unreasonable.

Buying shares

If you buy shares instead of assets the following advantages accrue:

- The business can continue uninterrupted.
- If you are an individual borrowing to buy shares in a close company, you could be eligible for income tax relief on the interest you pay (see page 200).
- The target company's tax advantages are acquired, for example:
  (a) carry forward of trading losses;
  (b) surplus advance corporation tax (ACT);
      These two advantages are not available if major changes are made to the trade, as explained below;
  (c) carry forward of capital losses.
- If your business is carried on by a company there are advantages in bringing the target company into the group, for example:
  (a) group relief for losses;
  (b) surrender of parent's surplus ACT;
  (c) capital gains relief on intra-group transfers of assets;
  (d) no balancing charges and preservation of trading losses where a trade is transferred between group members.

Because of the potential problems that you could be taking over when you buy the company's shares, it is essential that the vendors give you various warranties and indemnities. In addition to general warranties and indemnities relating to such matters as:

- proper provisions for all tax liabilities;
- submission of all relevant tax returns;
- accounting for VAT;
- proper application of PAYE;

it is usual to include a wide range of indemnities in respect of specific contingencies, many of which arise from complex anti-avoidance provisions. The vendor will, of course, wish to limit his exposure to matters within his control, or resulting from his actions.

Transfer of assets intra-group

Having taken over another company you may wish to transfer its trade or some of its assets to your parent company or another subsidiary. Where there is at least 75 per cent common ownership before and after the transfer, the trade is not treated as ceasing. This means that trading losses can continue to be carried forward and there is no clawback of capital allowances.

Provided the transfers of chargeable assets, including goodwill, are between members of a 75 per cent group, the transfer is deemed for capital gains tax purposes to be for a consideration that would produce neither a gain nor a loss. In other words, the acquiring company takes over the base cost plus indexation of the other group member.

Use of company losses

In the past, companies with trading and capital losses were often acquired as a tax saving device. The acquisition of the company enabled the purchaser to shelter trading profits and capital gains. Because of the loss of revenue the rules relating to the availability of trading and capital losses where there is a change of ownership have been tightened.

Following a change of ownership, trading losses can only be used where there is no major change in the nature or conduct of the trade or business. For example, if a company is acquired which has made losses selling carpets, the new owner cannot use the losses to shelter profits from selling cellular car phones. In the Inland Revenue's view, a major change does not occur simply because changes are made which increase the efficiency of the company's management or organisation, or are necessary to keep pace with modern technology.

Trading losses transferred with a trade between companies under common ownership may be restricted if the new owner does not also take over the liabilities. This rule was introduced because it had become common practice for a Receiver to transfer a saleable trade to a new subsidiary which would be sold leaving the original company insolvent. In the Revenue's view, tax relief for the loss was given twice, once when the creditors of the original company claimed deductions from income tax or corporation tax for bad debts and again when the company's trading losses sheltered future profits.

Stamp duty

For each asset you purchase (other than shares) using a written contract, stamp duty is payable on the purchase price at 1 per cent, although where the consideration for land is below £30,000 no duty is payable. This limit was increased to £250,000 for the period 19 December 1991 to 19 August 1992. Consider whether any assets can be transferred simply by delivery, in which case no stamp duty is payable.

Where you issue shares and/or debentures in exchange for the shares of a target company which give you control, stamp duty of 0.5 per cent of the value of the securities you issue is payable. However, stamp duty in respect of all property except land is to be abolished with effect from May 1993 to coincide with the introduction of TAURUS, a computerised paperless dealing system.

Selling your business

If you are a sole trader or in partnership you can choose to sell your business as a going concern or sell assets separately. The advantages of selling as a going concern rather than selling off individual assets are that:

- gains on the disposal can be deferred if the sale is to a company in exchange for shares;
- no VAT is payable on the sale if certain conditions are met;
- unused trading losses can be preserved; and
- where other conditions are met, retirement relief should be available.

If you sell a business there is normally a cessation of trade, stock is deemed to be disposed of at market value, balancing charges arise and losses cannot be carried forward. There is an exception to this rule if 75 per cent of the trade continues to be under common ownership. Carefully consider the timing of the sale to take advantage of the closing year rules where profits for certain periods drop out of assessment.

If you have a company and intend to sell its business assets you may be able to defer capital gains by investing the sale proceeds in other business assets (see page 67).

Exchanging shares

There are no reliefs from capital gains tax if you simply sell your shares, unless you qualify for retirement relief (see Chapter 30).

However, if your company is taken over and you are offered shares in the acquiring company in exchange for your present shareholding, you may be able to defer your capital gain.

This is because there is a capital gains tax relief where the shareholder in one company exchanges shares or debentures in that company for shares or debentures in another. The shareholder is treated as not having disposed of his original shares if the following conditions are met:

- The company issuing the shares or debentures holds or will hold, as a result of the acquisition, more than 25 per cent of the ordinary share capital of the target company or;
- the company issuing the shares or debentures does so in exchange for

shares as a result of certain types of offer made to the shareholders of the target company; and

* the exchange is effected for bona fide commercial reasons; and
* is not part of an arrangement to avoid tax.

You should use a clearance procedure to obtain confirmation from the Revenue that in their opinion the share exchange is for bona fide commercial reasons. Full details of the transaction involving the share exchange must be given, together with the reasons why the transaction is going ahead. It is necessary to ask for clearance more than a month before the exchange as the Revenue have 30 days to reply to your enquiry.

Example

On 31 July 1992 Mycroft New Trend Hotels Ltd (Mycroft) acquired from Mr Woolley the whole of the share capital of Ambridge Leisure Ltd (Ambridge), the consideration being an allotment of 4,000 shares in Mycroft. The acquisition was for bona fide commercial reasons and at the time the Mycroft shares had a value of £80 per share. The Ambridge shares had cost Mr Woolley £1,000 in May 1970 and at 31 March 1982 had a value of £1,800.

At the time of the take-over Mr Woolley is not treated as having made a disposal of his Ambridge shares. On a future disposal of his Mycroft shares his base cost will be £1,800 plus the indexation allowance.

If Mycroft disposes of its shares in Ambridge its base cost will be the value it gave at the time of acquisition, i.e. £320,000 (4,000 shares at £80).

It is not uncommon for the acquiring company in a take-over to withhold part of the consideration, whether cash or shares, until certain profit levels have been achieved. Depending on how such an arrangement is structured you could be liable to tax at the time when the contracts are exchanged on increased gains reflecting the future consideration which may not be received. If you are considering a sale on this basis you should seek professional advice.

Transactions in securities

The sale of shares is a transaction in securities. If the transaction is not carried out for bona fide commercial purposes income tax can be levied on the profit on the sale. However, before you sell you can make an application to the Revenue similar to that described above, explaining the circumstances and asking them to confirm they will not charge income tax on the profit.

Business property relief

After the sale your estate will include cash instead of shares which may have entitled you to business property relief (see page 263). Before contemplating a sale of your shares, consider whether to gift them outright or into a trust, enabling the family to benefit from the business property relief. The new owners can then decide to sell the shares. It would be preferable if the trust were already in existence. If you were simply to set up a trust for the purpose of holding the shares for a few months before the sale, the Revenue are likely to contend that the purpose of setting up the trust was tax avoidance and treat the transactions for tax purposes as a sale by you.

Capital gains tax retirement relief

You will be entitled to capital gains tax retirement relief if, at the time of the sale, you have reached 55 or are retiring through ill health. If you are likely to retire from the business in the next ten years consider the effect of any sale of shares on your retirement relief. You may be able to sell 75 per cent of the shares and retain 25 per cent to meet the conditions of the relief (see Chapter 30).

Reconstruction, amalgamations and demergers

The purpose or sale of a business may be part of scheme of reconstruction or amalgamation. A reconstruction may occur where a business is to be split between two or more companies or where the business is to be carried on broadly with the same ultimate ownership but by a new company with some changes to the share structure. Under a scheme of reconstruction a new company is formed or a dormant company is used to take over all or part of a business of another company. The majority, if not all of the shareholders of the acquiring company are the same as those of the target company and the consideration for the business is usually an issue of shares. After the take-over the target company is often dissolved.

An amalgamation occurs when the businesses (or a substantial part thereof), of two or more companies are merged. The consideration given to the shareholders of the target companies is an issue of shares by the acquiring company. The company that will carry on the merged business can be an existing company, or a new or dormant company, can be used.

If the reconstruction or amalgamation is for bona fide commercial purposes the shareholders' disposals will not trigger a CGT charge. Furthermore, if the whole or part of the target company's business is taken over by the acquiring company, the assets are treated as transferred at a consideration which gives rise to neither a gain nor a loss.

Where shareholders in one company receive an issue of shares in another company it can be said that their company has made a distribution to them. This would mean the company having to account for ACT and the shareholders being taxed on the value of the shares received at income tax rates. An exception is made for companies:

- which are to be liquidated; or
- where the demerger provisions apply.

The demerger provisions are designed to make it easier for large companies to split into smaller units.

28 Relocation of a Business

Introduction

During the life of a business there will be occasions when you need to decide whether to move to new premises or even to a new area. In arriving at such a decision it is important that you take into account the tax implications of each of the alternatives being considered.

We look first at some of the reasons why businesses might see a move as desirable:

- The business is expanding and its premises and plant are no longer adequate.

- In the present location there is either a shortage of employees generally or of employees with a particular skill.

- Its business units are widely dispersed, perhaps as a result of acquiring other businesses, and there would be benefits in centralising in one area.

- It is necessary to raise further capital and the business has valuable freehold property that could be sold.

- Rent, business rates and salaries in the area have increased to the point where the business cannot remain competitive.

- The business intends to change its product, service or method of trading, e.g. concentrate on a high price, high quality product or a low cost, high volume product or change from retail shop outlets to mail order.

- Its suppliers and/or customers are no longer in the same area.

- The market for the product or service is contracting and the premises and plant are surplus to capacity.

Capital gains roll-over relief

When selling your business assets you may inadvertently trigger a tax charge on gains that arise because the conditions for rolling over the gains into replacement assets have not been met (see page 67 for the detailed rules). Gains can crystallise where the business is buying cheaper premises because the gain available for roll-over will be reduced by the proceeds not reinvested.

Another potential problem associated with relocation is that you might purchase a business asset, but for a variety of reasons it may prove to be unsuitable. It is then sold on without ever being used for the business. Any gain realised could not be rolled-over.

Capital allowances

An unexpected tax charge could arise from the sale of assets if capital allowances which have been claimed in the past are clawed back. This has become a more serious problem since the abolition of the 75 per cent initial allowance on most industrial buildings. High allowances will be clawed back on the old building, but allowances on the new building will only be at the rate of 4 per cent per annum.

Individuals and companies may be able to avoid a clawback of capital allowances on buildings by retaining the interest in the property that was acquired. For example, if you had acquired the freehold, grant a 999-year lease, or if you had acquired a 21-year lease grant a sub-lease for the unexpected period less a few days.

When reviewing likely expenditure on buildings and plant it is important to consider whether that expenditure will attract capital allowances. In particular, one of the advantages of relocating in an enterprise zone is that 100 per cent of your capital expenditure on commercial buildings and fixtures (but not land) is deductible from taxable profits. This subject is considered in detail in Chapter 5. Grants are available for businesses relocating to certain areas of the UK (see Chapter 22).

Leasehold premises

If you are considering selling a leasehold interest in your business premises, whether it is owned by individuals or a company, there are several ways in which it can be done and they have different tax consequences. A lease can be granted if freehold premises are owned, but where the business only has a leasehold interest itself, the choice is between granting a sub-lease or assigning the existing lease. Furthermore, on the grant of a lease or sub-lease a lease premium may, but need not, be charged. What is common to each of these alternatives is that they result in a disposal of all or part of the interest in property. This means that if consideration is received, in addition to the rent payable under the lease, there will be a liability to pay tax on any gain that arises. If you are paid to surrender your lease the payment is liable to VAT. If you pay a landlord to allow you to surrender your lease the landlord will normally be obliged to charge VAT on top of the payment you make.

A further tax liability arises if a lease (or sub-lease) is granted at a premium for a term of less than 50 years. Part of the premium is taxed in the year of receipt as if it were rental income. The amount treated as rent is calculated by reducing the premium by one-fiftieth of the amount for each complete period of 12 months during the term of the lease except the first.

If you are the person considering taking on a lease of less than 50 years you should be aware that it is preferable from a tax point of view to be granted a lease at a premium rather than take an assignment of an existing lease. This is because part of the premium is deductible as rent over the term of the lease. An example showing the grant at a premium of a lease of less than 50 years is shown in Chapter 6 in the section 'Lease premiums'.

Sale and leaseback

If a major reason for relocating is to raise capital you should consider the possibility of staying where you are and entering into a sale and leaseback agreement. When considering the tax implications of a sale and leaseback it is assumed that the premiums are being used in your business. If under the terms of the sale and leaseback:

- your lease starts to run within one month of the sale; and
- the rent payable under the lease is not excessive

any gain on the sale will be calculated and taxed in the normal way and you will get relief for the rent paid. If the rent under the lease is excessive, your tax relief will be restricted to an amount equal to a commercial rent.

If you assign a valuable lease of 50 years or less in return for a lump sum and take back a lease of up to 16 years, the following proportion of the amount received will be taxed as income:

$$\text{Capital sum} \times \frac{16 - \text{Length of new lease}}{15}$$

Example

R Gillespie Computers Ltd is considering surrendering its 18-year lease to the landlord for £115,000 provided it is granted a new 10-year lease at a market rent of £26,000.

The company will be treated as having received:

- income of £46,000 (£115,000 × 6/15) and

- capital from the disposal of the lease of £69,000 and
- will be entitled to tax relief on the rent of £26,000 pa.

There are comparable provisions designed to achieve the same objective in relation to machinery and plant.

A sale and leaseback or lease and leaseback may be less attractive if industrial buildings capital allowances have been claimed, as these will be clawed back. This is because the business no longer has its original interest in the property even though it continues to occupy the premises under a lease.

VAT and the disposal of business assets

If certain conditions are met (see page 77) the transfer of a business as a going concern is outside the scope of VAT.

Normally, the sale of premises and its fixtures is exempt, in which case the VAT on selling costs must be counted as exempt input tax and can only be deducted if it is de minimis (see page 77). Where exemption has been waived or where a non-residential freehold under three years old is being sold the sale is taxable and VAT on selling costs is recoverable (see page 73). If the construction of a building was zero-rated on condition that the owner uses it for at least ten years for a relevant residential or charitable purpose, any disposal within ten years will be taxable unless the purchaser is to carry on the qualifying use.

The value of disposals of capital assets that have been used in your business can be excluded from taxable turnover for the purpose of the VAT registration limits.

If you dispose of goods which form part of the assets of your business and receive no consideration VAT must be accounted for on their cost.

'Reverse premiums'

There are occasions when a person receives a capital sum from a landlord as an inducement to take a lease. This is often referred to as a 'reverse premium'. Provided that the rent subsequently payable is at the market rate, and there are no other conditions attached to the payment of the capital sum (e.g., on condition that it must be used for improvements to the building), the reverse premium is not taxable under present legislation. A reverse premium is liable to VAT at the standard rate. Where an inducement takes the form of a rent-free period the tenant has no VAT liability unless he performs services which will benefit the landlord financially or commercially, e.g., undertaking building work which would normally be the responsibility of the landlord.

Removal expenses

Although the courts have decided that the cost to the business of moving into new premises is not deductible in arriving at a taxable trading profit, in practice the Revenue do allow a deduction for normal removal expenses on the basis that it is an expense wholly and exclusively incurred for the business. This includes the cost of transporting trading stock, equipment, office furniture, etc., the cost of installing or connecting supplies such as electricity, gas and telephone and notifying customers, suppliers, advisers and authorities of the change.

If your business is moving to a new area it will be necessary for the directors and employees to incur costs of moving their possessions. Before deciding whether the business should meet these costs it is necessary to consider the tax implications. The business should be able to get a tax deduction if it meets or reimburse the employees' and directors' domestic removal costs provided they are reasonable and were incurred wholly and exclusively for the business. This should not result in the individuals being treated as having received a taxable benefit. If the individuals bear the cost themselves they would not be eligible for tax deduction.

VAT incurred on relocation costs borne by a business will be deductible subject to the normal rules.

Partners' domestic removal expenses

There had been some doubt about the deductibility of such expenses where the individuals are partners in the business. In a recent case, partners of a large accountancy practice were requested to move to offices in different parts of the UK and were reimbursed by the firm for their domestic removal expenses. The Revenue refused to allow the expense as a deduction in computing the firm's profits because the expenditure had both a business and private purpose. The High Court decided that, as the domestic removal costs of a sole trader would not be a deductibility business expense because of the duality of purpose, the same principle should apply to a partner. In the Court of Appeal the decision went in favour of the taxpayer but this was reversed by the House of Lords in November 1989.

Employees who own houses

If it is necessary for any of your employees to sell their houses and buy new ones in a different location in order to come to work for you, or because they are required in another part of your organisation, there is a Revenue concession which allows you to reimburse the following costs without a tax charge arising to the employee:

- legal and professional fees, stamp duty, removal costs and insurance;

- the net cost (after tax relief) of any bridging finance taken out on the employee's old property, provided certain conditions are met;

- travel and hotel costs incurred when looking for a new property;

- a subsistence allowance to cover a period of waiting to move into the new home;

- a disturbance allowance (of perhaps between 10 per cent and 12.5 per cent of salary) to cover connection charges, replacement of curtains, carpets, school uniforms, etc.;

- any loss suffered on the employee's old property because a quick sale was necessary; and

- if the move was to a more expensive area, the reimbursement of additional annual costs for a number of years.

Payments must be for a limited period of time, and taper as the years progress. They should not be in the form of a lump sum at the time of transfer. The exemption for the total payments made over the entire period is limited to the maximum payable within the Civil Service which is £20,370 as from 1 June 1991.

Guaranteed price arrangements
It is understood that employees will not be assessed to tax under relocation schemes where the employer guarantees a price for the old house to the employee and makes up the difference if the house is sold below this price. The conditions which must be satisfied are:

- the guaranteed price must be based on the market value at the time the house is put on the market and should be arrived at by reference to the average of at least two valuations by qualified independent experts; and

- active steps should be taken to market the property with some control exercised over it, i.e. not simply left to the employee.

National Insurance
In order to avoid having to pay NIC on expenses payments you make to your employees you should ensure that all expenses are properly evidenced. If you pay round sum allowances you should do so through a scheme which complies with the DSS requirements listed on page 183.

Rented accommodation for employees

If the business has problems of attracting and keeping staff, thought should be given to providing them with living accommodation either near the present site or near to the new business location. If the accommodation provided is at a low rent or is rent-free, the employee is taxed on the benefit (see page 154 for further details).

The Business Expansion Scheme (BES) gives income tax relief for investment in rented residential accommodation and some employers see this as a solution to their staffing problem.

Example

Gilroy Garages Ltd is a family company which owns ten garages and workshops in Sussex. It has proved difficult to attract skilled labour to the area because of the shortage of rented accommodation. Tom Gilroy, together with his sister Joan and Kate and his cousin Jim and father-in-law Peter, will subscribe £40,000 each for ordinary shares in a new company. The new company will purchase four cottages for £160,000 and convert them into eight dwellings to be let on assured tenancies to employees of Gilroy Garages Ltd. Each of the subscribers will get a tax repayment of £16,000 on the £40,000 subscribed assuming they pay income tax at 40 per cent.

Further details of the BES are given in Chapter 23.

Assistance with house purchase

If you are moving to a more expensive area directors and employees may be reluctant to move unless you offer to help them buy more expensive houses. One possibility is to make interest-free or low interest loans to your employees (see page 154 for how the benefit is calculated).

Alternatively, you could offer to buy an equity share in your employee's house. This also gives rise to a taxable benefit as costs are incurred in providing accommodation, but where the employer's cost is below £75,000 the employee's tax charge is insignificant (see page 154). In such cases it is usual for the employee to be granted an option to buy the employer's interest at the acquisition price.

Trading losses

Relocation is often seen as an opportunity to make changes to the trade and this can create a tax problem. The Revenue may contend that you have ceased a trade and started a new one and not allow relief for earlier trading losses. For example, a brewing company which ceased to brew beer but continued to sell beer was denied relief for the losses of its brewing trade.

Care must be taken where the relocated business is carried on by a company which has recently changed ownership or is about to change. Where the relocation also results in a major change in the nature or conduct of the trade valuable trading losses can be lost. If there is both a major change in the trade and a change of ownership in a three-year period, trading losses incurred in an accounting period before the change of ownership cannot be set against income and profits of an accounting period ending after that time.

Example
Ambridge Garden Products Ltd was formerly a loss-making subsidiary of a large London based public group (losses of £200,000) but 18 months ago the shares were bought by its management. In its new factory in Newcastle the company intends to make only four out of ten of its current products and it will make them to wholesalers' orders rather than keep stocks. It also intends to sell some of its output through advertisements directly to the public.

Such a change in the trade would mean the loss of tax relief of up to £66,000 (£200,000 × 33%).

Redundancies

When a business relocates there are often directors and employees who do not make the move, and employees with over two years' service may be entitled to a statutory redundancy payment. For the tax treatment of golden handshakes, see page 142.

Notifying the tax authorities

Both Customs and Excise and the Inland Revenue must be notified in the event of a change in the principal place of business.

29 Pensions

Introduction

As part of your business planning, it is important not to overlook the need to provide for your retirement. Various pension arrangements are available, and in making your choice you must take into account whether you are employed or self-employed and the effect on your tax liability. In this chapter we examine the options and consider the tax position of each of them.

Personal pensions

If you are under 75 and receive 'relevant earnings' you can effect a personal pension plan. Relevant earnings would either be income which you receive as a sole trader or partner, or your salary if you are not in a company pension scheme.

The benefits under personal pension plans are determined by the contributions which you can make. If you are aged up to 35 you may contribute up to 17.5 per cent of your net relevant earnings (relevant earnings less certain deductions, up to a maximum of £75,000 for 1992/93 and receive an allowance for the premiums at your highest marginal rate of income tax. The maximum amount which can be paid increases with age as shown below.

Age	Percentage of net relevant earnings
35 or less	17.5
36–45	20.0
46–50	25.0
51–55	30.0
56–60	35.0
61 and over	40.0

Of the maximum contributions, up to 5 per cent of net relevant earnings can be used to provide life assurance. Banks may require life assurance for a key person within a business, to ensure that on death there are sufficient funds to pay off any creditors, or at least ensure that the business remains financially secure.

The income tax allowance is available against your income for the tax year in which you pay the premiums. Alternatively, you can claim for the relief to be given against your income for the previous tax year. If you do not pay the maximum premium the shortfall can be carried forward for up to six years, provided certain conditions are met.

The benefits which are available include:

- A pension which must commence between the ages of 50 and 75 or a combination of a tax-free lump sum and a reduced pension. The tax-free lump sum is limited to 25 per cent of the final fund.

- A pension payable to your widow or other dependants.

- If you die before you start to draw your pension, a lump sum equal to the value of the fund and any life assurance taken could be paid to your dependants free of inheritance tax provided the policy has been written under trust.

It is not a requirement that you take your pension from the office with whom the premiums have been invested. It is possible, at retirement, to take your retirement fund to the open market in order to 'shop around' for the best annuity rate available at that time. It may be, for example, that a pension company which has been extremely efficient in investment terms, does not offer the best rates at retirement. This planning point is often missed.

If you take out a personal pension you have the opportunity to borrow in a tax-effective way. Banks, and building societies, are often prepared to lend on the basis that you only pay interest on the loan. The tax-free lump sum from your personal pension plan is used to repay the loan.

Personal pensions which have been available since 1 July 1988 are similar to retirement annuity plans (RAPs) which were available until that date. However, there are the following differences:

- If you are employed, your employer can contribute to the scheme.

- The DSS can make a contribution to secure protected rights.

- An employee's contributions are paid after deducting income tax relief at the basic rate of 25 per cent.

- A wider range of institutions are permitted to offer schemes.

- The investments can be chosen and managed by yourself or your financial advisers.

- Benefits must be taken between the ages of 50 (compared with 60 for

RAPs) and 75. Earlier retirement is acceptable for certain individuals such as athletes.

- A higher tax-free sum may be available for those with RAPs.
- With regard to contribution limits for RAPs, there is no upper limit on net relevant earnings, but the maximum percentage for the over 35s is lower than it is for personal pension schemes.

Occupational pension schemes

Occupational pension schemes are arrangements set up by an employer to provide pensions for his employees. Provided the scheme is approved by the Superannuation Funds Office:

- employer's contributions are deductible for tax purposes and not assessed on the employees as a benefit;
- income and capital gains in the pension fund are tax-free.

An employee may contribute up to 15 per cent of his earnings to the scheme and obtain income tax relief for his contributions.

The maximum contributions which an employer can make are not related to his employee's salary, but are geared to the benefits which may be provided under the scheme.

In 1989 a maximum pensionable salary was introduced, for those starting pension arrangements after that date, which is currently £75,000. The maximum pension shown below can now be taken at age 50, or deferred until age 70, subject to the completion of 20 years' service with the employer. Funding for maximum benefits below the age of 60 is not permitted.

The maximum benefits which can be received are as follows:

- Members pension:

Years service	Percentage of final salary allowable as pension
1	3.33
5	16.66
10	33.33
15	50.00
20 or more	66.66

The maximum pension is now £50,000 under an approved scheme (66.6 per cent × maximum pensionable salary of £75,000).

- Tax-free cash:
The tax-free cash sum cannot exceed the higher of

3/80 of final salary for each year of service up to 40 years (i.e. 1.5 × final salary)

and

2.25 × amount of the pension before taking cash.

The maximum tax-free sum is therefore £112,500 (i.e. 1.5 × maximum final salary of £75,000).

- 4 times salary death in service life cover (maximum £300,000).
- Widow's and dependant's pension on death

    (a) in service – 4/9ths of salary

    (b) in retirement – 2/3rds of member's pension.

The Inland Revenue also permit benefits to be increased annually, so long as the overall increase does not exceed the rise in the Retail Prices Index. Final salary schemes are schemes which define benefits by reference to service and final salary. These schemes, from some date in the future yet to be announced, will be required to provide a 5 per cent per annum increase in the future entitlement to benefits. The Government has indicated that it will give 12 months' notice of the appointed day for this change.

If for any reason the pension fund is larger than is necessary to provide the promised benefits for the particular scheme, it is overfunded and the trustees are required to reduce the surplus. If it is a Final Salary Scheme the first call on the surplus will be to ensure that all benefits accrued to date, including future entitlement to pensions and deferred pensions (for ex-employees), will enjoy immediate increases of 5 per cent, after the appointed day.

If any surplus remains after this upgrading of benefits, and after making allowance for the *Barber* decision, explained below, the trustees are then required to reduce the surplus by:

- increasing benefits within the limits set out above; or
- reducing or suspending contributions for up to five years; or
- making refunds to the employer. Although such refunds are taxed at 40 per cent they are not income for tax purposes, so losses and other deductions cannot be set off against them.

Barber v Guardian Royal Exchange

This judgment of the European Court of Justice makes it illegal to impose any differences in the benefits granted to men and women. So, for example, if the scheme's retirement age for women is 60, then men must be able to take the same benefits as women at age 60, even though the scheme specifies a retirement age for men of 65. In equalising benefits it is necessary to equalise upwards, so from 17 May 1989 men in many schemes will have been entitled to a higher benefit than that funded for by their scheme. The Social Security Acts state that benefits accrued cannot be taken away so it is only possible to adjust future benefits. It is still not certain how service before 17 May 1989 is to be treated. If your scheme has not yet been reviewed it is suggested that you take action immediately. Although contributions can be relieved against tax, the additional costs may be unpalatable.

A protocol to the Maastricht Treaty has attempted to limit the costs of the *Barber* decision. However, this will need ratification by all members of the EC before it becomes effective, and there are indications that it will not obtain full ratification.

Self-administered schemes

Most pension schemes, whether retirement annuity or company pension arrangements, are managed by insurance companies either on a with-profits or unit-linked basis. However, a company pension scheme can be self-administered. The Revenue normally require that a person with experience of managing pension schemes, known as a pensioner trustee, be appointed when there are fewer than 12 members in the scheme.

The advantage of a self-administered scheme is that the directors of the company can be trustees and can, within Revenue rules, decide on how to invest the fund. New rules have been introduced which include a reduction of the permissible level of 'self-investment' to 5 per cent of the fund, for example, where the fund owns shares in the company. Special rules apply to small schemes with fewer than 12 members.

Trustees of small self-administered pension schemes can lend up to 50 per cent of the value of the fund to the company, provided the loan is for business. Under new rules recently introduced, the limit is reduced to 25 per cent for the first two years of the scheme. The interest on the loan is tax deductible to the company and tax-free in the pension fund. It is also possible for the trustees to invest in property occupied by the company.

Example
Currently the business premises used by Robinson, Ramsay and Clark Ltd are rented. If Paul, the controlling director, or the company purchases the property, then its eventual sale will result in tax on a capital gain. If, however, the trustees of the pension scheme were to purchase the property, then not only would the company obtain a corporation tax deduction for the rent it would pay, which would be

tax-free in the pension fund, but there would be no tax on the capital gain when the property is sold.

Small self-administered schemes are not necessarily more expensive to run than insurance company schemes but you should establish at the outset that the self-administered facility will be an advantage. You could start with an insured arrangement and switch at a later stage. Professional advice should be sought when considering any pension arrangement, but particularly if it is to be self-administered.

Additional voluntary contributions

If you are an employee and a member of a company pension scheme, you may be able to increase your pension entitlement by making an additional voluntary contribution (AVC), up to the maximum of 15 per cent of salary as mentioned above. If you are already required to make a contribution to the scheme that amount will be included in arriving at the 15 per cent limit. AVCs attract relief at your highest marginal rate of income tax. All members of occupational pension schemes are able to make 'free standing' AVCs to a separate pension company of their own choice, with the same limits stated above.

There is a tax on overfunded AVCs of 35 per cent for basic rate tax payers and 48 per cent for higher rate tax payers instead of reducing benefits allowed under the employer's scheme.

Portable pensions

The Government is keen to ensure that pension entitlements are not seen as a barrier to movement between jobs. It is now possible to transfer funds between personal and company pension funds. It is no longer possible to make membership of a company pension scheme obligatory and, indeed, existing members may opt out of their current schemes without seeking the permission of their employers or the pension trustees. However, advice should be sought before opting out of a scheme to ensure that significant benefits are not lost.

Non-approved pension arrangements

Those who feel that their current pension entitlement is too low can also make provisions through non-approved pension arrangements.

These arrangements which can be funded (i.e. employer puts specific funds aside for pension benefits) or unfunded, allow you to take all your benefits as cash at retirement.

If the scheme is unfunded, you will be subject to a tax charge on the money you receive, whilst the company will receive full tax relief on the payment.

If the scheme is funded, there will be an immediate tax charge on the employee, and tax relief for the company. There is no National Insurance charge. If the money is accumulated in a trust fund the income and capital gains will only be charged at the basic rate of tax, and there will be no tax charge on the eventual payment to the employee. Non-approved schemes are proving increasingly popular where directors and executives are looking for a beneficial tax regime for large bonuses.

30 Retirement

Introduction

It is important from a tax point of view to consider several years beforehand the ideal position to be in at the time you retire. The following would be areas for consideration:

- Whether you are in business as a sole trader, a partner or as a director of a family company, if you have met certain conditions when you dispose of your shares or your business, all or part of the gain you realise will be exempt. This relief is considered below.

- Pension contributions. How much are you going to receive as a tax-free lump sum and as a pension? Are these amounts sufficient and are you in a position to increase the contributions? Chapter 29 examines pensions in detail.

- If you are in business as a sole trader the date of ceasing to trade is important to enable you to take advantage of the closing year rules where profits for certain periods fall out of assessment (see Chapter 9). The point is also relevant for partnerships, although the opportunity exists to elect for the trade to be treated as continuing.

- Whether the business is to be sold on your retirement or gifted to the next generation of your family.

- Whether to plan to reduce inheritance tax on your estate, for example, by making gifts to individuals or to family trusts.

Capital gains tax retirement relief

The retirement relief provisions are generous but complex, and what follows is only a broad outline of the relief. If you are likely to realise a gain on the disposal of an interest in a business you are strongly advised to seek professional advice. Broadly, the relief is available if you are either at least 55 years of age or unable to continue because of ill health when you dispose of:

- your business;
- an interest in a partnership;

- shares in your family trading company of which you are a full-time working director; or
- assets which were used in your business or family company and their disposal is part of your withdrawal from the business.

Your family company is one in which:

- you hold at least 25 per cent of the voting rights; or
- you hold at least 5 per cent of the voting rights and more than 50 per cent is held by you together with members of your family.

For this purpose, your family includes your spouse, your children and grandchildren and both sets of parents, grandparents, brothers and sisters.

If you meet the conditions for the relief, the first £150,000 of gains are wholly exempt from capital gains tax as are half of any further gains between £150,000 and £600,000. If your spouse also meets the conditions these figures could be doubled. Assuming at the date of the disposal you are at least 55 years of age or are retiring through ill health (see below) what other conditions must be met? To obtain the full relief you will need to have owned the interest in a business or the shares in a family trading company for ten years. For a shorter period the relief is reduced proportionately, with a minimum, 10 per cent of the full relief, where the business interest was owned for at least one year before the disposal.

Example

Grace, who is 57, sells her 25 per cent holding in Ross Gifford and Simpson Ltd and realises a chargeable gain of £800,000. At the same time she resigns as a full-time working director of the company. She had bought the shares six years ago at which time she became a full-time director. The relief would be given as follows:

	£	£
Chargeable gain before retirement relief		800,000
Less: Retirement relief		
60% × £150,000	90,000	
60% × £450,000 × 50%	135,000	225,000
Reduced chargeable gain		£575,000

The length of a qualifying period may be determined by aggregating the current qualifying period with earlier business periods where, for example, you have been involved in two or more businesses at different times. You will only need to consider this where the current qualifying period is less than ten years.

Aggregation can be used where:

- the end of the earlier business period occurred less than ten years before the end of the current qualifying period; and
- not more that two years have elapsed between the earlier and the current periods; and
- the current period is of at least one year's duration.

If the business or shares in question were acquired by gift or were inherited from your spouse, your spouse's qualifying period may be taken into account in calculating your own period of ownership.

In order to allow the aggregation of the earlier spouse's business period:

- the whole of your spouse's interest must have been transferred;
- you and your spouse must have been living together in the year of assessment in which the gift or transfer on death occurred; and
- you (the transferee) must make an election in writing within two years of the end of the tax year in which the disposal on which you are seeking retirement took place.

There is a further restriction of the relief if the company owns assets that are not used in its business, such as quoted shares. This rule is illustrated by the following example.

Example

Alfred, who is 60, sells his 90 per cent interest in Roberts Coronation Products Ltd and realises a gain of £80,000. He has held the shares for 20 years and prior to the disposal had been a full-time working director for ten years. At that date the market value of the company's assets were as follows:

	£
Goodwill	40,000
Factory	100,000
Quoted securities	60,000
Staff cars	21,000
Current assets (including stock) less liabilities	10,000
	£231,000

Any disposal of the goodwill, factory or quoted securities could result in a chargeable capital gain so these are described as chargeable assets. Of these the goodwill and the factory are also business assets. The cars are exempt and trading stock would produce a trading profit. Only the following percentage of Alfred's gain on his shares qualifies for relief.

Chargeable business assets:	£140,000	=	70%
Chargeable assets	£200,000		

	£
Chargeable gain before retirement relief	80,000
Retirement relief 70% × £80,000	56,000
Reduced chargeable gain	£24,000

Had the company sold the quoted securities shortly before Alfred's disposal, the whole of his gain would have been covered by retirement relief.

This relief should be given automatically if all the conditions are met. It is, however, necessary to claim the relief if you retire from business because of physical or mental illness before you are 55 years old. The Revenue has stated that they would require such claimants to provide a medical certificate and that they would take advice from the Regional Medical Service. In some cases a further medical examination by the Regional Medical Officer will be required. To obtain the relief you must satisfy the Revenue that at the date of disposal you were incapable of engaging in work of a kind which you previously undertook, and it was likely that you would remain permanently so incapable. You will be glad to hear that the relief is not withdrawn if you later recover your health

Ill health under the age of 55 is the only circumstance in which actual retirement is necessary. Once you are 55, you can dispose of a business, obtain retirement relief and still acquire another business in which you may take an active role.

Retirement is an occasion when you might wish to make gifts of your business or personal assets and this is the subject of the next chapter.

31 Gifts and Trusts

Introduction

You may consider giving some of your business assets to younger members of the family. This could be achieved by an outright gift or a transfer into a trust. In this chapter we consider the capital gains tax implications of making gifts of business assets and the tax implications of using trusts. A gift is a disposal for capital gains tax and market value is used in calculating the gain, even though no consideration is received. This seems a bit unfair because you have no sale proceeds from which to pay the tax. Of course, if you are disposing of business assets you may be able to get retirement relief. But if retirement relief is not relevant, or your gain is not fully covered by retirement relief, you may wish to consider making an election to defer the chargeable gain.

No capital gains tax arises if you make a gift to your wife or husband or to a charity.

Gifts on which deferral is available

Before 14 March 1989, gains on giving away any type of asset used to qualify for hold-over (or gift) relief. Since then the scope of the relief has been substantially curtailed and it is now only available in respect of:

- gifts of business assets or heritage property; or
- gifts into and from discretionary trusts; or
- gifts to political parties; or
- gifts out of accumulation and maintenance trusts (see page 258) to beneficiaries under 25 years old.

In all cases the donor must be an individual or a trustee and both donor and donee must be UK resident.

'Business assets' include:

- assets used in the donor's unincorporated business;
- assets owned by the donor but used in his family trading company;

- shares and securities in trading companies which are neither quoted on the Stock Exchange nor dealt in on the USM;
- shares and securities in the donor's family trading company;
- certain agricultural property.

'Family company' is as defined for retirement relief (see page 249).

How hold-over relief works

If you make a hold-over election the gain is deferred until the new owner disposes of the asset. For the purposes of calculating a gain on the next disposal the acquisition cost is reduced by the held-over gain.

Example

For many years Joe has been running his own business, Maplin Equipment. In 1992 he decided that a warehouse which cost him £6,000 in June 1972 had become surplus to requirements and so in February 1992 he gave it to his daughter, Peggy, who had recently started in business making floor cleaning equipment. At 31 March 1982 the warehouse was worth £25,000 and in February 1992 the market value was £85,000. Joe and Peggy elect to hold over the gain on the gift of the property. RPIs are March 1982 79.44; February 1992 136.3.

	£	£
Deemed sale proceeds		85,000
Less: MV 31 March 1982	25,000	
Indexation allowance		
RPI increase March 1982 to February 1992		
0.716 × £25,000	17,900	
		42,900
Chargeable gain – held over		£42,100

When Peggy disposes of the property the capital gain will be calculated using an acquisition cost of £42,900 (£85,000 − £42,100). If she uses the proceeds to buy another business asset she will be able to roll over the gain.

For inheritance tax Joe has made an outright gift and no tax is payable if he survives for seven years. If he does not survive and this is the only gift he has made in the last seven years no tax is payable but part of his nil rate band is used.

If you make a gift you can only elect to hold over the total chargeable gain. It is not possible, for example, to hold over sufficient gain to leave in charge an amount that will be covered by your annual exemption. However, the same result can be achieved if you sell an asset at an undervalue.

Sales at an undervalue

The hold-over relief is also available where you make a qualifying disposal at an undervalue. If the actual proceeds you receive exceed the amount you can deduct as allowable expenditure (excluding indexation), the excess reduces the gain that can be held over.

Example
Simon purchased shares in an unquoted trading company for £1,000 in August 1980 which were worth £6,000 on 31 March 1982. He sold them to his daughter Pat for £11,500 on 10 December 1991 when they had a market value of £22,748. Simon and Pat elect to hold over the chargeable gain. RPIs are March 1982 79.44; December 1991 135.7.

	£	£
Deemed sale proceeds		22,748
Less: MV March 1982	6,000	
Indexation allowance		
RPI increase March 1982 to December 1991		
0.708 × £6,000	4,248	10,248
Gain		12,500
Less: Chargeable gain:		
Actual proceeds less allowable expenditure		
(£11,500 − £6,000), covered by		
annual exemption		5,500
Gain held over		£7,000

Time-limit

The time-limit for claiming hold-over relief is six years from the end of the year of assessment in which the gift is made. Therefore it is not too late to consider making a claim in respect of gifts made before 14 March 1989 of assets which would not qualify had they been gifted after 13 March 1989, e.g. paintings or second homes.

Emigration of donee

It would be a very generous relief, if having given an asset to your son and elected to hold over the gain, he could sell it when he is no longer resident in the UK and no longer subject to UK capital gains tax. In fact, what happens is, the held-over crystallises just before the donee becomes non-resident. It should be emphasised that it is only the held-over gain that crystallises, not the total gain that has accrued to the donee.

Example
After two years of ownership Susan gave Paul 200 shares in May 1986 when they were worth £50,000 and they elected to hold over the gain of £20,000. In August 1991 when the shares were worth £110,000 Paul emigrated to Australia.

Paul will be assessed in 1991/92 on £20,000, being the gain held over. The gain since 1986 will escape UK capital gains tax. But, on the other hand, if the shares in August 1991 were worth only £10,000, the held-over gain of £20,000 would still crystallise and there would be no relief for the unrealised loss.

The rule concerning the emigration of the donee does not apply if the donee is an individual who becomes non-resident:

- more than six years after the end of the year in which the gift is made; or

- because of his or her employment which requires all duties to be performed outside this country and the individual becomes UK resident again after three years.

In our example, the held-over gain would never crystallise if Paul were to emigrate after 5 April 1993. If the donee does not pay the tax on the held-over gain within 12 months of the date that it becomes payable, the donor, Susan in our example, can be made to pay the unpaid tax.

Relief for capital transfer tax and inheritance tax

Relief is available for capital transfer tax (CTT) or inheritance tax (IHT) that has been paid on a gift where the gain was held over. In computing the gain when the donee disposes of the asset, relief is given for CTT or IHT paid at the time of the gift although the deduction cannot create or increase an unindexed loss. Whether it is the donor or the donee who pays the CTT or IHT is not relevant. Details of when IHT becomes payable and how it is calculated can be found in Chapter 32.

Example
In April 1989 Paul gave his son Gordon shares in Collins Merseyside Properties Ltd when they were worth £45,000 and elected to hold over the gain of £32,000. As this was a potentially exempt transfer no IHT was payable at the time. However, Paul died in February 1992 and IHT

of £9,000 became payable on the gift. Assume Gordon sells the shares for £100,000 in June 1993. RPIs are April 1988 105.8; June 1993 say 150.0.

	£	£
Sale proceeds		100,000
Less: Acquisition cost	45,000	
Less: Gain held over	32,000	
	13,000	
Indexation allowance		
RPI increase April 1988 to June 1993		
0.418 × £13,000	5,434	
	18,434	
Add IHT payable	9,000	27,434
Chargeable gain		£72,566

Whether to claim the relief

There are several factors to consider before deciding whether you should be a party to a claim for hold-over relief:

- Where the donee is likely to be able to shelter the held-over gain on a future disposal the election should be made. If business assets are gifted the donee may qualify for replacement of business assets roll-over relief or retirement relief.

- As donor you should look at your tax position were you not to make the election. It may be that you have tax losses or an unused annual exemption which will cover a large part of the gain. If there is only a small tax saving for you it may be better not to make the election so that the donee takes over the asset with an acquisition cost equal to the full market value.

- Where the person contemplating making the gift is old and the gain represents a large part of the asset's value, it is worth remembering that there is no capital gains tax on death and that the deceased's beneficiaries acquire the assets at market value. Making a gift before death and claiming hold-over relief, on the other hand, is going to reduce the donee's acquisition cost on future disposals of the asset, which in turn reduces any indexation allowance.

    If you are the donee you may be able to persuade the donor to part with an equally valuable asset with a smaller gain or to let you inherit the first mentioned asset.

- Where CTT or IHT has been paid or is likely to be paid on the gift this may influence you in favour of making an election as this is the only opportunity for obtaining relief for the tax paid.

- The possibility of capital gains tax being abolished or the rate of charge being increased or decreased.

Use of trusts

Trusts are set up for some of the following reasons:

- To provide property which is to be used for
  (a) the young;
  (b) the disabled;
  (c) the old;
  (d) employees and their dependants; and
  (e) animals.

- To make provision privately for dependants such as a mistress and an illegitimate child.

- To tie up property in order to benefit different persons in succession.

- To protect family property from those members who are extravagant.

- To hold land for the benefit of those who cannot legally own it, for example an infant or more than four persons.

- To allow investors to invest in shares and property by owning units in trusts.

- To provide for a gift to be made in the future in the light of the circumstances a that time.

- To minimise the tax payable on income and gains and on transfers from a person's estate. Anti-avoidance provisions have been introduced which reduce or cancel the tax benefits of holding property in a trust rather than in an individual's free estate.

The person who provides the trust property and usually sets up the trust is known as the settlor. The settlor transfers the ownership of the property to trustees who hold the property for the benefit of beneficiaries. It is possible for the settlor to be one of the trustees and one of the beneficiaries. The terms of a trust can be extremely flexible, allowing the trustees to increase the class of beneficiaries and appoint capital back to the settlor. For tax purposes trusts are divided into three categories:

- *A life interest trust* or *interest-in-possession trust.* This is a trust where one or more persons have the right to receive the income from the trust property. This right can be for life or for a fixed period of time.

- *A discretionary trust.* With this type of trust no person has a right to the trust income. It is for the trustees to decide on the distribution of income and capital.

- *An accumulation and maintenance trust.* This is a form of discretionary trust, set up for the benefit of children, which is favourably treated under the IHT rules.

Residence of trusts

The residence of a trust depends upon the residence of its trustees. If all the trustees are resident in the UK, the trust itself is UK resident. If they are all resident overseas, the trust is non-UK resident. Where some trustees are UK resident and some are not, the position depends upon the tax being considered.

With income tax, the deciding factor is the status of the settlor when he provided the trust with the funds. If at that time he was resident or ordinarily resident or domiciled in the UK, the trust will be UK resident. Otherwise it will be non-UK resident.

For capital gains tax purposes, a trust is treated as being UK resident if its general administration is carried on in the UK and a majority of the trustees are resident in the UK.

Gifts to trusts

For many years tax has been avoided by the following device. A settlor would gift property into a UK resident trust and hold over any gain. The UK trustees (or a majority of them) would at a later stage be replaced by non-UK trustees and the administration would be transferred overseas. Because the trust had emigrated, the gain held over at the time the property was settled crystallised. However, any unrealised gain while the property was in the trust escaped UK CGT until such time as disposal proceeds were remitted to a UK beneficiary.

Provisions in the 1991 Finance Act are designed to stop such tax savings. For trusts emigrating since 18 March 1991 the trust's assets are deemed to have been sold and reacquired immediately before the emigration giving rise to a capital gains tax liability based on the gain to the date of emigration and assessable on the pre-emigration trustees.

Inheritance tax

No IHT is payable on transfers to interest in possession trusts and accumulation and maintenance trusts provided the donor survives for seven years.

Furthermore, in the case of accumulation and maintenance trusts, there is no IHT payable when a right to receive the income is created or when capital is distributed by the trustees to the beneficiaries.

For the purposes of IHT the person who has a right to the income of an interest in possession trust is treated as owning the settled property which produces the income.

For discretionary trusts there is a charge to IHT when assets are transferred into the trust, if the value of those assets, plus the value of any other gifts made by the settlor in the last seven years exceeds the nil rate band which is £150,000 for 1992/93. The charge is calculated at half the death rate (this lower rate is known as the lifetime rate) but is likely to be increased if the donor dies within seven years. There is a tax charge every ten years on the value of the trust property at 30 per cent of the lifetime rate, i.e. maximum 6 per cent, and an exit charge when the property leaves the trust.

Although there are several occasions when discretionary trust property could be taxed this does not mean that such trusts are not very useful vehicles. In fact, they are often used where the chargeable value of the property going into the trust does not exceed the nil rate band and the trust is likely to be wound up before the tenth anniversary.

Example

Eric, who is 32, is married with no children and has made no gifts in the last seven years. He owns shares in Ross Gifford and Simpson Ltd which are currently worth £150,000. It is anticipated that the company will seek a Stock Exchange listing during the next 18 months. Eric sets up a discretionary trust with himself, his wife and other relatives as beneficiaries. Assume that the shares remain in the trust for just under ten years, at which time they are worth £500,000. A decision is then made to transfer some of the shares to certain individuals including Eric and his wife; the remaining shares are put into an accumulation and maintenance trust for Eric's children.

No IHT charge arises when the trust is set up as the value of the gift does not exceed the nil rate band of £150,000. The charge which applies when the property leaves the trust before the ten-year anniversary is calculated by reference to the initial IHT rate, which being nil would mean that no IHT is payable. One effect of this exercise is that the growth in value of Eric's shares over ten years has occurred outside his estate free of any IHT charges.

32   Inheritance Tax

Introduction

In general terms inheritance tax (IHT) is payable when the value of your estate, i.e. your capital, is reduced whether this occurs as a result of gifts made during your lifetime or on death. However, there are a considerable number of exceptions to this rule which are considered below. Further reliefs are available in arriving at the value of certain types of property, for example business and agricultural property. If you are UK domiciled the transfer of your capital is chargeable wherever it is located. If you have a foreign domicile transfers of property situated abroad will not be chargeable.

The increase in the number of exemptions and reliefs in recent years has meant that for individuals who are aware of them and are willing to plan ahead this is a tax that can largely be avoided. Furthermore, for those who do pay IHT the rates of tax have been reduced in recent years.

Non-chargeable transfers

The following transfers are specifically exempted from IHT:

- Transfers to a spouse. If the person making the transfers is UK domiciled and the spouse is not, up to £55,000 of the total of all transfers is exempt.

- The first £3,000 of gifts each year is exempt. If you do not use the exemption it can be carried forward for one year only.

- Gifts to individuals limited to £250 per gift per person per year.

- Where the transfer is normal expenditure out of income, i.e. you can demonstrate that you are left with sufficient income to support your normal lifestyle. Examples are covenants and insurance premiums.

- Gifts in consideration of marriage:

  (a) Parents can give £5,000 each.

  (b) Grandchildren and great grandparents £2,500 each.

  (c) Friends and relatives £1,000 each.

- Gifts to charities.

- Gifts of land to registered housing associations.

- Gifts to the major political parties.

- Gifts to certain public bodies. For example, if you gift amenity land to a local authority or a painting to the National Gallery.

- Heritage property if transferred to an approved body. If you transfer it to another person the exemption is conditional on the new owner agreeing to meet certain conditions which would include allowing access to the public and allocating funds for the property's maintenance.

- Foreign currency accounts with UK banks are exempt on death where the deceased was not deemed to be UK domiciled.

In the following instances you are not treated as having reduced the value of your estate and therefore no tax is chargeable:

- Where there was no intention to make a gift. For example, if you have unintentionally sold property at an undervalue.

- Where the transfer was made for the maintenance of your family.

- Where the item would have been deductible in computing profits or gains for income tax or corporation tax.

- Where your pension contributions benefit another person.

- Where you waive remuneration.

- Where you waive dividends within the 12 months before the right to the dividends accrues.

- Where you grant an agricultural property tenancy for full consideration.

- Where you disclaim a legacy or enter into an agreement with other beneficiaries to vary the destination of inherited property.

- Where you transfer excluded property which consists of:

  (a) Any reversionary interest in settled property so long as you did not purchase it, nor was an earlier entitlement to the interest held by you or your spouse.

  (b) Property situated outside the UK and certain Treasury securities if you are not UK domiciled. If the property is in a trust you must have had a foreign domicile at the time the trust was created.

  (c) If you are domiciled in the Channel Islands or the Isle of Man, war savings and national savings certificates and National Savings Bank deposits.

Potentially exempt transfers

The following lifetime gifts are initially treated as exempt from IHT but tax is payable if the donor dies within seven years of making the gift. In each case it is a condition of the exemption that the donor does not continue to enjoy the property gifted:

- Outright gifts to individuals.
- Gifts into accumulation and maintenance trusts.
- Gifts into trusts for the disabled.
- Gifts into interest in possession trusts.

There are therefore opportunities to spread wealth among members of the family without incurring a charge to IHT. It is worth considering transferring capital to your spouse during your lifetime so that both estates can benefit from the nil rate band. There is, however, little point in equalising estates if your wills are made out in favour of each other. Where there is reluctance to transfer capital outright to younger members of the family, consider setting up an accumulation and maintenance trust or a trust in which they will have a life interest.

Valuation of property

Where a transfer of capital is chargeable to IHT it is valued on the basis of the loss suffered by the donor rather than the value gained by the person receiving the property.

Example

Sinclair, who owns 51 per cent of the shares of RM Yates Ltd, a property dealing company, gifts 2 per cent of the shares into a discretionary trust. The market values are as follows:

2 per cent	£300
49 per cent	£12,250
51 per cent	£38,250

For IHT the value of the gift is £26,000 being the difference between the value of Sinclair's holding before and after the gift.

If the donor pays the IHT on the gift this also reduces his estate. Therefore, in calculating the tax, the value transferred is grossed up to reflect this.

Related property

Another feature of the valuation rules is that all related property is taken into account in arriving at the value of what is being transferred. Property is related property if it:

- is owned by the spouse;
- is held in a trust in which the donor or the spouse has an interest in possession; or
- was transferred to a charity or other exempt body during the last five years.

Example

Pauline owns 5 per cent of the shares in Fowler Garden Produce Ltd and her husband Arthur owns 46 per cent. If Pauline gifts her shares and dies within seven years the shares will be valued at 5/51 of the market value of a 51 per cent holding.

Business property relief

To be eligible for this relief you must have owned the business assets for the two years immediately preceding the transfer. It is not necessary for you to work full-time in the business, e.g. the assets of a Lloyd's underwriter may qualify. Businesses which mainly deal in land or securities or hold investments are excluded. The relief, which was substantially increased from 10 March 1992, is given by reducing the value of the property transferred by one of the following percentages:

100 per cent

- A sole trader's business assets.
- An interest in a partnership carrying on a business.
- Unquoted shares giving a controlling interest in the company just before the transfer.
- Unquoted shares which carry more than 25 per cent of the voting rights.

The effect of this 100 per cent reduction (which was 50 per cent before 10 March 1992) is to take many business assets and unquoted shares, including shares dealt in on the Unlisted Securities Market, outside the charge to IHT.

Example

	9 March 1992	10 March 1992
Date of death	£000	£000
House and other assets	650	650
Shares – 30% interest in unquoted company	2,500	2,500
	3,150	3,150
Business property relief 50%, 100%	(1,250)	(2,500)
Taxable estate	£1,900	£650
IHT payable	£704	£200

50 per cent

- Business assets owned by:
  - (a) a partner and used in his partnership;
  - (b) a controlling shareholder and used by the company; or
  - (c) trustees of settled property used by the life tenant who is carrying on the business.
- Unquoted shares which carry 25 per cent or less of the voting rights.
- Quoted shares giving a controlling interest in the company just before the transfer.

Shares dealt in on the Unlisted Securities Market are now treated as unquoted shares for business property relief.

Related property is taken into account when determining whether a person has control of an unquoted or quoted company.

Example

Mr and Mrs Arnold own shares in Belax Ltd.

	Voting control	Voting control
	%	%
Mr Arnold	24	25
Mrs Arnold	2	—
Others	74	75
	100	100
Business property relief	100%	50%

Agricultural property relief

A relief similar to business property relief is available to reduce the agricultural value of agricultural property such as land, buildings and plant.

To be eligible you must either have used the property in your farming business for the two years prior to the transfer or have owned it for seven years, during which time it has been used for agricultural purposes. If your land is worth more than its agricultural value (e.g. it has development potential) you can obtain business property relief on the additional value if you own or have an interest in the business which farms the land. The agricultural property is reduced by one of the following percentages:

- 100 per cent where you have a right to vacant possession of the property; and

- 50 per cent in other cases (e.g. where the property is subject to tenancy).

Gifts with reservation and debts

Where a person makes a gift with the intention of continuing to enjoy the property it is described as a gift with reservation and is treated for IHT as remaining in the estate of the donor. An example of such a gift is where you give a painting to your son but stipulate that it is to remain hanging in your home during your lifetime. Where a gift is made with reservation and later the donor releases his interest the gift is treated as made at that later time.

A gift of a family business or farm or shares in a family company will not necessarily amount to a gift with reservation merely because the donor remains in the business, perhaps as a director or partner. It would be necessary to show that the remuneration or other benefits received were linked with or affected by the gift.

The value of a person's estate is normally net of liabilities. However, debts which were not incurred for full consideration cannot be deducted; for example, if you gave property away and then bought it back from the donee leaving the debt outstanding.

Calculating the tax payable

The chargeable amount of the property being transferred is added to the value of any chargeable transfers made by the donor in the previous seven years. No tax is payable if the cumulative total is less than £150,000 (for transfers after 9 March 1992) and this 'nil rate' band increases annually in line with inflation. Lifetime gifts are taxed at 20 per cent, being half the rate applying on death. The current transfer is taxed assuming it represents the top slice of the cumulative total.

If the transferor dies within three years of making the gift, the full rate of tax applies. Tapering relief is available where the transferor dies between three and seven years after making the gift (see Appendix 16).

Example
In addition to the transfer of shares described in the earlier example, Sinclair had made chargeable transfers of £140,000 in the previous seven years. Assume that the tax on the gift of shares will be paid by the trustees and Sinclair has used his annual exemptions.

	Gross £	IHT £
Previous transfers	140,000	Nil
Gift of shares – value transferred	26,000	
	£166,000	
£16,000 (£166,000 − £150,000) × 20%		3,200
IHT payable		£3,200

Accounting for inheritance tax

There is no requirement to make a return for gifts that are exempt or potentially exempt. Chargeable transfers must normally be reported to the Inland Revenue Capital Taxes Office within 12 months from the end of the month of transfer.

IHT is normally payable six months after the event which gives rise to the tax. The exception is lifetime chargeable transfers which are made between 6 April and 30 September where tax is payable on the following 30 April. Tax on death will often be paid earlier where probate is required. Interest runs from the date on which payment of tax is due. The current rate of interest is 8 per cent per annum.

On lifetime chargeable transfers where the donee agrees to pay the tax and on death transfers, IHT may be paid by instalments provided the assets are in certain categories and an election is made. The tax is paid in equal annual instalments starting six months from the date of death or from the normal due date. The assets must be:

- land;
- a business or an interest in a business;
- shares in a company which the donor controlled; and
- unquoted shares (including shares quoted on the USM) where certain conditions are met.

Any outstanding interest on overdue instalments is added to the next instalment due. On a sale of the property any outstanding tax (and interest) is payable immediately.

The tax on lifetime chargeable transfers is usually paid by the donor but can be paid by the donee. The primary responsibility for the payment of IHT on death is that of the donee but where it remains unpaid it can be collected from the deceased's estate. It is worth considering at the time a potentially exempt transfer is made, the amount of IHT that would be payable should the donor die during the following seven years. If appropriate, term assurance could be taken out on the donor's life to pay the tax.

Settled property

IHT is payable on the transfer of capital from a person's estate. Included in the estate is deemed to be the value of settled property in which the deceased had an interest in possession, i.e. a right to receive the trust income. Any tax relating to the transfer of that interest is calculated by reference to the beneficiary's cumulation of transfers, but is payable by the trustees from the settled property. The IHT aspects of trusts are considered in Chapter 31.

Appendixes

The forms reproduced in Appendixes 2, 3, 4, 11 and 12 are Crown Copyright and are reproduced with the kind permission of the Controller of Her Majesty's Stationery Office.

1   Business Economic Notes (BEN)

Type of business	Publication date
BEN No.	
1 Travel Agents	1987
2 Road Haulage	1987
3 Lodging Industry	1987
4 Hairdressers	1987
5 Waste Materials, Reclamation and Disposal	1987
6 Funeral Directors	1987
7 Dentists	July 1988
8 Florists	July 1988
9 Licensed Victuallers	July 1988
10 Jewellery Trade	January 1990
11 Electrical Retailers	January 1990
12 Antiques and Fine Art Dealers	January 1990
13 Fish and Chip Shops	October 1990
14 Pet Industry	October 1990
15 Veterinary Surgeons	October 1990
16 Catering – General	October 1990
17 Catering – Restaurants	October 1990
18 Catering – Fast Food Cafes and Snack Bars	October 1990

Notes 1–12 cost 60p each and notes 13–18 cost £1 each (post-free). Copies can be obtained by writing to:

The Reference Room
Inland Revenue Library
Room 8, New Wing
Somerset House
London
WC2R 1LB

2   Starting a Business: Enquiry Form 41G

Inland Revenue
Income Tax

Reference

Dear Sir/Madam

I understand you may now be self employed (this includes subcontracting in the Construction Industry). If so please let me have the information asked for below and over the page as soon as possible.

If this is the first time you have been self employed, you may find booklet IR28 'Starting in Business' helpful. You can get this from any Tax Office. If you need any further help I shall be pleased to arrange an appointment for you to see me.

When you become self employed, you normally pay National Insurance Contributions (Class 2). Please get in touch with your local Social Security Office about this.

Yours faithfully,

District date stamp

H.M. Inspector of Taxes

Enquiries about yourself and any business partners

Yourself

Your surname

Your first names

Your private address

Postcode

Tax Office to which last
Income Tax Return made

Reference in that Office

National Insurance Number

Date of birth   ...   ...

Business partners

	Partner 1	Partner 2	Partner 3
Partner's surname			
Partner's first names			
Partner's private address			
	Postcode	Postcode	Postcode

If you have more than three business partners please give the names and addresses of any other partners on a separate sheet

41G(1989)

Please turn over

Enquiries about the business | Replies

1. In what name is the business carried on, if not in your own name?

1. _____

2. What is the business address, including postcode, if different from your private address?

2. _____

Postcode

3. What is the nature of the business?

3. _____

4. When did you start in this business?

4.   19

5. If you took over an existing business, who did you acquire it from?

5.

Name

Address

Postcode

6. To what date do you propose to make up your business accounts?
If they are to be prepared by a firm of accountants, please give their name and address including postcode.

6.   19

Name

Address

Postcode

7. If you are not already operating PAYE as an employer, have you any employees earning
   • more than £53.50 a week or £232 a month?
   • more than £1 a week who have other employment?

7.   Yes   No

   • [ ]   [ ]   *Please '√' appropriate box.*

   • [ ]   [ ]

Personal enquiries | Replies

8. Were you employed or were you self employed before you started this business?

   What was the name and address of the business or employer. Please give this information even if you had a period of unemployment between leaving employment and starting your own business.

   If you still have the leaving certificate form P45 handed to you by your last employer, please attach it and give the leaving date.

8. Employed [ ]   Self employed [ ]   *'√'one box*

   Name

   Address

   Postcode

   19

9. If this is your first occupation since leaving full time education on what date did the education finish?

9.   19

10. If as well as running your business you are in paid employment, or are continuing an existing business, please give the name and address of the employer/existing business.

10.

   Name

   Address

   Postcode

   Is this an existing business or employment?

   Existing business [ ]   Employment [ ]   *'√'one box*

Signature _____   Date   19

Please say whether you are single, married, widowed, separated or divorced

3   Starting a Business: Enquiry Form CT41G

**Inland Revenue
Corporation Tax**

Reference

The Secretary

Dear Sir/Madam,

I shall be grateful if you will supply the information requested overleaf and at the same time **forward a copy of the Company's Memorandum and Articles of Association for me to retain.**

May I remind you that -

• the company should

 - operate Pay As You Earn in respect of all remuneration paid (including fees, etc., paid or credited to directors)

 - deduct National Insurance Contributions

• the company is required to make returns to the Collector of Taxes

 - of all qualifying distributions and the Advance Corporation Tax payable in respect of them

 - of certain amounts of Franked Investment Income received, and

 - of all annual payments etc. and the income tax deducted from them

• the company should return this form in order to avoid the possibility of estimated assessments being issued.

You may like to take a photocopy of this form as a record of your reply.

Yours faithfully

District date stamp

HM Inspector of Taxes

CT41G

7287/0870L Dd 8154570 200M 4/89 TP Gp607

Information requested	Replies
1. The nature of the activities to be carried on by the company.	1.
2. (a) The address of its Registered Office *including postcode*.	2. (a)
(b) The address of the place of business (if different from the address at (a)).	(b)
3. The date of commencement of business.	3.
4. The company registration number.	4.
5. If the company is a member of a group, (a) the name of the group (b) the District which deals with the parent company of the group, and, if known that company's tax reference number.	5. (a) (b) District Reference
6. If an existing business has been taken over, (a) the name and address of that business, and (b) the name and address of the person from whom it was acquired.	6. (a) (b)
7. The date to which the first accounts will be prepared.	7.
8. The name and address *including postcode* of the accountants or other agents who will be dealing with the company's tax affairs.	8.

9. If Pay As You Earn is already being operated, the name of the tax district concerned and the full PAYE reference number	9. _____ District Reference _____

10. Details of Directors

To help in allocating correct codes to the directors of the company, will you please give their full names, addresses and National Insurance numbers.

Separate enquiries to the directors may be avoided if they can tell you their previous Tax Offices and references for entry below.

Surname, first name(s) and private address	National Insurance number	Tax Office and reference
Post Town County Postcode		
Post Town County Postcode		
Post Town County Postcode		
Post Town County Postcode		
Post Town County Postcode		
Post Town County Postcode		
Post Town County Postcode		
Post Town County Postcode		
Post Town County Postcode		

A copy of the company's Memorandum and Articles of Association is enclosed

Signature _____ Date _____

4 The Taxpayer's Charter

You are entitled to expect the Inland Revenue

To be fair

- By settling your tax affairs impartially
- By expecting you to pay only what is due under the law
- By treating everyone with equal fairness

To help you

- To get your tax affairs right
- To understand your rights and obligations
- By providing clear leaflets and forms
- By giving you information and assistance at our enquiry offices
- By being courteous at all times

To provide an efficient service

- By settling your tax affairs promptly and accurately
- By keeping your private affairs strictly confidential
- By using the information you give us only as allowed by the law
- By keeping our costs down

To be accountable for what we do

- By setting standards for ourselves and publishing how well we live up to them

If you are not satisfied

- We will tell you exactly how to complain
- You can ask for your tax affairs to be looked at again
- You can appeal to an independent tribunal
- Your MP can refer your complaint to the Ombudsman

In return, we need you

- To be honest
- To give us accurate information
- To pay your tax on time

5   Rates of Income Tax, Personal Allowances and Reliefs for 1992/93

Lower, basic and higher rates

Taxable income	Tax on full band	
Up to £2,000	£400	20%
£2,001–£23,700	£5,425	25%
Excess over £23,700		40%

Additional rate

Discretionary trust	10%
Accumulation and maintenance trust	10%

Personal allowances

	£
Personal	3,445
Married couple's	1,720
Single parent addition	1,720
Widow's bereavement	1,720
Blind person	1,080

Age allowance

	Aged 65–74	75 years and over
	£	£
Personal	4,200	4,370
Married couples	2,465	2,505
Income limit	14,200	14,200

Important reliefs

Mortgage interest (relief restricted to basic rate)
On the first £30,000 of a loan to purchase a main residence. For loans made after 31 July 1988 the relief is shared in the case of joint borrowers.

Business Expansion Scheme
Maximum relief in a year £40,000. Husband and wife are each entitled to maximum relief.

6   Enterprise Zones

Enterprise zone	Came into operation
The Lower Swansea Valley	11 June 1981
Corby	22 June 1981
Dudley	10 July 1981
Langthwaite Grange (Wakefield)	31 July 1981
Clydebank	3 August 1981
Salford Docks	12 August 1981
Trafford Park	12 August 1981
City of Glasgow	18 August 1981
Gateshead	25 August 1981
Newcastle	25 August 1981
Speke (Liverpool)	25 August 1981
Belfast	21 October 1981
Hartlepool	23 October 1981
Isle of Dogs	26 April 1982
Delyn	21 July 1983
Wellingborough	26 July 1983
Rotherham	16 August 1983
Londonderry	13 September 1983
Scunthorpe (Normanby Ridge and Queensbury)	23 September 1983
Dale Lane and Kingsley (Wakefield)	23 September 1983
Workington (Allerdale)	4 October 1983
Invergordon	7 October 1983
North-West Kent	31 October 1983
Middlesbrough (Britannia)	8 November 1983
North-East Lancashire	7 December 1983
Tayside (Arbroath)	9 January 1984
Tayside (Dundee)	9 January 1984
Telford	13 January 1984
Glanford (Flixborough)	13 April 1984
Milford Haven Waterway (North Shore)	24 April 1984
Milford Haven Waterway (South Shore)	24 April 1984
Dudley (Round Oak)	3 October 1984
Lower Swansea Valley (No. 2)	6 March 1985
North-West Kent (No. 2)	10 October 1986
Inverclyde	3 March 1989
Sunderland (Castleton and Doxford Park)	27 March 1990
Sunderland (Hytton Riverside and Southwick)	27 March 1990

Note that the first enterprise zones, designated in 1981 and 1982, have now expired.

7 Improvements for Interest Relief

Interest relief is available where a loan is taken out to make improvements to property. The following are examples of improvements:

(1) Home extensions and loft conversions.

(2) Central and solar heating installations (excluding portable radiators and night storage radiators not fixed to a permanent spur outlet). The cost of replacing one form of heating with another, for example changing from oil to gas heating, is included.

(3) Installation of double glazing even though it is in a detachable form.

(4) Insulation of roof or walls.

(5) Installation of bathrooms and other similar plumbing.

(6) Kitchen and bedroom units (for example sink units) which are affixed to and become part of the building. In practice, a range of matching units may be treated as qualifying as a whole even though only some of them qualify (but always excluding cookers, refrigerators and similar appliances).

(7) Connection to main drainage.

(8) Erection and cost of garages, garden sheds, greenhouses, patios and fences.

(9) Recovering and reconstructing a roof.

(10) Construction or landscaping of gardens.

(11) Construction of swimming pools.

(12) Reconstruction of property, e.g. conversion into flats.

(13) Underpinning a house.

(14) Rebuilding a facade.

(15) Insertion or renewal of damp-proof course. Dry and wet rot treatment.

(16) Replacement of electrical installations.

(17) Extensive repointing, pebble-dashing, texture coating or stone cladding (but excluding painting).

(18) Installation of fire or burglar alarms.

(19) Installation of water softening equipment forming a permanent part of the plumbing system.

(20) Construction of driveways and paths.

(21) Extensive replacement of guttering.

Source: Leaflet IR 11 (1985), since discontinued.

8 Retail Prices Index

The Retail Prices Index (RPI) also known as the 'cost of living index' reflects the price movements of certain items in the family's budget. An index number is calculated for each month and is published by the Department of Employment approximately 15 days after the end of the month.

	1982	1983	1984	1985	1986	1987	1988	1989	1990	1991	1992
January		82.61	86.84	91.20	96.25	100.0	103.3	111.0	119.5	130.2	135.6
February		82.97	87.20	91.94	96.60	100.4	103.7	111.8	120.2	130.9	136.3
March	79.44	83.12	87.48	92.80	96.73	100.6	104.1	112.3	121.4	131.4	136.7
April	81.04	84.28	88.64	94.78	97.67	101.8	105.8	114.3	125.1	133.1	138.8
May	81.62	84.64	88.97	95.21	97.85	101.9	106.2	115.0	126.2	133.5	139.3
June	81.85	84.84	89.20	95.41	97.79	101.9	106.6	115.4	126.7	134.1	
July	81.88	85.30	89.10	95.23	97.52	101.8	106.7	115.5	126.8	133.8	
August	81.90	85.68	89.94	95.49	97.82	102.1	107.9	115.8	128.1	134.1	
September	81.85	86.06	90.11	95.44	98.30	102.4	108.4	116.6	129.3	134.6	
October	82.26	86.36	90.67	95.59	98.45	102.9	109.5	117.5	130.3	135.1	
November	82.66	86.67	90.95	95.92	99.29	103.4	110.0	118.5	130.0	135.6	
December	82.51	86.89	90.87	96.05	99.62	103.3	110.3	118.8	129.9	135.7	

9   Depreciation Table for Leases

Years	%	Years	%
50 (or more)	100	25	81.100
49	99.657	24	79.622
48	99.289	23	78.055
47	98.902	22	76.399
46	98.490	21	74.635
45	98.059	20	72.770
44	97.595	19	70.791
43	97.107	18	68.697
42	96.593	17	66.470
41	96.041	16	64.116
40	95.457	15	61.617
39	94.842	14	58.971
38	94.189	13	56.167
37	93.497	12	53.191
36	92.761	11	50.038
35	91.981	10	46.695
34	91.156	9	43.154
33	90.280	8	39.399
32	89.354	7	35.414
31	88.371	6	31.195
30	87.330	5	26.722
29	86.226	4	21.983
28	85.053	3	16.959
27	83.816	2	11.629
26	82.496	1	5.983
		0	0

Percentages taken from Schedule 8 to the Taxation of Chargeable Gains Act 1992.

10 Car Scale Benefits 1992/93

Age of car on 5 April 1993	Use of company car		Petrol	Diesel
	Under 4 years	4 years or more	Age not relevant	
	£	£	£	£
CARS UP TO £19,250				
Cylinder capacity				
1,400cc or less	2,140	1,460	500	460
1,401 to 2,000cc	2,770	1,880	630	460
Over 2,000cc	4,440	2,980	940	590
No cylinder capacity				
Price under £6,000	2,140	1,460	500	460
£6,000 to £8,499	2,770	1,880	630	460
£8,500 to £19,250	4,440	2,980	940	590
CARS OVER £19,250				
£19,251 to £29,000	5,570	3,870	940*	590*
Over £29,000	9,300	6,170	940*	590*

*Petrol £500 up to 1,400cc and £630 between 1,401cc and 2,000cc. Diesel £460 up to 2,000cc.

Employers are liable to pay NICs at 10.4 per cent on these charges.

Applies to employees earning £8,500 or more per annum and most directors.

Car scale charge increased by 50 per cent if business use does not exceed 2,500 miles per annum.

Car and fuel scale charges halved if business use at least 18,000 miles per annum.

11   VAT on Car Fuel 1992/93

Table A (average or low business mileage)

Cylinder capacity of vehicle	3 month period				1 month period			
	Scale charge diesel	VAT per car	Scale charge petrol	VAT per car	Scale charge diesel	VAT per car	Scale charge petrol	VAT per car
	£	£	£	£	£	£	£	£
1,400cc or less	115	17.13	125	18.62	38	5.66	42	6.26
1,401–2,000cc	115	17.13	158	23.53	38	5.66	53	7.89
More than 2,000cc	148	22.04	235	35	49	7.30	78	11.62

Table B (high business mileage, i.e. more than 4,500 miles a quarter)

Cylinder capacity of vehicle	3 month period				1 month period			
1,400cc or less	58	8.64	63	9.38	19	2.83	21	3.13
1,401–2,000cc	58	8.64	79	11.77	19	2.83	26	3.87
More than 2,000cc	74	11.02	118	17.57	25	3.72	39	5.81

12   Return by Employer of Expenses and Benefits: Form P11D

Inland Revenue
Income Tax

Employer's name _____ PAYE reference _____

Director's/employee's*
name _____ NI number

*delete as appropriate

Return of expenses payments and benefits etc - directors, and employees earning at a rate of £8,500 a year or more.
Year ended 5 April 1992

Please read form P11D (Guide) before completing this form.

You are required to make a return by 6 June 1992 of all benefits (such as cars and car fuel, beneficial loans, medical insurance, home and mobile telephones etc) provided to
- directors - *for certain exceptions see form P11D (Guide)*
- employees who are paid at a rate of £8,500 or more including expenses and benefits.

You should also show details of all expenses payments other than those covered by a dispensation *see form P11D (Guide).*

A   Cars and car fuel

1. Cars made available for private use

If more than one car made available during the year, give details of each car at (a) and (b)

Make and model   (a) _____ cc   (b) _____ cc

		(a)	(b)
Value when new	£19,250 or less	[ ]	[ ]
	£19,251 - £29,000	[ ]	[ ]
	more than £29,000	[ ]	[ ]
First registered on or after 6.4.88		[ ]	[ ]
	before 6.4.88	[ ]	[ ]

Made available to director/employee   from _____ to _____   from _____ to _____

Please indicate the annual business mileage travelled

2500 or less	[ ]
2501 - 17,999	[ ]
18,000 or more	[ ]

The amount of any wages paid to a driver provided for the director/employee in respect of private journeys   £ _____

Payment received from the director/employee for the private use of the car   £ _____

You may wish to show the scale charges that you calculate apply to the car(s) provided using these boxes. Enter the taxable benefit   (a) £ [_____]   (b) £ [_____]

2. Car fuel "scale charges" - cars available for private use   Yes   No

Was fuel for the car(s) provided other than for business travel?   [ ]   [ ]

If yes was the director/employee required to make good the cost of all fuel used for private motoring including travel between home and normal place of work?   [ ]   [ ]

If the director/employee was required to make good the cost did he actually do so?   [ ]   [ ]

You may wish to show the scale charges that you calculate apply to the car fuel provided using these boxes. Enter the taxable benefit   (a) £ [_____]   (b) £ [_____]

3. Car owned or hired by director/employee

Allowances paid to the director/employee in respect of the use of the car and/or running and overhead expenses   £ _____

Sum contributed by you towards the purchase price, depreciation or hire of a car   £ _____

For official use

P11D(1991)

Printed in the UK for HMSO 12/91 Dd. FAL0101059 C50,000 (11037).

B   Beneficial loans

4. Enter details of loans made to, or arranged for, a director/employee (or any of his relatives) on which no interest was paid or on which the amount of interest paid was less than interest at the official rate (see P11D (Guide)). Include Miras loans under £30,000 and loans to directors from overdrawn or current accounts with the company. Complete a separate column for each loan. **Note:** If the only loan(s) provided is within (c) below (eg season ticket loan) and the benefit does not exceed £300 there is no need to complete this section. Where you know the purpose of the loan please tick the box applicable. Otherwise tick the 'Don t know' box

(a) loan for purchase or improvement of a main residence on which interest is eligible
    for relief (see Booklet 480 Appendix 4)

(b) loan for a purpose eligible for interest relief, other than loans covered by (a)
    (see Booklet 480 Appendix 4)

(c) loan not eligible for interest relief

                                                            Don t know

You need not provide any further details for a loan within (b) above. For each loan not within (b) please enter

- amount outstanding at 5 4 91 or date loan was made (if later)   £ _____   £ _____
- amount outstanding at 5 4 92 or date loan was discharged (if earlier)   £ _____   £ _____
- total amount of interest paid by the borrower in the year to 5 4 92 (enter nil if none was paid)   £ _____   £ _____
- date loan was made or discharged in year to 5 4 92 (where applicable)   _____   _____

If any loans made by you were waived or written off in the year to 5 4 92 what was the amount waived or written off?   £ _____

C   Other expenses payments and benefits etc

		Gross Amount £	Amount made good by director/employee or amount from which tax has been deducted under PAYE £
5	Private medical dental etc attention and treatment or insurance against the cost of such treatment		
6	General expenses allowance		
7	Travelling and subsistence		
8	Vans made available for private use		
9	Entertainment		
10	Home telephone expenses paid or reimbursed { Rental / Calls		
11	Mobile telephone. Tick box if available for private calls. Indicate number of appliances		
12	Subscriptions		
13	Goods or services supplied free or below market value		
14	Vouchers and credit cards not returned elsewhere		
15	Cars, property, furniture and other assets given or transferred to the director/employee		
16	Nursery places provided for children of the director/employee		
17	Educational assistance provided for the director/employee or members of his family		
18	House, flat or other living accommodation provided for the director/employee *Please show address _____ Cost £ _____*		
19	Income tax paid to the Collector in the year to 5 April 1992 which a company failed to deduct from a director s remuneration		
20	Other expenses and benefits eg National Insurance contributions, holidays, private legal, accountancy etc expenses; contributions towards house purchase and other household expenses such as wages and keep of personal or domestic staff and gardening expenses. *This is not an exhaustive list. Please consider whether you provide any expenses payments or benefits which are not mentioned here. Please give details _____*		
	Totals		

Declaration

I declare that all particulars required are fully and truly stated according to the best of my knowledge and belief

Signature _____   Date _____

Capacity in which signed _____

13 Leaving Certificate: Form P45

P45 **New employee** **Part 3**
Details of previous employment

1. Previous PAYE reference

2. National Insurance number

Mr. Mrs. Miss. Ms.

3. Surname

First two
forenames

	Day	Month		Year
4. Date of leaving			**19**	

5. Code at date of leaving — Code — Week 1 or Month 1
   'X' means Week 1 or Month 1 basis

6. Last entries on Deductions Working Sheet | Week or Month number | Week | Month |
   If there is an 'X' at item 5, there will be no entries here | Total pay to date | £ | p |
   | Total tax to date | £ | p |

New employer *Please complete items 7 to 14 below and send this form to your Tax Office* **IMMEDIATELY**. *Please also read the 'New Employee' instructions on the form P8.*

7. New PAYE reference

	Day	Month		Year
8. Date employment commenced (in figures)			**19**	

9. Tick '✓' here if you want these details to be shown on code notifications | '✓' | Works number |
   | | | Branch, Dept. |

10. Write 'P' here if this employee will not be paid by you between the date shown at item 8 and the next 5 April. | 'P' |

11. If tax entered at item 6 does not agree with tax entered on Deductions Working Sheet from the Tax Tables, write the Tax Table figure here. | £ |

12. Employee's private address _____ Postcode _____

13. Nature of employment _____

14. **Declaration**
    I have prepared a Deductions Working Sheet in accordance with the above details.
    Employer _____

    Address _____

    _____ Postcode _____ Date _____

P45

14   The Schedular System

	What is charged	Basis of assessment
Schedule A	Rents under lease of UK land and buildings	Income to which entitled in the year
Schedule C	Interest on Government securities and certain overseas public revenue dividends	Tax deducted at source
Schedule D	There are six cases	*Normally profits of accounting period which
Case I	Profits of a trade	ended in previous tax year. Special rules when business begins or ends
Case II	Profits of a profession or vacation	Ditto
Case III	Interest received gross	*Normally income arising in previous tax year. Special rules when source of income begins or ends
Case IV	Interest from foreign securities	Ditto
Case V	Income from overseas possessions	Ditto
Case VI	Income not assessed under another schedule or case	Income in the year
Schedule E	Wages, salaries, benefits and pensions. There are three cases	
Case I	UK resident employee working in the UK	Earnings received in the year
Case II	Non-UK resident employee working in the UK	Earnings from UK duties
Case III	UK resident employee working abroad	Earnings remitted to the UK
Schedule F	Dividends and other distributions from UK companies	Tax deducted at source

*Income within Schedule D, Case I, III, IV and V which is received by a company is assessed in the accounting period in which it arises.

15 Assured Tenancies – Grounds for Possession

Grounds where, if there is a periodic tenancy, the court *must* order possession of the dwelling:

(a) Where the tenant is more than three months in arrears with the rent both at the date of serving notice for possession and at the date of the hearing.

(b) Where the landlord intends to demolish or reconstruct the whole or a substantial part of the building.

(c) Where a periodic tenancy has occurred following the death of the former tenant and recovery proceedings have begun within 12 months of the death.

(d) Where the dwelling is subject to a mortgage taken out before the tenancy and the mortgagee wishes to exercise his right to sell the property.

Further grounds where the court *may* order possession:

(e) Where some rent due from the tenant is unpaid both when the landlord serves notice for possession and when the proceedings are begun.

(f) Where the tenant has persistently delayed paying the rent.

(g) Where suitable alternative accommodation is available for the tenant.

(h) Where any obligation of the tenancy (other than rent) has been broken or not performed.

(i) Where the tenant has caused a nuisance or annoyance to the neighbours or has used the dwelling for immoral or illegal purposes.

(j) Where the condition of either the dwelling, the common parts, or the furniture has deteriorated because of ill-treatment by the tenant, his subtenants or lodgers.

(k) Where the tenant occupied the premises in consequence of his employment and he has ceased that employment.

The court may also order possession on the grounds (a), and (d) to (j) where there is a current fixed term tenancy which includes a provision for it to end in those circumstances.

The landlord has to give the tenant notice that he intends to begin proceedings for possession. If the grounds are (c), (d), (g) or (k) the notice is two months, and in the other cases it is two weeks. If it considers it is just and reasonable the court can dispense with the notice requirements except when the ground is (a).

16   Inheritance Tax Rates Payable on Death

At death the value of a person's estate is increased by any chargeable transfers made in the last seven years. If the total value is £150,000 or less the tax rate is nil. If it is greater the excess over £150,000 is taxable at 40 per cent.

Taper relief

Where potentially exempt transfers have been made and death occurs after three years but within seven years there is a tapering of the tax rates.

Years between death and gift	Reduction of rate %	Effect of reduction %
0–3	Nil	40
3–4	20	32
4–5	40	24
5–6	60	16
6–7	80	8

Successive transfers

There is relief for IHT payable on death where IHT has been levied on the same property within the previous five years. A deduction is given from the tax payable on the second occasion equal to a percentage of the tax paid earlier.

Period between first and second event Years	Percentage of the tax charged on first event %
0–1	100
1–2	80
2–3	60
3–4	40
4–5	20
Over 5	Nil

17   Useful Addresses

Tax and law

Capital Taxes Office

England and Wales
  Minford House
  Rockley Road
  London W14 0DF
  071-603 4622

Northern Ireland
  Law Court Buildings
  Chichester Street
  Belfast BT1 3JF
  (0232) 235111

Scotland
  16–22 Picardy Place
  Edinburgh EH1 3NF
  031-556 8511

Inland Revenue

HMIT Telford
  Crown Buildings
  Walker Street
  Wellington
  Shropshire TF1 1LE
  (0952) 641146

Public Enquiry Room
  West Wing
  Somerset House
  London WC2R 1LB
  071-438 6420/5

Pension Schemes Office
  Lynwood Road
  Thames Ditton
  Surrey KT7 0DP
  081-398 4242

Profit Related Pay Office
  St Mungo's Road
  Town Centre
  Cumbernauld
  Glasgow G70 5TR
  (0236) 736121

Valuation Unit
  Westminster 2 District
  2 Fouberts Place
  London W1V 2HE
  071-434 2211

Inland Revenue Savings & Investment
(Employee Share Schemes)
  Room 127
  New Wing
  Somerset House
  London WC2R 1LB
  071-438 6288

Operations Divisions
  Room 837 South West Wing
  Bush House
  Strand
  London WC2B 4RD
  071-438 6622

Claims Branch
  St Johns House
  Merton Road
  Bootle L69 9BB
  051-922 6363

Accounts Office
  St Mungo's Road
  Town Centre
  Cumbernauld
  Glasgow G70 5TR
  (0236) 736121

Accounts Office
  PO Box 111
  Freepost
  Bradford
  BD98 8RR
  (0274) 594141

Stamp Office Information Service
  Ridworth House
  Liverpool Gardens
  Worthing
  West Sussex BN11 1XP
  (0903) 50928

Customs and Excise
  New King's Beam House
  22 Upper Ground
  London SE1 9PJ
  071-620 1313

Department of Social Security

DSS Class 4 Group
  Newcastle Central Office
  Benton Park Road
  Longbenton
  Newcastle upon Tyne
  NE98 1YX
  (0912) 135000

DSS Leaflets
  PO Box 21
  Honeypot Lane
  Stanmore
  Middlesex HA7 1AY
  (0895) 238601

DSS Overseas Branch
  Newcastle upon Tyne
  NE98 1YX

Registrar of Companies

England and Wales
  Companies House
  Crown Way
  Maindy
  Cardiff CF4 3UZ
  (0222) 388588

Companies House
  55–71 City Road
  London EC1Y 1BB
  071-253 9393

Northern Ireland
  Dept of Economic Development
  IDB House
  Netherleigh
  Massey Avenue
  Belfast BT4 2JP
  (0232) 763244

Scotland
  100–102 George Street
  Edinburgh EH2 3DJ
  031-225 5774

The Patent Office
  Cardiff Road
  Newport
  Gwent NP9 1RH
  (0633) 814000

**Home Office Immigration and
Nationality Department**
  Lunar House
  Wellesley Road
  Croydon CR9 2BY
  081-686 0688

Assistance for business

*Department of Trade and Industry;
Regional Offices*

North East
  Stanegate House
  2 Groat Market
  Newcastle upon Tyne NE1 1YN
  091-235 7292

North West
  Sunley Buildings
  Piccadilly Plaza
  Manchester M1 4BE
  061-236 2171

  Graeme House
  Derby Square
  Liverpool L2 7UP
  051-224 6300

Yorkshire and Humberside
  25 Queens Street
  Leeds LS1 1TW
  (0532) 443171

East Midlands
  Severns House
  20 Middle Pavement
  Nottingham N81 7DW
  (0602) 506181

Northern Ireland
Industrial Development Board
for Northern Ireland
IDB House
64 Chichester Street
Belfast BT1 4JX
(0232) 233233

South East
Bridge Place
88–89 Eccleston Square
London SW1V 1PT
071-215 0572

South West
The Pithay
Bristol BS1 2PB
(0272) 272666

Scotland
Alhembra House
45 Waterloo Street
Glasgow G2 6AT
041-248 4774

Wales
Welsh Office Industry Dept
New Crown Buildings
Cathays Park
Cardiff CF1 3NQ
(0222) 823185

North Wales District Office
Government Buildings
Dinerth Road
Colwyn Bay
Clwyd LL28 4UL
(0492) 544261

West Midlands
Ladywood House
45–46 Stephenson Street
Birmingham B2 4DT
021-632 4111

British Coal Enterprise Ltd
Hobart House
40 Grosvenor Place
London SW1X 7AE
071-235 2020

British Steel Corporation (Industry) Ltd
Bridge House
Bridge Street
Sheffield S3 8NS
(0742) 731612

Enterprise agencies
Ask at your local library or Jobcentre
for the address of your nearest agency

Highlands and Islands Enterprise
Bridge House
20 Bridge Street
Inverness IV1 1QR
(0463) 234171

Scottish Enterprise
120 Bothwell Street
Glasgow G2 7JP
041-248 2700

European Commission (London Office)
8 Storey's Gate
London SW1P 3AT
071-973 1992

Loan Guarantee Unit
1st Floor
St Mary's House
c/o Moorfoot
Sheffield S1 4PQ

LEDU Business Centre
25–27 Franklin Street
Belfast BT2 8DT
(0232) 242582

Small Firms Centres
Dial 100 and ask for Freefone Enterprise

Mid Wales Development
Ladywell House
Newtown
Powys SY16 1JB
(0686) 626956

Rural Development Commission
11 Cowley Street
London SW1P 3NA
071-276 6969

14 Castle Street
  Salisbury
  Wiltshire SP1 3TP
  (0722) 336255

Welsh Development Agency
  Pearl House
  Greyfriars Road
  Cardiff CF1 3XX
  (0222) 222666

European Investment Bank
  68 Pall Mall
  London
  SW1Y 5ES
  071-839 3351

Index

References are to page numbers